THE New Shape OF Suburbia

TRENDS IN RESIDENTIAL DEVELOPMENT

Primary Authors

Adrienne Schmitz

Pam Engebretson

Frederick L. Merrill

Sarah E. Peck

Robert L. Santos

Kristin Shewfelt

Debra Stein

John Torti

Marilee A. Utter

**Urban Land
Institute**

About ULI–
the Urban Land Institute

About ULI–the Urban Land Institute is a non-profit education and research institute that is supported by its members. Its mission is to provide responsible leadership in the use of land in order to enhance the total environment.

ULI sponsors education programs and forums to encourage an open international exchange of ideas and sharing of experiences; initiates research that anticipates emerging land use trends and issues and proposes creative solutions based on that research; provides advisory services; and publishes a wide variety of materials to disseminate information on land use and development. Established in 1936, the Institute today has more than 17,000 members and associates from some 60 countries representing the entire spectrum of the land use and development disciplines.

Richard M. Rosan
President

Recommended bibliographic listing:

Schmitz, Adrienne, et al. *The New Shape of Suburbia: Trends in Residential Development.* Washington, D.C.: ULI–the Urban Land Institute, 2003.

ULI Catalog Number: N26
International Standard Book Number: 0-87420-897-1
Library of Congress Control Number: 2003102380

Copyright 2003 by ULI–the Urban Land Institute
1025 Thomas Jefferson Street, N.W.
Suite 500 West
Washington, D.C. 20007-5201

Project Staff

Rachelle L. Levitt
Senior Vice President, Policy and Practice
Publisher

Gayle Berens
Vice President, Real Estate Development
Practice

Adrienne Schmitz
Director, Residential Community Development
Project Director

Nancy H. Stewart
Director, Book Program
Managing Editor

Sandy Chizinsky
Manuscript Editor

Betsy VanBuskirk
Art Director

Helene Y. Redmond/HYR Graphics
Cover and Book Design/Layout

Karrie Underwood
Digital Images Manager

Diann Stanley-Austin
Director, Publishing Operations

Cover image: Belle Creek, Commerce City, Colorado.
Cover site plan: Evergreen, San Jose, California, courtesy of Dahlin Group.

Authors

Principal Author and Editor

Adrienne Schmitz
Urban Land Institute
Washington, D.C.

Primary Contributing Authors

Pam Engebretson
Interra Strategies
San Diego, California

Frederick L. Merrill
Sasaki Associates
Watertown, Massachusetts

Sarah E. Peck
Progressive Housing Ventures
Malvern, Pennsylvania

Robert L. Santos
Lennar Communities
Mission Viejo, California

Kristin Shewfelt
McStain Neighborhoods
Boulder, Colorado

Debra Stein
CGA Strategies, Inc.
San Francisco, California

John Torti
Torti Gallas and Partners
Silver Spring, Maryland

Marilee A. Utter
Citiventure Associates
Denver, Colorado

Contributing Authors

André Bald
Consultant
Washington, D.C.

Sam Begner
Consultant
Atlanta, Georgia

Steven Fader
Steven Fader Architect
Los Angeles, California

Leslie Holst
Urban Land Institute
Washington, D.C.

Jennifer LeFurgy
Metropolitan Institute at Virginia Tech
Alexandria, Virginia

Robert L. Miller
Robert L. Miller Associates
Washington, D.C.

Sam Newberg
Maxfield Research, Inc.
Minneapolis, Minnesota

Advisory Committee

Pete Halter
Halter & Associates
Smyrna, Georgia

Brent Herrington
DMB Associates
Scottsdale, Arizona

Kim M. Morque
The Spinnaker Companies
Stamford, Connecticut

Daniel Van Epp
The Howard Hughes Corporation
Las Vegas, Nevada

Reviewers

Kim Calomino
Denver Metro Home Builders Association
Denver, Colorado

James Charlier
Charlier Associates
Boulder, Colorado

Craig Cox
Colorado Coalition for New Energy
   Technologies
Denver, Colorado

Steven Coyle
Lennertz Coyle & Associates
Portland, Oregon

Michael Dobbins
City of Atlanta Bureau of Planning
   and Development
Atlanta, Georgia

Ann V. Edminster
Design AVEnues, LEED Homes
Pacifica, California

Robert Engstrom
Robert Engstrom Companies
Bloomington, Minnesota

James Heid
Urban Green
San Francisco, California

Melissa Knott
Forest City Development
Stapleton, Colorado

Robert Lang
Metropolitan Institute at Virginia Tech
Alexandria, Virginia

Kathleen O'Brien
O'Brien & Company
Bainbridge Island, Washington

Duncan Prahl
IBACOS, Inc.
Pittsburgh, Pennsylvania

Roger Reinhardt
Denver Metro Home Builders Association
Denver, Colorado

James Wentling
James Wentling/Architects
Philadelphia, Pennsylvania

Acknowledgments

Many professionals contributed their expertise and hard work to the research, writing, and production of this book. First and foremost, many thanks go to the chapter authors: Marilee Utter, Fred Merrill, Bob Santos, Pam Engebretson, John Torti, Sarah Peck, Kristin Shewfelt, and Debra Stein, all of whom approached the task with enthusiasm and dedication. Thanks, also, to Leslie Holst, researcher, writer, reviewer, and all-around critic, who greatly improved the quality of every aspect of the book.

The authors of the case studies deserve credit for their research and writing. Thanks to André Bald, Sam Begner, Steve Fader, Leslie Holst, Jennifer LeFurgy, Robert Miller, and Sam Newberg. Other writers who had a hand in the book include Dan Burden, William Lieberman, Clark Mercer, and Melissa Weberman. Thanks also go to Lori Hatcher, who both helped to conceive a book that would reach the right audiences and defined the audiences that would appreciate the book. Much credit goes to Gayle Berens, who expertly guides every ULI book, including this one, from conception through completion.

ULI staff members Geoffrey Booth, Bob Dunphy, Anne Frej, Jo Allen Gause, and Rick Haughey offered constructive comments. Karrie Underwood provided technical support in this rapidly changing electronic age, and Clark Mercer assisted with research and writing. Thanks also go to Sandy Chizinsky, who ensured that the text was clear and grammatically correct, to Nancy Stewart, who tirelessly guided the production process, and to Helene Redmond, who designed the book with careful attention to every page.

I also want to acknowledge the many architects, planners, and developers who generously shared their beautiful photographs and illustrations, adding immeasurably to this publication. And to all others who had a hand in this book, I offer my appreciation.

Adrienne Schmitz
Principal Author and Editor

Contents

The New Shape of Suburbia

1 Suburbia in the 21st Century

DAHLIN GROUP

"I know it's important to be aware of what's going on in suburban America, but you know, who cares?"

—*Herbert Muschamp, architecture critic*

Those who dismiss the suburbs as unimportant are dismissing the places where the majority of Americans live, work, play, shop, and learn. At the turn of the 21st century, the rate at which Americans are moving to suburban developments far outpaces any "back to the city" trend. The suburbs also merit attention because they are no longer the plain-vanilla pods that once sprawled across the landscape. Today's diverse and demanding population calls for better homes and neighborhoods, and developers are meeting the challenge.

The suburbanization of the United States began well before World War II, but it was after the war, when returning veterans required unprecedented numbers of new homes, that suburban development really exploded, fueled by federal highway and housing subsidies. For many families, the suburban communities of the 1950s—symbolized by the "Levittowns" of Long Island and New Jersey—epitomized the American Dream. These communities offered young, middle-class families the chance to own their own homes, and plenty of space to raise children. And they were largely populated by other traditional families who were raising children and forming community ties.

Much has changed since those times. The population is older, and minorities, including recent immigrants, make up a much larger proportion of the mix. A majority of women now hold jobs outside the home. In many ways, American suburbs have become more urban: traffic congestion, overcrowding, and social problems have worked their way into the suburbs, as have a number of other formerly urban issues like growth, aging infrastructure, poverty, and pressure for more sustainable planning and development practices. Further, declining tax bases at the federal, state, and local levels mean that little is left to spend on the roads and infrastructure that are needed for growth. The cost of development is being shifted to the homebuyer, a fact that will change the shape of new communities in ways that have yet to become clear.

In the past half-century, much rural open space and agricultural land has been engulfed by the expanding suburbs; since 1950, the percentage of the population living in the suburbs has steadily increased (23 percent in 1950 versus 50 percent in 1998), and the rural population has decreased accordingly (44 percent in 1950 versus 20 percent in 1998).[1]

The suburbs of the early 21st century are different from their predecessors in several ways. They offer higher development densities, a greater mix of land uses, more mass-transit options, more primary employment centers, better access to educational and medical services, and more cultural amenities. The new urbanism (also called "traditional neighborhood development") and smart growth policies are having a major impact on suburban planning and development. The results include denser development; more infill development; smaller, clustered residential lots that conserve open space; mixed-use town centers; residential developments in commercial locations; shared parking arrangements; and the integration of public transit into development. While some older, inner-ring suburbs are declining and losing population, many others are being transformed into walkable, higher-density, mixed-use districts that are the equals of the best urban neighborhoods.

Who Are the New Suburbanites?

American households have changed dramatically since the mid-20th century. They are increasingly made up of smaller families, nonfamilies, and single people. According to demographer William Frey, in 2000, "traditional" households—married couples with children—made up only 27 percent of all suburban households; married couples with no children made up 29 percent, nonfamily households made up 29 percent, and "other" kinds of families made up the remaining 15 percent. By 2010, traditional families will make up only 20 percent of all suburban households.[2] Frey has studied the ethnic makeup of suburban populations as well. According to the 2000 census, 27 percent of the suburban population in large metropolitan areas is made up of minorities, up from 19 percent in 1990. In fact, minorities were responsible for the bulk of the population growth in many suburban regions.[3]

Facing page: With the advent of higher densities and more mixed-use development, the suburbs are becoming increasingly urban.

A report by Lend Lease Real Estate Investments notes that Hispanic Americans, who make up 12.5 percent of the population, are the largest minority. African Americans make up 9 percent of the population, and Asian Americans another 9 percent. A majority of Asian Americans, half of all Hispanics, and 39 percent of African Americans live in the suburbs.[4]

More than 11 percent of the population is foreign born, up from 8 percent in 1990.[5] Although immigrants enter the country at the gateway cities of Los Angeles, Miami, and New York, many of them do not stay in those cities, as the immigrants of the past did. Instead, they move to where the best job opportunities are, which means that—again unlike immigrants of the past—many head for suburban locations, where they often settle among others from their native countries.

Age is another factor that is changing the suburbs. Like the country as a whole, the suburbs are graying. Once catering largely to young families raising school-aged children, today's suburban communities house the full range of age cohorts. Young families continue to move into suburban neighborhoods. Middle-aged empty nesters continue to live in the neighborhoods they've grown to love. And a majority of retirees prefer to remain in the communities where they've spent their lives. Many older suburbs are populated by residents who have aged in place.

Not only have demographics changed, but lifestyles have changed as well. Many people have more money but less free time than ever; consequently, they value time over money. Some people have grown tired of the maintenance that comes with home-ownership; others never want to settle into that routine to begin with. Fewer people want to spend large chunks of their day commuting from remote locations or driving to one errand after another. And increasing numbers of people work at home: between 1997 and 2001, the number of people who worked at home at least part of the time increased from 22.4 million to 25.0 million.[6] More people are concerned about environmental and health-related issues. All these trends spell changes in suburban communities—changes that will affect where they are located, how they are developed, what kinds of services and amenities they include, and what kinds of homes they provide.

What Do People Want in Their Communities?

As recently as the early 1990s, it was easy to build developments that appealed to the majority of consumers: just pack the developments with more amenities. Master-planned communities competed by including expansive parklands, ballfields, bigger and better recreation centers, and above all, golf courses. Multifamily developments followed suit, with business centers, lap pools, and indoor racquet-ball courts. But today's homebuyers are bored with the "old" kinds of communities. They are demanding that developers find new ways of accommodating their busy lifestyles.

"Suburban sprawl" is a term once used only by planners and environmentalists. Today everyone talks of sprawl. Suburban residents complain about long commutes on congested roadways. They vehemently protest new developments in their communities because they believe that more development will only exacerbate existing problems. They are concerned about the loss of open space and about declining environmental quality.

Many observers assume that because household size has declined, so has the demand for square footage. But between 1987 and 2001, the median size of new homes increased nearly every year: from 1,755 square feet (163 square meters) to 2,100 square feet (195 square meters).[7] Averages, however, fail to reveal the complexity of the changes in the marketplace. For example,

Duany Plater-Zyberk & Company designed Prospect New Town, in Longmont, Colorado, to include single-family homes, town-houses, live/work lofts, and accessory apartments. The homes were built in both tra-ditional and contem-porary architectural styles.

while an admittedly substantial share of the housing market is still buying large houses in greenfield locations, some important—and growing—market segments are settling into townhouses or into houses on smaller lots, or exploring new types of housing. Similarly, although ownership continues to rise overall, some households are renting homes, either by necessity or choice. Still others are not even making housing decisions because what they want—or can afford—does not exist.

Just as averages do not tell the whole story, old assumptions cannot be used to predict future trends. "Minorities live in inner-city neighborhoods." "Retirees prefer gated, golf-oriented communities." "Single women rent suburban apartments." Consumers, who are far more diverse than the conventional wisdom acknowledges, contradict all the old stereotypes.

The good news is that the broad diversity of today's population means a broad diversity of opportunities for developers and builders.

Markets exist for housing in inner cities; in close-in suburbs; in older, middle-ring suburbs; and in outer suburbs and rural areas. Demand exists for rental apartments, for loft units above commercial space, for rowhouses, and for single-family houses. Every location, community type, housing type, and price range offers some potential for developers who understand who the buyers are and what they want. While the majority of developers try to satisfy the majority of buyers, niche markets offer astute developers untapped opportunities.

"Often, what buyers want is not what they get," according to Brooke Warrick, of American LIVES, a consumer research group in Oakland, California. "One of the main reasons behind this is that they couldn't find what they wanted in their market."[8] Market research conducted for builders and developers provides feedback from current shoppers and recent buyers of new homes, but such efforts often bypass those who buy older homes and those whose expectations are not being met by the marketplace. Developers who explore these ignored market segments might find untapped opportunities. American LIVES's surveys reveal, moreover, that many of the features people want most are relatively inexpensive and easy to provide. About two-thirds of respondents, for example, want sidewalks on all streets, walking and biking paths, and natural open space—all of which are fairly inexpensive when compared to an on-site golf course, which typically elicits fairly low interest. Successfully addressing other demands may be a more elusive goal, however: nearly 90 percent of those surveyed want a "quiet, low-traffic area."[9]

In 2001, the National Association of Home Builders (NAHB) published the results of a survey of 1,180 people who were shopping for or had bought new homes.[10] Those surveyed had an average age of 44 and a median income of $45,500 (just above the national median). When asked which of 22 community amenities would seriously influence their decision to move to a new community, the highest percentage of respondents selected parks (62 percent) and walking trails (58 percent); these results are similar to those obtained by American LIVES and other surveys. About one-third of those surveyed said that they would be seriously influenced by the availability of public transportation.

When asked how concerned they were about the environment, 50 percent said that they wanted an environment-friendly home, and 14 percent were willing to pay more for such a home. Only 10 percent were not concerned about the impact of a home on the environment. Sixty-two percent rated "natural undeveloped lands" as important.

DMB, an Arizona-based developer of master-planned communities, has conducted its own consumer research. The firm has noted that recent results differ markedly from those of the early 1990s, when respondents' main interest was amenities—in particular, golf and other recreation. Today, respondents are looking for less tangible characteristics. The desires cited most often are the following:

- A sense of community;
- A sense of connection;
- Diversity;
- Pedestrian access.

Brent Herrington, of DMB, says that "time poverty" is a major issue for homebuyers. For developers, the task is to foster community for people who have no time to do it themselves. Often, new residents have relocated from outside the region and crave a sense of connection. Herrington suggests that developers hire staff to help establish clubs and other organizations that people want, and that they also provide places for such groups to meet.

As more people work at home either full- or part-time, homes have changed to accommodate work spaces. But communities need to change as well. Work-at-homers often feel isolated in typical suburban communities and would like access to the amenities that are available to downtown office workers. The corner coffee bar, a nearby copy center, handy lunch spots and carry-outs, and convenience retail facilities all serve the daily needs of workers. Residential communities that best serve those who work at home must include such amenities.

Astute developers recognize the importance of women in the housing market. In most married couples, the woman either makes the renting or the homebuying decision on her own or plays a major role in the decision. And growing affluence among single women has dramatically increased homeownership rates for that market segment. Many developers report that more single women than single men buy new homes; men, they conclude, either rent or continue to live with their parents. Census data bears this observation out: the most recent American Housing Survey reveals that 62 percent of all single-person owner-occupied housing is owned by women. Among nonmarried homeowner households of two or more people, 64 percent are headed by women.[11]

Because women are so important in home-buying decisions, developers must understand their needs. Pete Halter, of the Atlanta-based consultant V.R. Halter & Associates, cites security and a good location as key factors in women's homebuying decisions. Women also tend to be more concerned than men are with social infrastructure and with environmental issues.

Niche markets share some characteristics and demands with the market as a whole. In other ways they are different. The following three sections highlight the characteristics of market segments that bear watching.

Smaller Households

In one respect, buyers that are considered a niche are actually the majority: nearly three-quarters of all suburban households are *not* married couples with children but some kind of "nontraditional" household. Of these, most are made up of only one or two people. While some of these smaller households do gravitate to four-bedroom suburban homes with rolling lawns, many are looking for alternative product types. In many regions, the existing stock of traditional suburban housing will meet the demand for years to come, but there is a shortage of attached housing (both for rent and for sale), of affordable units, and of other kinds of smaller housing types. Opportunities exist for creative developers who can detect what is missing in the marketplace and can develop innovative product types to meet the demand.

Ethnic Minorities

What are now considered to be ethnic minorities will account for 40 percent of the U.S. population by 2010. As minority populations grow and prosper, they are becoming increasingly important market segments. Recent immigrants have been responsible for the revitalization of many inner-ring suburban com-

Luxury rental apartments satisfy a market niche that includes affluent young professionals and empty nesters.

munities. Neighborhoods that had begun to deteriorate are now thriving "Little Saigons," "Korea Towns," and "Little Havanas." Drawn by jobs, schools, and other quality-of-life factors, immigrants are also entering mainstream suburban communities in unprecedented numbers.

Hispanic Americans are the largest—and fastest-growing—minority in the United States; hardly a monolithic group, they come from many countries—Mexico, Cuba, the Dominican Republic, El Salvador, and Puerto Rico, among others. In gateway cities like Miami, Latin Americans are a major economic force—accounting, for example, for about 50 percent of the new condominium sales, many of which serve as second or third homes. Some Miami-based developers have opened sales offices in Latin America to cater to these buyers.

In many ways, minority homebuyers are no different from others in corresponding economic and age cohorts. But there are subtle differences in what minority homebuyers want in their communities and homes. On the West Coast, for example, where many Asian Americans live, feng shui increasingly influences the design of new homes. A broader difference is that immigrants at all income levels are more accustomed to living in closer quarters than Americans are, and are therefore more likely to accept attached housing types.

Baby Boomers and Echo Boomers

Because the baby boom (the cohort born between 1945 and 1966) is so large, it will be an important market segment for years to come, and its demands will continue to shape all kinds of new communities in every region. While many suburban baby boomers will maintain their current homes, some will add a second home, either in a resort location or in a downtown. Baby boomers are helping to fuel a small back-to-the-city trend;

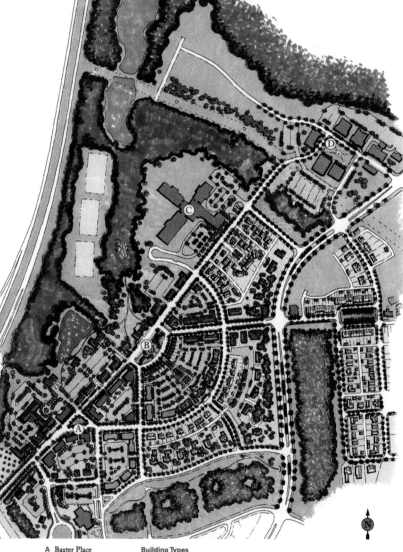

A	Baxter Place	**Building Types**		
B	Close Park	■	Mixed-use Office & Retail	■ Apartments
C	Elementary School	■	Mixed-use Office & Residential	□ Residential
D	Medical Campus	■	Civic Buildings	

at the same time, many suburban regions are developing new, urban-style communities that are designed to meet baby boomers' lifestyle demands as well as to control sprawl.

According to a recent study that explores what baby boomers want in their communities, households made up of people who are older than 45—which will account for almost one-third of the growth in the total number of homeowners between 2000 and 2010—tend to be interested in homes in denser, more central locations.[12] "As the percentage of childless households increases, the market for smaller lots—if not smaller homes—is expected to increase. The declining presence of children suggests a growing market for denser, more walkable neighborhoods that adults find interesting."[13] The study also cites data from a 1996 survey conducted by the American Association of Retired Persons, which found that older households are especially receptive to decreased auto dependence and easy access to public transportation.

Pete Halter has found that empty nesters typically prefer to stay in their current neighborhoods but want to downsize. Halter uses the term "down-aging" to describe the group of older Americans who are not living the way that older people used to. They have much more active lifestyles and demand communities that accommodate busy lives.

The children of the baby boomers are as large a force as the baby boomers themselves—but, boosted by a wave of immigration, are more ethnically diverse. This cohort, sometimes called the echo boom, or Generation X, Y, or Z, is now moving through adulthood. In the early years of adulthood, affordability is usually important, and some experts predict that the demand for rental apartments will increase as the echo boom grows up and ages. There are broader implications as well. DMB's Herrington finds that this generation "does not enjoy the suburbs"—an important piece of information for large-scale develop-

ers whose projects evolve over a long period, and who will still be marketing when echo boomers reach their homebuying years. Moreover, as current baby boomers become empty nesters, they, too, will start to prefer more urban lifestyles. Herrington concludes that it will be important to develop more diverse, urban-style communities that provide the lifestyle that the next wave of consumers will demand.

Affordability

Most of the trends outlined so far spell new opportunities for developers, but housing affordability presents a difficult challenge. While those in the highest income brackets continue to make gains, lower- and middle-income households are losing ground. In 2001, the mean inflation-adjusted household income of the top quintile rose to $146,000, up from $143,000 in 1999. But the overall mean household income declined to $42,100, down from $43,100 in 1999.[14] During the same time period, the median price of a new home increased from $139,000 to $158,000 —far below the average price for housing in the most active and sought-after markets.[15] Affordability has reached crisis proportions in much of California, for example, where the average cost of a new home in some markets is approaching $500,000. Statewide, only 30 percent of households can afford a median-priced home.[16]

Affordability will be a continuing problem, not only for lower-income households but for the middle class as well. New strategies must be developed to create housing that is affordable and that meets the needs of middle- and lower-income households.

How Are Communities Changing to Meet Demands?

All these market demands translate to the need for different kinds of housing, neighbor-

Facing page: Baxter Village, a 1,033-acre (418-hectare) development in Fort Mill, South Carolina, combines single-family homes, townhouses, retail and commercial development, a school, a library, a medical campus, and more than 400 acres (162 hectares) of open space.

hoods, and development types. Frustration with traffic congestion is leading to more transportation options. The increasing costs of land and infrastructure are forcing developers to find more efficient ways to use these resources while maintaining quality of life for residents. Environmental concerns on the part of both residents and local governments are encouraging developers to preserve open space to enhance the desirability of their communities. A shortage of affordable housing is leading to partnerships focused on the creation of mixed-income housing developments.

Expanding Mobility Options

As suburban dwellers demand relief from traffic, some developers are responding. Transit-oriented development and pedestrian-friendly design are two ways to expand transportation options. Connectivity is another. Better linkages between developments are crucial for improved access. Developers and planners should consider how a given project will connect with both existing and future developments. Instead of designing isolated pods, developers should consider creating contiguous development. Connectivity can actually add value to a development. Street systems can be linked to enhance walkability, improve bike access, and support bus service. Better street connections can even help to reduce traffic on arterials. Civic spaces and commercial districts can augment rather than compete with adjacent developments. To protect linear habitats, natural landscapes can be extended through multiple developments. In some cases, it may be possible to protect natural features and views for the benefit of several developments. Infill projects typically take advantage of contiguous development in these ways, and some new greenfield development is beginning to do so as well.

Public transportation solutions work in some markets but not in others. In Arizona, for example, developers have had a difficult time

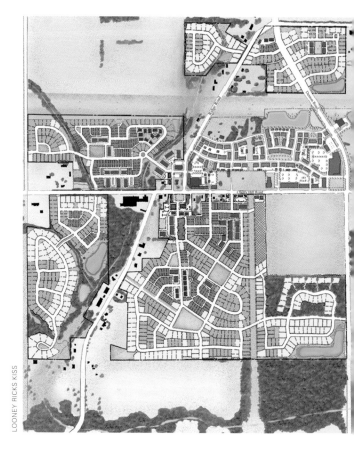

LOONEY RICKS KISS

getting the public—or the public sector—interested in transit. They find that consumers do not like buses, and that rail is too expensive to implement. Other regions are more amenable to transit solutions. Boulder, Colorado, for example, has developed an extensive network of bus routes that serves the town and student population. In most regions of the country, the majority of suburbanites no longer work in downtowns but in offices that are scattered throughout low-density suburban locales, which public transit cannot efficiently serve. Nevertheless, planning "transit-ready" development could make public transportation more workable in suburban districts.

Developers need to be aware of emerging transportation technologies, which may offer alternatives for mitigating traffic. The sometimes-maligned, sometimes-heralded Segway Human Transporter, for example, might soon become a viable alternative to

LOONEY RICKS KISS

driving for some trips. Although they may prove unsuitable for today's sidewalks or roads, Segways may ultimately take their place alongside bikes in bike lanes, or even in separate Segway lanes, thus changing how new streets are planned.

Using Infrastructure Efficiently

Reducing lot sizes has a major impact on infrastructure and other costs without necessarily decreasing demand or homeowner satisfaction. Reid Ewing, in *Best Development Practices*, notes that according to surveys, "residents are as satisfied with housing at six or seven units per acre [15 or 17 per hectare] as they are at three or four units per acre [seven or ten per hectare]."[17] Herrington has found that buyers are interested in higher density, but only if smaller lots are offset by first-rate amenities and public spaces.

Smaller lots decrease the amount of infrastructure and road surface required per resi-

dential lot. Narrowing street widths lowers the amount of road surface per lot even further. As jurisdictions have come to realize that the old roadway standards are unnecessarily expensive and add a sprawling, unappealing character to communities, many are beginning to reduce their standards for street widths. Smaller lots, narrower streets, and other ways of increasing the efficiency of development are discussed in chapter 3.

Using Open Space as an Amenity

Increasingly, what draws newcomers to a community is not just jobs, but also a high quality of life. Communities that preserve their scenic, ecological, and recreational assets have a competitive edge over those that do not. People are drawn to parks and to walking and biking trails, public squares and gardens, tree-lined streets and sidewalks, water features, and sports facilities. It is thus important to integrate open space into the overall plan for a community. It should provide a variety of natural and developed recreational spaces in readily accessible locations; it should also provide attractive views.

Open space can be an effective marketing tool. For maximum impact, attractive open space should be visible to prospective homebuyers. A park or other open area creates an appealing entrance for residents and guests, and can insulate homes from a busy road. Open space can add value throughout the community—or, where it is distributed among individual lots, can add value in the form of lot premiums.

Building for Diversity and Addressing Affordability

Designing a project to incorporate homes that appeal to several market segments strengthens initial and long-term marketability. In order to ensure that the communities will retain value over time, developers of large-scale, multiuse communities that are phased in over many years have learned to consider evolving needs. Other developers, who move from one small project to another, building their reputations as they go, should be just as concerned with long-term viability.

Building in flexibility to accommodate changing needs, maturing markets, and successive uses can help projects to avoid obsolescence in future years. At Disney's Celebration, for example, first-floor apartments can be reconfigured as retail space as the market evolves. At King Farm, in Maryland, the developer worked with the local government to keep the master plan flexible in terms of the number and types of units.

As prices escalate, higher densities, smaller lots, and smaller unit types are helping to keep housing more affordable. Including a mix of housing types is one strategy that developers are using to incorporate affordable housing into their projects. Mixing product types can be difficult, however. Production builders usually prefer to buy large tracts of raw land and develop large sections of similar housing types, taking advantage of economies of scale. Some smaller and medium-sized builders, however, have been successful at creating mixed-housing communities. And, although developers have found it difficult to attract financing for vertical mixing (housing above retail, for example), as more and more vertically mixed projects succeed, lenders are becoming increasingly willing to fund them.

Infill Development

Renewed interest in city living has brought about a rebirth of many inner-ring suburbs. (It has also created demand for more urban-style development in farther-out suburbs, where residents want some of the benefits of an urban lifestyle but in a greenfield location.) With infill development, the key to success is fitting the project to the location—and location is still the primary factor driving market potential.

Most infill and redevelopment activity occurs in neighborhoods located in the favored quarter, or most desirable section, of a metropol-

A high-density, mixed-use environment, the town center at Abacoa, in Jupiter, Florida, exemplifies many of the trends in suburban development today.

itan region. Historically, cities have evolved clusters of higher-income residents and high-end employment that, in combination, create a particularly desirable sector. Demand for locations in the favored quarter drives up land prices but also creates incentives for infill and redevelopment. Vacant lots that were skipped over during the first wave of development become choice building sites. Properties with steep slopes or oddly shaped lots attract developers who are willing to tailor plans to site constraints.

Locations outside the favored quarter also can attract infill and redevelopment. For example, areas along transportation corridors can benefit from their proximity to those facilities. Other areas that have a distinctive character can generate interest from niche markets. Some infill sites, however, still present impediments to cost-effective development: land assembly may be too difficult, or site conditions—such as the presence of toxic waste—may make development too expensive.

Recycling old buildings has also become a significant market niche in many districts, including older, inner-ring suburbs, where historic areas and buildings that offer unusual spaces and design features attract consumers and developers alike. Old buildings and neighborhoods are so desirable that many new projects emulate old ones. Witness the growing popularity of "loft apartments," which have the look and feel of rehabilitated old industrial buildings but are newly constructed. The ambience of old neighborhoods—their storied pasts, and their unique character—is a quality for which consumers are often willing to pay significant premiums. Infill opportunities are discussed in chapter 6.

Broad Trends

This book is about developing residential communities, but the best new developments are much more than that: they are places where people can build their lives—where they can make social connections, educate their children, obtain the goods and services that meet their daily needs, and even earn their livelihoods, all within the community.

Chapter 9 includes 11 case studies of some of the best recent suburban developments. They range from a tiny, 1.5-acre (0.60-hectare) infill project of 22 homes to a new, 4,000-acre (1,620-hectare) master-planned community that features 8,100 homes, nearly 1 million square feet (92,900 square meters) of office and retail space, and all the other elements of a full-fledged town. While the projects depicted are diverse in size, type, and location, they share several key characteristics and point to some broad trends occurring throughout the country:

- The ideal of "live-work-play-shop-learn" shapes the most interesting projects. People want to live full lives in their communities, not shuttle from one pod to another for work, relaxation, or family activities.
- The new urbanism has become a mainstream way of designing communities. While not all projects follow the new urbanist approach to the letter, most have moved in that direction, providing more walkable street patterns, more mixed uses, smaller residential lots—and, often, alleys to keep driveways, trash collection, and utilities off the more formal streets.
- Extra dollars spent on design and planning lead to savings in marketing. The best projects require very little marketing, relying instead on word of mouth and positive press.
- Higher density sells if it is well done. Buyers are open to trading large lots for high-quality public spaces and amenities. In fact, many busy homebuyers actually prefer homes without labor-intensive yards.
- Demographically mixed neighborhoods are a goal for many developers—and they

ADRIENNE SCHMITZ

work. An approach that integrates affordable housing into market-rate projects has succeeded in many places.

- Developers who plan carefully, and who understand and work with current residents, can often mitigate "not-in-my-backyard" responses.
- Jurisdictions are beginning to see the value of reduced street widths and rights-of-way. New standards improve aesthetics, enhance auto and pedestrian safety, and reduce costs. Although local governments often need to be persuaded that emergency vehicles can maneuver the narrower streets, many developers have found that this is a battle worth fighting.
- The public is beginning to demand greater environmental responsibility. "Green" approaches to development, including separate systems for potable water and new, environmentally friendly methods of stormwater management, are being used in many parts of the country with great success.

Developers and consumers alike are reaping the benefits of the more efficient use of resources.

All the case studies provide useful examples and lessons learned for developers of new residential communities.

Notes

1. U.S. Department of Commerce, Bureau of the Census, "Census of Population and Housing" (http://ceq.eh. doe.gov/ nepa/reports/statistics/tab1x4.xls [January 24, 2002]).

2. William Frey, "Census 2000," *Urban Land*, May 2002, 75–80.

3. William Frey, speaking at a ULI housing forum, March 1, 2002, Washington, D.C.

4. Leanne Lachman and Deborah Brett, "Commentary: A Nation of Niches; Real Estate's Demand Demographics," White Paper Number 7 (New York: Lend Lease Real Estate Investments, 2002).

5. U.S. Department of Commerce, Census Bureau, *Profile of the Foreign-Born Population in the United States: 2000* (Washington, D.C.: Census Bureau, December 2001).

6. Bureau of Labor Statistics, "Work at Home in 2001," News Release 02-107 (http://www.bls.gov/cps/ [March 1, 2002]).

7. National Association of Home Builders, "Characteristics of New Single-Family Homes (1987–2001)" (http://www.nahb.org/generic.aspx?genericContentID=374).

8. American LIVES, *Community Preferences: What the Buyers Really Want in Design, Features, and Amenities* (Oakland, Calif.: American LIVES, February 1999), 6.

9. Ibid., 21–25.

10. National Association of Home Builders Economics Group, *What 20th Century Home Buyers Want* (Washington, D.C.: National Association of Home Builders, 2001).

11. U.S. Department of Commerce, Census Bureau, "American Housing Survey, 1999 Detailed Tables for Owner-Occupied Housing Units" (http://www.census.gov/hhes/www/housing).

12. Dowell Myers and Elizabeth Gearin, "Current Preferences and Future Demand for Denser Residential Environments," *Housing Policy Debate* 12, no. 4 (2002): 642.

13. Ibid., 645.

14. U.S. Department of Commerce, Bureau of the Census, "Historical Income Tables" (http://www.census.gov/hhes/income).

15. National Association of Home Builders, "Housing Opportunity Index, Median Price and Interest Rates" (http://www.nahb.org/assets/docs/files/HOI_Historical_813200283323PM.xls).

16. California Association of Realtors, "Housing Affordability Index" (http://www.car.org/index.php?id=MzE2MzU=).

17. Reid Ewing, *Best Development Practices* (Chicago, Ill.: American Planning Association, 1996), 137.

2 Transportation Choices Enhance Livability

Most of all, suburbanites are tired of traffic—the congestion, the pollution, and the hectic and unfulfilling lifestyle it promotes.

—Lend Lease Real Estate Investments, *Emerging Trends in Real Estate 2000*

Why Worry about Traffic?

"Location, location, location" is still the mantra of real estate, but as traffic and congestion erode people's quality of life, the market has reevaluated the definition of a premium location. Since the 1950s, the success of the American suburbs has been driven by suburbanites' ability to have it all: an affordable, spacious home removed from the hubbub of the city—and, at the same time, easy access to jobs and amenities. The wildly successful product known as the suburbs has virtually recreated the American landscape and lifestyle, earning premium values for property owners and developers alike. And, thanks to an ever-expanding roadway system un-

Mockingbird Station, a transit-oriented village located at a Dallas Area Rapid Transit (DART) station north of Dallas, offers an urban lifestyle in a suburban setting. The development includes 211 luxury loft apartments, an office building, 220,000 square feet (20,440 square meters) of retail space, and an eight-screen independent film center.

COURTESY OF UC URBAN

matched anywhere in the world, American suburbs have flourished at an ever-increasing distance from the city core.

Initially, the interstate highway system, a growing number of regional freeways and tollways, and improved street networks facilitated and sustained the move out to the suburbs. However, in a shift that was probably unforeseeable in the mid-20th century, more Americans now live in suburbs than in cities. This enormous increase in the suburban population has put a great deal of stress on the existing transportation infrastructure. Public funding alone cannot solve the nation's transportation crisis; developers must be proactive by creating new suburban communities that apply proven techniques to the problem of congestion.

Despite the enormous effort and investment of the past half-century, America's roadway system has been unable to keep up with population growth and dispersion. A number of factors have contributed significantly to the current predicament: changing demographics and consumer habits, flaws in the design of suburban road systems, and inefficient land use patterns that separate land uses from one another.

Changing Demographics

The American population has grown enormously in the past half-century: from 151 million in 1950 to 281 million in 2000. More important, however, is the even more rapid growth in the rate of household formation. Households are key generators of travel, and

as they have gotten smaller over the past half-century (the average household now consists of fewer than 2.6 people), the same population is generating more trips. America today has about 100 million households—about 20 million more than if the rate of household formation had stayed at the 1960 level. Household formation alone has added more than 50 million vehicles to the road.

Changing Consumer Habits

The suburban lifestyle has changed consumer habits and behavior. The 1950s' infatuation with the freedom represented by the automobile has evolved into economic dependency. In all but a few cities, automobiles are virtually inescapable elements of American life. The average household includes approximately 1.77 licensed drivers and 1.77 automobiles. Car ownership rates in the United States are among the highest in the world, and the average cost of owning and driving an automobile is about $7,000 a year. In highly populated and dense areas such as New York City, the costs of owning, driving, and parking a car are exceptionally high: parking fees alone can be as high as $900 a month. As a result, car ownership rates in New York City are well below the national average; in 1990 there were only 0.6 cars per household.

Eastside Village, a mixed-use, transit-oriented development in Plano, Texas, is being developed by Amicus Partners. The project includes apartments, shops, offices, and structured parking for residents and commuters.

In contrast, vehicle ownership in sprawling metro areas such as Houston, Phoenix, and Atlanta is well above the national average, and is largely responsible for the growth in the number of vehicles in the past few decades. In Atlanta's 20-county metro area, for example, the number of motor vehicles increased by 178 percent between 1970 and 1995, compared with only a 134 percent increase in population. With the growth in the number of vehicles outpacing the growth in population, it is no wonder that regions such as Atlanta face seemingly unmanageable gridlock.

One important reason for these increases is the automobile's changing role in family life. Trips to the store, to school, and other errands account for an average of five trips per day per household—four times the number of trips to work. Traffic analysts and street-system designers never imagined this level of use, and it is not surprising that overcrowding is causing suburban road systems to fail.

The Design of Suburban Road Systems

Most suburban developments of the past half-century have featured a hierarchical street system, in which the grid network of intersecting streets—typical of cities—was replaced by a system of major arterials, complemented by cul-de-sac streets and smaller looping streets. This design communicated an important message to buyers about the privacy and security of these new, nonurban communities. It also saved developers precious upfront dollars by reducing the lineal feet of pavement, drainage, lighting, and landscaping while still meeting the projected capacity requirements. The collective assumption was that travel demand would not increase materially, and that neither the dispersion nor the capacity offered by a traditional street grid would be necessary. But with the unexpected growth in households and auto usage, the suburban model has often proven disastrous—and difficult to remedy.

During evening rush hour, home-bound commuters limited to a few points of access into their developments overwhelm suburban intersections on regional arterial roads. The arterials—which commuters use to reach the similarly overwhelmed highway system—are already over capacity. If land is available, it is sometimes possible to create a grid by adding more street connections, but such retrofits are politically difficult because residents resist the creation of new streets, and the encroaching traffic and reduced privacy that they bring.

Land Use Patterns

Suburban land use patterns are perhaps the most fundamental problem. The combination of outdated zoning ordinances and the tendency toward specialization in the development community has fostered the proliferation of single-use developments. Employment centers, retail venues, and residential districts are disconnected, and travel between them is impossible without an automobile. Whereas grocery stores and houses of worship were once located in neighborhoods so that they would be convenient to pedestrians, they are now located on major arteries and highways so that they will be convenient to drivers. The increase in VMT (vehicle miles traveled), which is growing twice as fast as the population, is caused less by commuting than by the four to six stops that people average each day for errands and activities.

Moreover, each destination requires parking. An average of five parking places are required to accommodate each automobile in a community: one space at home, one at work, and three others at theaters, shopping malls, doctors' offices, grocery stores, health clubs, parks, schools, and other destinations. Thus, each auto on the road requires about 1,600 square feet (150 square meters) of paved surface for parking alone—a highly expensive, unattractive, and inefficient use of land.

A shortage of affordable housing is among the effects of the separation of land uses. As

New Car-Sharing Options

Throughout the 1990s, Zurich, Berlin, Amsterdam, and a number of other European cities developed car-sharing organizations that provide access to cars on demand, without the responsibilities and costs of ownership. Now car sharing has arrived in the United States. Several new organizations—City CarShare, in the San Francisco Bay area; FlexCar, in Seattle, Washington; Portland, Oregon; and Washington, D.C.; and ZipCar, in Boston—are trying to change the way that Americans think about the private automobile.

Although environmentalists are credited with the original idea of car sharing, the practice has gained enough of a cachet to be regarded as a mainstream transportation option. Unlike earlier activists who focused on the evils of driving, car-sharing organizations embrace automobiles, offering on-call vehicles that are scattered around the city in "pods." Any member of a car-sharing organization can reserve one of the cars online, then walk to the closest pod, pick up a vehicle, and be billed for its use at the end of the month. The idea behind car sharing is to approximate the convenience of private ownership while spreading the large fixed capital costs of owning a car among many people.

Americans often underestimate the true cost of driving because they pay attention only to the variable costs, like gasoline and parking tickets. In fact, the majority of the costs—buying the car, insuring it, and maintaining it—are fixed, no matter how much or how little one drives. Many cars sit idle for 22 hours a day, but their owners are still paying for them. And because the marginal costs of using a car for a given trip are so small, car owners tend to think that it makes sense to hop in the car for every single trip in order to "get their money's worth" out of the upfront investment that they have already made by owning a car.

Car-sharing organizations, in contrast, convert fixed to variable costs: the large fixed costs of owning a vehicle are spread across many trips and many members, and members pay according to how much they drive, usually on the basis of both time and mileage. People who do not need to commute by car but still occasionally need to use one can save a great deal of money. Moreover, because the marginal costs of each trip are higher, members of car-sharing organizations tend to drive less over time, either by combining multiple errands into one trip or substituting other modes of transportation. A recent study by the Swiss Office of Energy Affairs found that car owners who switch to car sharing reduce their driving by an average of 30 percent over three years.

For private companies, car sharing can also be more cost-effective than maintaining a fleet of cars. Through membership in a car-sharing organization, employees can have access to cars for work purposes, such as visiting clients or attending off-site meetings. In addition, instead of driving their own cars to work, employees can commute to their jobs via public transit and then use car sharing as needed for errands and the like. For residential tenants, car sharing can be an alternative to owning a car—or to owning a second car. In addition to the cost savings, car sharing can enable households to choose different cars for different purposes.

Finally, car sharing can be developed as an amenity to increase the value of commercial and residential properties. Depending on the expected level of vehicle ownership in the target market, housing units can be provided with access to car sharing in place of a second parking space—or even in place of the first parking space.

Although Americans have become accustomed to the convenience of unlimited point-to-point mobility, traffic congestion has become epidemic. Car-sharing organizations recognize that people need access to cars, but they hold the promise of greatly reducing the number of cars that must be stored in a city; they may also encourage people to seek alternative modes of transportation. Because 20 or so people can essentially "share" a single vehicle, the amount of space devoted to parking could decrease, which could open up new ground uses in buildings and increase street-level activity. Car sharing won't bring about the end of the automobile, but it just might encourage Americans to drive less—and not to own the cars that they drive. ▲

Source: Gabriel Metcalf, deputy director, San Francisco Public and Urban Research Association.

---

land values and housing costs rise around employment centers, workers are forced to commute greater distances in order to find residential neighborhoods that they can afford. The result is longer commutes, higher transportation costs, less money to spend on housing, and reduced quality of life. This downward spiral for working families also creates costs for communities in the form of increased traffic, congestion, and infrastructure and service costs.

And the cost to consumers, in terms of time lost to commuting, is ever increasing. The average commuting time in America is about 25 minutes, but in many areas, figures of over

King Farm, in Rockville, Maryland, is a mixed-use transit-oriented development. The community provides shuttle service to the nearby Shady Grove Metro Station. The shuttle runs weekdays from 6:30 a.m. to 7:30 p.m.

an hour are not unusual. According to the 2000 U.S. Census, workers in the Houston metro area can expect one-way commutes of 29 minutes, in Atlanta 31 minutes, and in and around our nation's capital 35 minutes. Today, the average American spends 70 minutes per day in his or her car. In *Bowling Alone,* Robert Putnam describes the social costs of this time—and notes, for example, that most Americans spend more time each day in their car than with their children.[1] And suburban children spend increasing amounts of time strapped in their car seats.

Suburban land use patterns—and the resulting congestion on roads and highways—have jeopardized the viability of many suburban communities. Metropolitan areas with major traffic problems are losing their competitive edge in attracting new businesses and residents. Quality of life has become an increasingly important criterion in skilled workers' choice of location, and therefore in the success of business enterprises. Under the scrutiny of both workers and their employers, congestion and sprawl are more and more likely to be viewed as intolerable.

At the same time, consumers are reconsidering and revaluing older, closer-in neighbor-hoods and suburbs, in light of their appeal as full-service communities. Oakland, California, for example, is rapidly revitalizing because it offers easier access to San Francisco than do most Bay Area suburbs. Long-neglected Chicago neighborhoods along the "El" rail line are seeing dramatic redevelopment and increases in land prices. In overlooked mixed-use neighborhoods around Metro stations in and near the District of Columbia, reinvestment levels are unprecedented and property values are rocketing past those of gridlocked outlying suburbs.

What is the fate of suburban America, and of thousands of master-planned communities (MPCs)? Will the nation's growing transportation crisis make them obsolete? Are new communities doomed? Not necessarily.

The Future of Suburban Development

While America's love affair with—and dependence on—the automobile is alive and well, an interesting new phenomenon is also emerging. Americans feel increasingly isolated in their cars, and more and more cut off from their communities. Although the shift is more likely to take the form of a subconscious leaning than an open rebellion, one of the most interesting indications of its strength is where people go on vacation. People typically do not vacation in the suburbs but in some type of village or urbanized locale such as Paris, Venice, New York, or New Orleans. Even Disney World fits the village mold. All these places are mixed-use environments that are easy to navigate and that offer a high quality of life (as evidenced by their high property values), and visitors who do arrive by car park *once.* The problem is that American villages are too few, and have therefore become too precious and pricey. The challenge is to make the amenities typical of villages more broadly available, and at a variety of price points, styles, and locations. The future of suburban communities rests on their ability to meet this challenge.

Successful communities start first, and most profoundly, with the transportation system. Land use, density, architecture, cost structure, and marketability all flow from how people will move around the community: who can get where, and when, and how. Better access equals more value. The ability to move around comfortably and easily is as closely tied to land values as scenic views and lake frontage. Access and connections—on a national, regional, and local level—will drive the success and sustainability of communities in 21st-century America.

Accordingly, successful communities are now developing transportation strategies that are specifically designed to maximize national, regional, and local mobility. This effort begins with rethinking the best sites for growth, and extends to the careful evaluation of local master plans and infrastructure capacities.

Transportation Connections

National and regional connections are essential. Freeway interchanges have long been recognized as assets to a community. No less valuable for upcoming generations is access to the airport and to intercity bus and rail.

Airport connections are particularly critical, as both professional and recreational travel have become increasingly common elements of daily life.

Rail—whether commuter rail, light rail, or subway—is the rising star of metropolitan areas. Rail systems are found in only about 30 American cities, and in most of those, ridership is strong and demand threatens to exceed capacity. Unlike traditional city buses, light rail appeals to virtually every demographic group, including professionals and higher-income residents. And, to the extent the system allows, residents use light rail not only for commuting but also for entertainment and voluntary trips. The positive response to rail in the sprawling and auto-dominated cities of the West—such as Dallas, Denver, and Salt Lake City—has been particularly surprising.

Many cities are jumping into the fray, and are seeking federal funds (which now require a 40 to 50 percent local match) to initiate rail systems. Given the scarcity of federal funding, the competition is intense, and most cities must wait a decade or more for funding. As

The Burnham Building, a 121-year-old historic structure located in Irvington, New York, is situated directly across from the Metro North railroad station. The redevelopment of the 40,000-square-foot (3,720-square-meter) building, which had been vacant for ten years, yielded a public library on the first floor and 22 units of affordable housing on the upper floors.

a result, lower-cost alternatives are gaining support. One such system is bus rapid transit (BRT), rubber-tired vehicles that operate in a dedicated right of way, independent of auto traffic, and are therefore capable of faster travel times. Since the initial capital costs for BRT are significantly lower than those for rail systems, it is an attractive alternative for many communities. Moreover, the buses can be specially designed to be similar in character to rail cars—that is, to have sleek exteriors, nondiesel fuel systems, and a low floor, for easier entry.

Transit-Oriented Development

Because people seek to be close to transit— especially within walking distance of it—the presence of transit can dramatically shape land use. In fact, compact, mixed-use, transit-oriented developments (TODs), also known as transit villages, are popping up around stations all over the country and are routinely enjoying significant value premiums over similar products without transit access. In San Francisco, for example, TODs are the most valuable properties in the entire metro area, commanding an average premium of 20 to 25 percent over comparable nontransit sites.

The basic goal of transit-oriented development is to get as many people as possible living and working as close as possible to the transit connection; a TOD is essentially a zone of compact, mixed-use development in a 360-degree ring surrounding a transit hub. TODs are most successful when they incorporate a variety of uses and approach the status of "18-hour" communities. Hence, rail stations or busy shuttle or bus stops should not be surrounded with park-and-ride lots but with a comparatively dense "village" of people, with parking stored in structures or below grade.

TODs are rapidly gaining popularity nationwide, and several localities are making it a high priority to get plans approved and projects built. Washington's King County, for example, has recently completed three TODs (Northgate,

the Village at Overlake Station, and the Metropolitan Apartments) and has 30 more projects in the planning stages. Cities such as Washington, D.C.; Portland, Oregon; San Diego; and St. Louis are finding that mixed-use transit villages are an optimal way to reduce traffic and increase land value around existing train or bus corridors.

Even in the county of Los Angeles, an area defined by its love of the automobile, projects such as the Village Green are receiving national recognition for breakthroughs in transit-based housing. With 186 single-family homes, the Village Green—adjacent to the Sylmar/San Fernando Metrolink transit station—is one of the largest TODs in the Los Angeles area. Residents are just a short walk from the regional rail network and are able to leave their cars behind and commute to work. In the same complex as the transit station is a child care facility, Transit Tots, where parents can easily drop off or pick up their children as they travel to and from work.

Built in 1972, the Pleasant Hill BART (Bay Area Rapid Transit) station has long been a destination for commuters using the San Francisco Bay area's BART trains. While the station has been successful in providing access to buses, trains, and cabs, it has yet to develop into a community, complete with shops and services. Through an interactive planning process called a charrette, which involved more than 500 neighbors, community activists, BART commuters, and high-ranking public officials, a new plan has been put forth for the 18-acre (7.3-hectare) site. Under the Pleasant Hill BART Station Area Community Plan, the station and the surrounding area would be transformed into a five-block, mixed-use community that will include a civic center, office buildings, park space, townhouse units, and a public square—dubbed Station Square—at the heart of the project. Station Square will not only be a connecting point for BART commuters but will also include an ample

amount of retail space, outdoor dining, and widened, pedestrian-friendly sidewalks.

Whatever regional transportation connections a project enjoys, they are most beneficial when brought together in a transit center that is attractive, clearly designated, and convenient to local facilities such as shuttles, tour buses, taxis, bike stations, and parking. When the transit center is in the heart of the community, rather than isolated from other uses, it can be equally convenient for pedestrians and drivers. Although a transit center should offer adequate parking, that is not enough: it should also be surrounded by residential and commercial uses. Developers should lobby hard for the creation of such a facility; a transit hub establishes the entire community as a regionally valuable location and will pay dividends over the years.

Projects must reflect market realities, of course, but initiatives around the country offer substantial evidence of what works:

■ Multifamily housing of all types is generally successful at rail stations, whether the products are for rent, for sale, affordable, premium, or designed for seniors. (The lofts at Mockingbird Station, in suburban

Dallas, and Strathmore Park Condominums, in Rockville, Maryland, are priced at the top of those markets and have surpassed the developers' sales projections.)

■ Offices with high employee counts, such as government agencies, telephone-answering centers, and engineering firms, do very well. Employees avoid the expense and hassle of commuting and parking, and employers gain an additional tool to attract staff. (When Bell South consolidated its offices at a rail station in Atlanta, it received strong support from employees.)

■ Convenience retail, to reduce the driving that commuters often do on their way home from work at night, is also a key component.

Banks, child care, video stores, food stores, and dry cleaners, for example, do very well when they are convenient to transit nodes.

- Theaters, cinemas, and other entertainment venues benefit from the presence of transit riders and offer a great opportunity for shared parking. If commuter parking is used mostly during the day, sharing those spaces with restaurants and other evening venues can reduce overall development costs.
- Civic uses such as libraries, museums, post offices, and schools create traffic and demand throughout the day. They also differentiate a development and give it a civic identity and legitimacy that is crucial to success.

Research shows that people within walking distance (five minutes, or about one-quarter mile—0.4 kilometers) of a station are three to five times more likely to ride transit. This figure is not surprising, given the amenity value of a transit system: whether it is a big-city subway, a convenient bus system, or a cute local shuttle, people like the option transit provides.

Land values in and near TODs reflect both their higher density and the higher demand for pedestrian villages, where nonauto mobility is a prime amenity. While every project and every market is different, stabilized values for transit-village properties across the country are routinely at least 20 percent higher than for similar products a mile (1.6 kilometers) away. This pattern is consistent with evidence from around the globe: transportation access consistently determines value, and the highest property value is generated by the option of not using an auto.

The Pedestrian Village

Every European city has its historic square; the pedestrian area surrounding this square —"the village"—generally commands the area's highest property values. Introducing transit to the village extends the "pedestrian experience" of those who can get to the vil-

lage by transit and expands the high-value zone. Because autos are a basic element of today's communities, it is important to provide adequate, centralized, clearly designated parking in areas adjacent to the village. But once this accommodation is made for autos, then every street connecting to the village should be made friendly for pedestrians and bicycles. Creating pedestrian- and bike-friendly streets means more than just providing sidewalks: the goal is to create a high-quality village experience. Clear paths, adequate and attractive lighting, appealing landscaping, interesting street-facing architecture, buffers from traffic, and pedestrian-oriented intersections can make walking and biking enjoyable and can encourage residents to use them as the preferred modes of transportation.

Connections between neighborhoods are crucially important: walled and gated subdivisions prohibit walkability. Developments should not be self-contained islands, but should mesh with adjacent communities, linking streets, sidewalks, parks, and trails in ways that allow people to move freely. Connectivity not only brings better access, but also makes retail centers more viable, by increasing the number of residents that can support them.

When sidewalks run parallel to homes, homes have open porches, and common play areas are accessible to all neighborhood residents, community interaction is encouraged. Carefully designed small streets add character and value to a neighborhood; when arranged in grids, they also create a means of alleviating congestion. While pedestrian- and bike-friendly streets are more expensive to build at the outset, each such street will be viewed as an extension of "the village"—and will command price premiums to match. Through the use of new safety tools such as speed tables, residents can remain confident that although traffic flow may increase, it will remain at speeds appropriate to residential districts.

Local Transportation Systems

To make developments most successful, regional transportation systems should be interwoven with a system of local transit that "brands" the community. The system should be tailored to fit the lifestyle and travel patterns of residents, workers, and visitors alike. Whatever mode best suits the community should be considered: small customized buses and vans, "call-n-ride" services, electric vehicles, golf carts, trolleys, water taxis, ferries. The "fleet" should have a local identity; it should be entertaining and unique to the locale. What would San Francisco be without the trolleys?

Ten Keys to Walkable Communities

1. *A compact, lively town center (or many compact villages located within a larger development).* Buildings are close to the street, block lengths are short, merchants take pride in their properties, and a great variety of stores cater to local residents. The mix of uses includes a significant amount of housing.
2. *Many links to neighborhoods, including walkways, trails, and roadways.* All sidewalks are at least five feet (1.5 meters) wide, and most are buffered from traffic by planting strips, bike lanes, or on-street parking. Sidewalks are located on both sides of most arterial and collector roadways and on many neighborhood streets, are well maintained year-round, and are cleared of snow during the winter months. Most streets have access for handicapped users to and from each block in all directions.
3. *Low speed limits.* Many downtown and neighborhood streets have speed limits of 20 to 25 miles (32 to 40 kilometers) per hour. Most motorists obey traffic laws and yield to pedestrians.
4. *Neighborhood schools and parks.* Most children can walk or ride their bicycles to schools and small parks. Most residents live within one-half mile (0.80 kilometers)—preferably one-quarter mile

(0.40 kilometers)—of a small park or other well-maintained and attractive public space.
5. *Public spaces that attract a variety of users.* Public places, such as parks and squares, offer services and facilities that attract a variety of users, including children, teenagers, older adults, and people with disabilities. Public restrooms, drinking fountains, and seating are common in many parts of town, especially in the town center.
6. *Convenient, safe, and easy street crossings.* Pedestrians rarely have to travel more than 150 feet (45 meters) out of their way to reach a crossing. At an intersection, whether signalized or not, pedestrians rarely have to wait more than 30 seconds to start their crossing.
7. *An abundance of well-tended public space, green streets, and a heritage of trees.* Large shade trees line many streets, the development plan calls for planting strips with trees, homes are clustered to maximize green space, and natural trails and passageways are featured in many parts of town.
8. *Wise land use and transportation planning.* People understand and support compact development forms, infill development, mixed uses, economic diversity,

and the integration of affordable homes into most neighborhoods. Transit services connect centers of attraction, and transit runs frequently enough so that times need not be posted. All residents feel that they have a choice of travel modes to most destinations. Most people live within one-half mile (0.80 kilometers) of 40 percent of the products and services that they need.
9. *The celebration of public space.* Streets, plazas, parks, and waterfronts are festive, safe, convenient, efficient, comfortable, and welcoming. The community includes an appealing place to hold a parade, and many people take part in outdoor public events. Public space is well kept, respected, and loved.
10. *Lots of pedestrian activity.* People walk throughout the town. There is no such thing as "loitering." Lingering in town centers, schools, civic centers, waterfronts, and other public places is encouraged and celebrated. Street musicians and entertainers are welcomed. Children rarely need to ask parents for a ride to school, to parks, or to the town center. ▲

Source: Dan Burden, Transportation for Livable Communities Network, www.tlcnetwork.org.

Planning for Bus Lines

Designing an effective transit system—or, more likely, just a single bus line to serve a new community—requires a thorough understanding of the wants and needs of the residents and workers in that community. Unfortunately, until people actually move in, these wants and needs are purely speculative. But by then it may be too late: residents and workers may already have become accustomed to the same autocentric way of life that they had in their previous locale. Nonetheless, some rules of thumb can help a new transit line meet the needs of the more demanding market segments.

- Travel routes should be direct and follow a relatively straight path. Through-riders get impatient with the delays caused by deviations from the main route. Although such deviations will sometimes be necessary to serve a major destination (see the next point), they should be minimized on any single transit route.
- Major destinations such as workplaces, shops, schools, and medical facilities should be located within an easy walk of the transit line. The practical walking distance is one-quarter of a mile (0.40 kilometers) from a bus stop, and one-third to one-half of a mile (0.53 to 0.80 kilometers) from a rail stop. However, these guidelines apply mainly to residential areas. The more important the destination, the closer to a stop it should be. For example, a major hospital would not be well served at the very edge of the quarter-mile (0.40-kilometer) catchment area of a local bus line and probably should have a stop at its front door. If the hospital is already in place, the bus route may have to be diverted to serve it. If not yet built, the hospital's location should be planned to minimize diversions from the main bus path.
- Some streets may be too narrow for full-sized buses. It is best to anticipate during the planning stage where buses will travel so that the streets can be designed accordingly. Buses should not operate on streets that are so narrow that one vehicle must pull over to let an oncoming vehicle pass. A minimum lane width for full-size buses is ten feet (three meters); 12 feet (3.7 meters) is desirable. Thus, a two-lane street with parking on both sides would be a minimum of 36 feet (11 meters) wide from curb to curb; 40 feet (12 meters) would be desirable. Smaller buses may not require such wide streets, but such buses may not be appropriate for the anticipated volume of riders, or may not be operated by the transit agency providing the service.

Municipal officials are often concerned that small curb radii (i.e., sharp corners) will hamper buses. However, on streets where there is on-street parking, buses begin their turns some distance out from the curb, which negates the effect of a sharp corner. Charles Brewer, of Green Street Properties, has shown that on streets with parallel parking on both sides, a five-foot (1.5-meter) curb radius is sufficient for a full-size bus. According to Brewer's Law, "For every foot of increase of the starting/ending

---

Venice without the gondolas? Zermatt without the sleighs?

Developing a transit system is not for amateurs; it is an expensive and technically complex process. Given the coordination and level of expertise required, the recent emergence of transportation management organizations (TMOs)—groups dedicated to the design and support of transit services—is not surprising. Rapidly gaining in popularity, TMOs bring expertise in determining transit system feasibility, establishing transit systems, and managing funding and operations. Once a TMO consultant is hired, he or she will work with residents, existing transit agencies, local jurisdictions, principal employers, and landowners to assess existing demand and resources, determine what form the system should take, and decide how it should operate and be funded. Under the consultant's guidance, a nonprofit TMO will be established to act as the transit agency for the new service so that no one party is solely responsible. That said, those who stand to benefit from the system must be ready to make a substantial initial commitment to successfully launch a shuttle or other transit service.

Virtually all transit is subsidized by the returns on the resulting economic development. The beneficiaries of such returns should jointly invest in the system. Hence, to the extent that tax revenue increases, government should participate. Owners or developers of adjacent property where values are appreciating are also appropriate participants, as are employers who benefit from reduced parking costs

distance from the curb, the required curb radius is reduced by 3.415 feet (one meter), which is equal to 1.414/.414."

The ideal turning radius will prevent a vehicle from encroaching into the oncoming lane of the street that it is turning into. However, on a street with very low traffic volumes, the chance that a bus will encounter a vehicle in the oncoming lane is low as well, making it permissible, on occasion, for a bus to take up some of the space in the oncoming lane.

■ Frequency and the span of service (the first and last trip each day) are very important factors in attracting auto users to public transportation. The hours of 6:00 a.m. to 7:00 p.m., Monday through Saturday, are a suggested minimum; 5:00 a.m. to midnight every day is desirable. If a line will serve mainly workers and students, it is acceptable to start out with service only during peak hours. Such "commuter runs" generally operate from 5:00 a.m. to 8:00 a.m. and from 3:00 p.m. to 6:00 p.m., Monday through Friday.

With respect to frequency, the suggested minimum is every 30 minutes (as opposed to the one-hour frequency often used by transit systems). To attract the more demanding market segments, a frequency of every 15 minutes (or less, if patronage demands it) should be the goal. Of course, the more frequent the service and the longer the span of service, the better for passengers.

The problem is that both cost more money. And, because municipalities are loath to spend any more than they have to on public transportation, they tend to offer only the minimum in terms of frequency and span of coverage—and to attract only those patrons who are seeking minimal service. Municipalities fail to break through to higher ridership because the services they offer do not have the attributes that the more demanding travelers want.

■ Transfers can make or break transit ridership. In many cases, travelers cannot reach their destination on a single route, so the process of transferring to a second route should be fast, convenient, and comfortable. If service is offered less frequently than at ten- to 15-minute intervals on one or both routes, then transfer times should be coordinated whenever possible. Even then, the stops involved should be equipped with benches, illuminated shelters, and posted timetables—or better yet, real-time information displays.

Starting a brand-new transit route is a time-consuming endeavor that requires prior experience. If the community is located in or near the service area of an existing transit agency, that agency should be approached to initiate a service or to extend an existing line nearby. These rules of thumb can assist the community in negotiating the kind of service that best fits its needs. ▲

Source: William Lieberman, AICP, transit planning consultant.

and improved access for their employees. Increasingly, communities are using TMOs to sort out the value added by transit and to determine a funding strategy.

Disney World offers an excellent illustration of how transit can be transformed into an amenity. The area is so large that walking between the hotels and the various attractions, particularly on hot Florida days, is prohibitive. The challenge was to tie Disney World together and make it feel like a village, so that visitors wouldn't feel the need to drive. (Experience shows that once visitors get into a car, they tend to leave the area—which results in substantial retail "leakage.")

The answer was a transit system. A monorail circles the area and is the most visible transportation element. Buses and vans are the workhorses, and the water shuttles are key as well. But Disney did more. The company treated each transportation mode as a "ride" and made sure that the experience was fun. Vehicles are attractive and in top shape, and arrive frequently and dependably. Stations are easy to find and access, and the staff is friendly and helpful. The result? Driving is the more complicated, more expensive, and less convenient option. Visitors keep their cars parked and gladly use the shuttle systems.

Transit systems can and should be expanded as demand grows; but from the outset, they must be convenient, dependable, frequent, and affordable—even free, when appropriate. A common mistake is to underfund an initial experimental route, limiting the number and frequency of stops. When low use results, the enterprise is deemed a failure and abandoned. Especially in an existing community, transportation habits change slowly and must be given a reason, and reasonable time, to change. Since transit is competing with personal vehicles, it must somehow be made better than driving. Transit can compete, for example, with the financial cost of owning, parking, insuring, fueling, and maintaining a vehicle; it can also compete by reducing the time cost of travel delays and by reducing the emotional cost of driving in congested, intense traffic.

Boulder, Colorado, offers an example of a particularly successful transit system. Like other established communities, Boulder already had longstanding land use and transportation patterns. But in the mid-1990s, when traffic congestion and deteriorating walkability became critical political issues, the city of Boulder decided to take drastic measures. City lead-

ers approached the Regional Transit District (RTD) and requested a new shuttle service to connect two key pedestrian districts: the University of Colorado campus and the Pearl Street Mall. But the city didn't want the RTD's standard, 40-foot (12-meter) diesel bus. It wanted a smaller, van-style vehicle. And city leaders wanted the design and colors of the exterior, the interior upholstery, and the driver's uniform to coordinate. They wanted a CD player, and the freedom to pick the music that would be played. They wanted to pick the pricing, the route, and the schedule. And they wanted to name it "the Hop." Despite the unconventional requests, the RTD agreed to fund half the operating costs of the experiment if the city would fund the other half.

The customized system, so clearly responsive to the community, has been an unbridled success. Within six years, Boulder had expanded the system to include the Skip, the Jump, the Leap, and the Bound, all connecting different districts of the city. Not only has the program

NextBus

NextBus uses the latest technology to solve an age-old problem: waiting for the bus to come. One reason that more people do not take public transit is that it is considered unreliable: buses often fail to arrive when they are scheduled to, and passengers have no way of knowing whether they have time to run home or to grab a cup of coffee—or whether they should find an alternative means of transportation. Relying on a high-tech system that makes use of global positioning technology, NextBus shows passengers when the bus will actually arrive, instead of just showing them when it is scheduled to.

To build the historical data on which the system is based, each bus is equipped with a global positioning system (GPS) tracker

and monitored for four to six weeks. The vehicle's locations are transmitted (via cellular digital packet data) to a receiving computer, which builds a database that compares the actual to the scheduled arrival times. Once the initial monitoring period is over, the current GPS tracking information for each bus is sent to the central computer as the bus travels along its route; the arrival time is predicted on the basis of the relationship between the bus's current position and the historical data collected during the monitoring phase.

The projected arrival time is displayed on a sign at the bus stop and is continuously updated. Passengers can also obtain the predicted arrival times through other means: on the Internet (at www.NextBus.com), and via Internet-enabled phones, two-way mes-

saging units, and wireless-enabled personal digital assistants.

So far, NextBus seems to be a success. Systems are currently operating in more than ten areas nationwide, including Arlington, Virginia; Rehoboth Beach, Delaware; and San Francisco, California. NextBus has won many awards and has been recognized as a leader in both the transportation and Internet industries. Most important, it has made the transit experience more reliable, decreased passengers' exposure to harsh weather conditions, increased passengers' control over their arrival and departure times, and reduced the frustration of dealing with delays. ▲

Source: Melissa Weberman, Urban Land Institute.

"The Bound" is one of Boulder, Colorado's customized transit vehicles, which run routes every six to 20 minutes, from 7 a.m. to 6 p.m., weekdays. Using a fleet of vehicles, Boulder was able to create a grid system of routes instead of the traditional hub-and-wheel arrangement still in use in many areas. The grid system enables riders to change buses efficiently, without having to go into the downtown to wait at a central bus station.

succeeded in attracting riders, but neighborhoods served by the system have also seen significant increases in land prices—which are certainly due, in part, to the convenience and cachet of being part of such a pedestrian-oriented community.

New Haven, Connecticut, has also recognized the advantage of a local transit system that has a distinct identity. As part of its Clean Cities program, the U.S. Department of Energy recently awarded New Haven $1.2 million to create a fleet of trolleys to connect the city's downtown employment centers to retail and housing. The four 22-passenger trolleys are reminiscent of those that served New Haven in the 1950s, though they run on rubber wheels and are completely electric powered. Rides are completely free, and are paid for primarily through parking fees and local business fees. United Illuminating, for example, will pay approximately $56,000 a year to run a route from the parking facility at the New Haven Coliseum to the Green, the center of downtown activity.

Planning Transportation First

New master-planned developments have the advantage of being able to plan pedestrian and transit zones from the beginning. This brings them a number of advantages:

- *Land use and transportation can be optimally integrated.* From the outset, connections for pedestrians, bikes, autos, and shuttles can be mapped out in an efficient, easy-to-use pattern. Optimal access can be planned for key roads and regional transit nodes. The transportation center can be strategically sited in the heart of the community, ensuring its success and adding value to surrounding properties. To further add to the potential of the transit center, it can be connected to existing communities, improving access for residents of those communities.

- *Commercial districts can be created from the outset.* A shuttle system can be developed, which will effectively increase the number of residents located within a ten-minute trip of the transit center and will thereby increase the viability of the mixed-use development. When communities establish transit management systems, the jurisdictions within which they are located often reduce parking requirements and allow shared parking, which can lower construction costs and further increase the feasibility of the MPC's commercial development.

- *The overall development pattern can be more compact and efficient.* Buildings can be placed closer together, enhancing connectivity. When development is compact, business, residential, and commercial uses all gain convenient access to amenities. Residential structures can be designed in such a way as to protect privacy. Resort communities, where land is scarce, have demonstrated the attractiveness of such a development pattern. Vail, Colorado, for example, has a compact land development program offering premium, single-family, and multifamily residences interspersed among shops, offices, and community services, all linked by a free shuttle—an arrangement that leaves land available for additional development and profit. The same fundamentals of transit-oriented development can be applied to nonresort communities to make them distinctive and successful.

- *A strong village identity can be established to raise property values.* As MPCs struggle to differentiate themselves to consumers, a pedestrian identity adds significant perceived value. People will willingly pay premiums to be part of a community where they feel they belong, where they know their neighbors, where they feel safe, and where they can walk or bike to a town center. Although suburban developments in virtually every metropolitan area run Norman Rockwell–inspired ad campaigns that attempt to capitalize on the pervasive

desire for this way of life, a true system of connectivity for walking or shuttling around the neighborhood is far less common. When planners from Forest City Enterprises designed the master plan for the redevelopment of the 4,700-acre (1,902-hectare) former site of Denver's Stapleton Airport, they started with the transportation system. They fought for a light-rail station in a central spot, with easy access to the site's residential, retail, and commercial districts. They designed the street system to accommodate a free shuttle to the residential district and the "main street" development. Bike trails; wide, pedestrian-friendly sidewalks; and a hierarchy of predominantly two-lane streets were all carefully planned. The result, despite the formidable physical distances associated with such a large property, is a highly connected new neighborhood where residential sales and prices have topped the market and beat all projections.

- *Transit construction costs can be minimized.* Even if sidewalks, paths, and transit are implemented in a later phase, anticipating

West Ridge Market, in Minnetonka, Minnesota, is a 63-acre (25-hectare) mixed-use community with 418 housing units and 256,000 square feet (23,780 square meters) of retail space. The development includes a 500-car park-and-ride, which provides express and local bus service to and from major employment and retail locations.

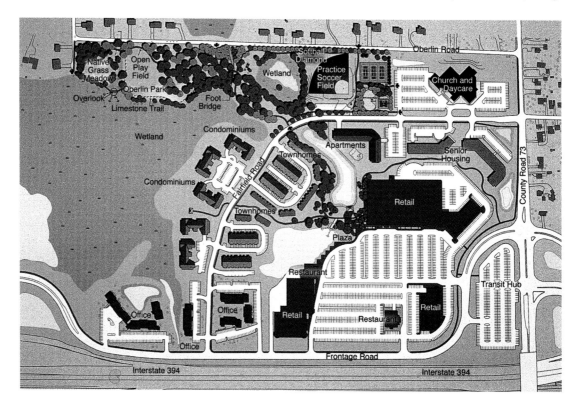

the connections can minimize retrofitting and construction costs. Jurisdictions commonly require a project to be of a certain size before they will implement all the connections and transit systems. Nonetheless, planning for transit upfront alleviates the need for expensive retrofitting and allows a more cost-effective phasing plan.

Summary

Mobility is a growing priority for consumers—and a growing source of frustration. The auto-oriented infrastructure built over the past half-century is expensive to maintain, let alone expand. At the same time, auto usage is skyrocketing as Americans seek more flexibility and mobility than ever before.

Transportation access has always been important to real estate values. Locations with convenient access to freeways, airports, and regional rail systems will increasingly command a premium. But proximity without access is useless; thus, transportation systems and land use must be carefully planned and integrated.

Beyond connecting to the regional systems, developers can add value to their projects by creating pedestrian-oriented communities. People pay a premium to live in neighborhoods and villages where they can live, work, shop, earn, and play without auto dependence. Walkability is enhanced by wide sidewalks, convenient and safe street crossings, and pedestrian connections between neighborhoods and communities. When such an environment is layered with transit options, demand and property values increase even more. Establishing transit systems is expensive and complicated, but the investment can bring substantial returns. TMOs are often used to organize, fund, and operate shuttle, bike, ridesharing, and similar systems. Developers should consider partnering with local jurisdictions and other landowners to add a transit amenity to their projects.

Whether located on infill sites or in outlying communities, the most successful communities of the future will be those that reflect an understanding of the dynamics and value of mobility, and of the formidable premiums that residents are willing to pay to recapture their commuting time, and to feel reconnected in a sprawling nation.

This chapter was written by Marilee Utter, president, Citiventure Associates, Denver, Colorado.

Note

1. Robert D. Putnam, *Bowling Alone: The Collapse and Revival of American Community* (New York: Simon & Schuster, 2000).

The redevelopment of the 4,700-acre (1,900-hectare) former Stapleton International Airport, in Denver, is the largest project of its kind: Stapleton will eventually include 12,000 residences and 17,000,000 square feet (1,580,000 square meters) of office and retail space. To ensure that the new community will be well connected, pedestrian-friendly, and cost-efficient, the developer, Forest City Enterprises, planned for transportation first.

3 More Efficient Use of Land and Infrastructure

Since their creation, the suburbs have been evolving and changing. From bedroom communities to edge cities, the trend has been toward more complex and complete places. In the past two generations, employment and retail have followed housing to the suburbs. Now, market forces are diversifying the mix of housing types and calling for alternatives to the car. Walkable neighborhoods and urban centers are emerging as socially desirable, environmentally sound, and economically profitable. The once segregated places of the suburbs are beginning to be connected by strategic mixed-use projects on infill and redevelopment sites. A network of centers that are urban in the best sense of the word is beginning to overlay and transform the suburban landscape.[1]

—*Peter Calthorpe and William Fulton,*
The Regional City

As the suburbs continue to push outward, regions such as Atlanta must plan more efficiently. Continuing the development trends of the past half-century will only ensure that traffic remains at a standstill.

As metropolitan areas continue to grow, the efficient development of land and the efficient use of new and existing infrastructure are becoming high priorities for purposes of sustainable development as well as cost efficiency. It is anticipated that by 2025, the U.S. population will have increased by 63 million, which translates into approximately 30 million new dwelling units of all types—including single-family homes, apartments, condominiums, and other niche products, both attached and detached. Moreover, household formation is changing as well; whereas in 1990 the average size of a household was 2.68 persons, by 2025 that figure will have decreased to 2.10. This significant decrease in household size reveals that while the population will continue to grow, housing options will have to adapt.

Some of the population growth will occur in urban areas, but the suburbs will continue to grow as well. Despite criticisms that the suburbs are economically stratified, socially isolated, culturally boring, and automobile dependent, suburbs still offer many people the American Dream of owning a new home. Thus, suburbs will remain highly attractive when people choose where to live, work, and play. And, as suburbs change to reflect social, economic, and demographic trends, it will be necessary to use suburban land and infrastructure more efficiently than ever before, in order to control costs, to accommodate a greater diversity of community and housing types, and to help achieve economic and environmental sustainability. This chapter examines the reasons for improving the efficiency of development, and describes some successful techniques for doing so.

GEOFFREY BOOTH

The suburban land-scape is changing as baby boomers retire and demand new and innovative housing alternatives. At Soli-vita, Avatar's 6,500-unit active-adult com-munity in Poinciana, Florida, the 105,000-square-foot (9,750-square-meter) village center and other amenities were built with the needs of res-idents well in mind.

When development becomes more efficient and more cost-effective, everybody wins—consumers, local governments, and private developers alike. What does it mean to use suburban land and infrastructure more effi-ciently? In terms of land planning and devel-opment, efficiency is generally achieved by increasing density, mixing land uses, and making more intensive use of existing infra-structure, including streets, utility systems, parks, open spaces, and public facilities. Unfor-tunately, development trends of the past half-century suggest that we still have a long way to go toward improving the efficiency of land and infrastructure use. In 1950, 70 million Americans lived in the nation's urbanized areas, which covered approximately 13,000 square miles (33,670 square kilometers). During the next 40 years, as land use patterns and land use per capita changed, the population living in urbanized areas more than doubled, while the land area occupied by that population quintupled—to more than 60,000 square miles (155,400 square kilometers).[2]

Why Increase Efficiency?

Many factors compel real estate developers, planners, designers, and public officials to seek more efficient use of land and infrastructure

—economic, financial, political, social, and environmental considerations all play a part.

Changing Suburban Demographics

As noted in chapter 1, today's suburban pop-ulations are older, more socially and ethnically diverse, and comprise a broader range of household types. Moreover, suburbanites' expectations are greater: they demand hous-ing, amenities, and services that fit their specific needs.

Seniors are more often inclined to age in place. Instead of retiring to Florida, many of the nation's empty nesters are choosing to stay close to family and friends, and are remaining in their primary home or moving to a nearby active adult retirement commu-nity. Because empty nesters require less household space, and perhaps own a vaca-tion home, they may prefer smaller homes —possibly a product type not typically found in traditional suburbs, which are predominantly single-family in character. The result is increas-ing demand for alternative housing types—whether multifamily, multiplex, assisted living, granny flat, or carriage house. To address the need for such alternatives, suburban planning commissions are increasingly allowing zon-

Ford's Landing, in Alexandria, Virginia, overlooks the Potomac River and was built on one of the last developable pieces of land in Old Town Alexandria. Featuring 136 townhouses on seven acres (2.8 hectares), the development caters to the affluent.

BOB NAROD

ing changes that permit higher densities and the adaptive use of existing buildings, and that encourage infill development and the redevelopment of underused parcels.

Similarly, the increasing percentage of minority and immigrant households in the suburbs creates significant demand for new housing types, including products that can accommodate multigenerational families, and live/work spaces that provide opportunities for start-up businesses, niche retail, and services.

Land Economics in Existing Suburbs

As metropolitan areas continue to expand outward from downtowns, it is becoming less and less desirable to work in a central business district. And, as traffic congestion and commuting times increase, many homebuyers are choosing to live closer to work. At the same time, many companies are moving near their suburban employees to more effectively compete for labor. As a result of such trends, commercial land values and rents in many suburban areas are equal to or approaching downtown rates.

New suburban commercial development broadens opportunities for local tax revenues, but it also places greater demands on infrastructure. To meet the needs of new devel-

opment—in particular, to manage transportation demands—existing infrastructure will have to be improved and upgraded. In some cases, public transit may need to be added.

Desirable, developable land is increasingly scarce and expensive. According to the conventional wisdom in the real estate community, "the best land is already developed, and only the marginal and unsuitable land remains." In mature suburban communities, particularly in the metropolitan areas of the Northeast and the West Coast, there is indeed a scarcity of developable land. What remains undeveloped typically includes wetlands or steep topography, or is inaccessible, geologically unsuitable, protected open space or habitat, or fragmented by multiple ownership. As the continued demand for new development drives up the price of the few remaining developable sites, developers may feel pressured to develop the remaining sites at higher densities than they are zoned for, or to develop extremely expensive single-family homes.

As suburbs have matured, land acquisition and site development costs have risen as a percentage of total project costs for both housing and commercial development. In some parts of the country, land price can easily account for 40 to 45 percent of the cost of a new residence, versus 10 to 20 percent where land is more readily available. Typically, when developers are forced to pay more for land, they can build homes only for a limited number of high-income residents. The result is unmet demand for housing for first-time buyers, empty nesters, people with low or moderate income levels, and people who require assisted-living facilities.

Today's suburban communities are filled with examples of inefficient land and infrastructure uses—from the construction of culs-de-sac and large-lot homes to the squandering of water resources and the creation of gated communities. From a business perspective, it is necessary to use suburban land and infrastructure more efficiently in order to address the economic pressures caused by land scarcity. Well-coordinated planning and development strategies can alleviate these economic pressures.

Cul-de-Sac Streets

Culs-de-sac are an inefficient use of land and roadway dollars. Once the trademark of the suburban realm, culs-de-sac are now being criticized for contributing to growing traffic problems. They force everyone out onto crowded arterial roads, creating more con-gestion. At the same time, residents are locked within their cul-de-sac subdivisions, with little or no access to the surrounding community by foot, bicycle, or public transit.

Instead of culs-de-sac, planners are now promoting connectivity: more gridlike street patterns with shorter blocks, many intersections, and narrower streets, usually lined with side-walks. (Narrower streets slow traffic and increase the safety and comfort of pedestrians.) Planners in Olympia, Washington, have outlawed culs-de-sac unless there are topographical restraints such as wetlands or bodies of water. Baltimore County, Maryland, is trying to balance the number of culs-de-sac and grid streets by permitting culs-de-sac only where there are topographical restraints or if they "provide a balance of street elements."[3]

Utilities

Higher-density and infill development allow for the more efficient use of existing utilities, including sewer and water. Although it seems obvious, a recent study confirmed that the costs associated with providing sewer and water service are higher for large-lot homes than for small-lot homes, because of the longer distribution mains needed to link the

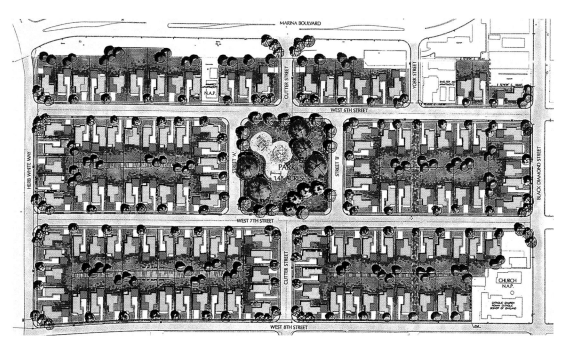

A key element in the revitalization of Pittsburg, California, Marina Walk offers 120 single-family homes and a street system in the traditional grid pattern. A neighborhood park serves as the focal point for the 23-acre (9.3-hectare) development, which is located on a former brownfield.

lots. Currently, less compact areas pay less than the true cost of services.[4] Communities are rectifying this imbalance by increasing the developer's share of the cost of new service lines—a strategy that is expected to help promote higher-density development.

The efficient management of water resources is a critical need for many communities. Across the country, state and local governments are stopping projects in their tracks because they are unable to provide sufficient water to support the development. In January 2002, California passed a law requiring developers of projects with more than 500 residential units to prove that water can be supplied to the development for at least 20 years, with government approval of the project contingent on the developer's ability to provide such proof.[5] While most common in western states, water shortages have hit the East as well: cities in Massachusetts, Maryland, and North Carolina have rationed water and limited development. Water resource management will affect every suburban developer over the coming decades.

Gated Communities

Once the bastions of the elite, gates and walls now surround even middle- and lower-income developments. Although some residents believe that the gates deter crime, this theory has not been proven. In fact, gates may encourage crime by lulling residents into a false sense of security. Moreover, gates slow the response time of police and other emergency vehicles. In a more general sense, gating isolates segments of a community from one another and does nothing to address the social problems that the gates are attempting to shut out. While some developers believe that buyers prefer gated communities, others believe the demand is developer driven.

Local governments may welcome gated communities because such developments do not require public funds to build or maintain infrastructure, and may not even require emer-

gency services. However, there is also a growing backlash against gated developments. Local governments can ban gated communities by invoking local police powers; more often, however, planning commissions simply make the approval of a development contingent on the removal of gates and walls from development plans.[6]

Broader Market Opportunities

By using land and infrastructure more efficiently to reduce project development costs, developers can provide residential opportunities for a broader cross section of the population. They may begin by seeking zoning changes to increase density in selected districts. Higher density will drive down the lot-to-home cost ratio that can price middle-income buyers out of the market. For example, a higher-density single-family zoning district, with 5,000-square-foot (465-square-meter) lots, could be amended to allow for medium-density attached units—such as townhouses at six units per acre (14.8 per hectare)—and still be compatible with a surrounding single-family community.

In mature suburbs, particularly those with commercial uses, infill sites can also be used for more intensive development. Infill development is often especially suitable for housing for seniors, students, and moderate-income households, and can also accommodate housing products designed for empty nesters downscaling from larger homes. Infill sites are often quite attractive to homebuyers and renters because they provide convenient access to employment, shopping, entertainment, and services. Where all or part of an infill site is classified as a brownfield, federal and state monies may be available to reduce the developer's costs and liability. (See chapter 6 for further discussion of brownfields.)

To make infill projects feasible, developers must often seek density increases. But, as is evident at planning commission meetings, approvals for higher densities do not come

Newington, which served as the Athlete's Village during the 2000 Olympic Games in Sydney, Australia, has received more awards than any other project in the country. Highly regarded for its well-planned central parks and strong sense of community, the development houses over 5,000 people in a mix of housing types.

easily in most established suburban communities. To persuade planning commissions of the need for increased density, the developer should be prepared to discuss public policy and site-specific benefits and to explain how potential negative impacts, such as increased traffic volume, will be addressed. Often, the community's main concern is that greater demands will be placed on local services, particularly public schools. In response, developers should prepare municipal impact studies that quantify the potential effects of the development. Fiscal impact studies are also helpful in persuading the neighborhood and the planning commission of the project's potential for beneficial impact; for example, the developer could propose that tax any revenues that exceed the cost of extending municipal services to the project be earmarked for a "pet project" of the existing neighborhood.

The preservation of open space is the universal mantra of suburban planning commissions and neighborhood associations. The desire for open space manifests itself in a variety of ways, including intense opposition to the development of remaining greenfield sites. Despite community resistance, however, parklands and other open spaces are, in fact, often underused, creating havens for criminal activity and causing municipalities to expend unnecessary funds on upkeep. To ensure that excess open space is put to best use, devel-

opers should be aware of both development industry standards and planning agency standards for open-space acreage per capita.

Increasingly, developers are proposing mixed-use developments as a means of providing a range of commercial, residential, retail, and civic benefits while minimizing the impact on the community. In addition to impact fees and proffers, the standard methods for collecting funds for the provision and maintenance of infrastructure, municipalities are now trying linkage fees. Linkage fees are paid by the developer on the basis of density: as density increases, so do the fees.

Smart Growth: Changing Ideas about How Communities Should Grow

Smart growth is now a recognized term among members of the planning and development community. Although it takes many forms, smart growth is, in its essence, economically sound, environmentally responsible, and supportive of community livability. Thus, it is growth that adds value and enhances quality of life.

The smart growth agenda, as articulated by ULI and other organizations, is influencing land use policy makers and regulators at all levels of government. At the federal level, land use planning and quality of life are gain-

Boston's Urban Ring

The Urban Ring is a planned 15-mile (24-kilometer) transit line that will wrap around Boston and connect its four rapid-transit lines, more than half the city's bus routes, and all its major highways. Designed to provide access into and out of downtown, the "T"—Boston's mass-transit system—is often likened to the spokes of a wheel. Planners hope that, as Route 128 did for the suburbs in the mid-20th century, the Urban Ring will connect the "spokes" —and thereby ease congestion in the core, improve circumferential access, and stimulate development in inner-ring suburbs. In the past few decades, most transit projects have been designed to improve service from the suburbs to downtown, and have generally taken the form of costly commuter rail, and its associated parking garages. But the construction of the Urban Ring represents a shift in emphasis and intent—to better serve users living and working in the city and older inner suburbs.

When built, the Urban Ring will focus development on brownfields in the working-class neighborhoods and industrial centers of Boston, Chelsea, Everett, Cambridge, and Somerville, and in income-diverse Brookline. Even without the development of the

Urban Ring, the corridor through which it will pass is projected to grow three times faster than the Boston metropolitan region as a whole: between 1990 and 2025, the population is expected to grow 34 percent, versus 11 percent for the region; and employment is expected to rise 81 percent, versus 26 percent for the region.[1] According-ing to Jay Wickersham, director of the Massachusetts Environmental Policy Act Office, the Urban Ring "epitomizes smart growth by putting infrastructure where it benefits our cities, and thus easing development pressures on natural resources outside of the city."[2] By building on existing infrastructure, the Urban Ring will foster growth in more central, already developed areas rather than on greenfields. By promoting the cleanup and redevelopment of brownfields and underused parcels and by revitalizing industrial areas in the inner suburbs, the Urban Ring will also help preserve open space in the outer suburbs. Within the Urban Ring are 3,674 acres (1,486 hectares) of vacant or underdeveloped land, much of which is in close proximity to already developed activity centers.

In older inner cities and suburbs, small blocks, limited parking, and high densities

CONSERVATION LAW FOUNDATION/ INFOGRAPHIC: DG COMMUNICATIONS; AMANDA WAIT

The Urban Ring, in Boston, Massachusetts, will connect existing bus and train lines the way that the rim of a wheel connects its spokes. It will link major employment centers (MIT, Boston University Medical Center, Longwood Medical) with neighborhoods such as Roxbury, Chelsea, and Cambridgeport.

encourage walking and the use of public transportation. In 1990, car ownership in the ring was 0.8 per family, versus 1.37 in

ing priority. At the state level, policies and funding are being used to discourage suburban sprawl, redevelop brownfields, and rebuild urban centers. Many states are purchasing, or assisting conservation groups in purchasing, uninterrupted open spaces. Regional planning, where it is effective, focuses on directing growth to locations that have adequate or underused infrastructure capacity. Strategies used to accomplish this goal include interlocal agreements, the transfer of development rights (TDRs), regional transportation planning, regional impact reviews, land buildout analyses (to determine appropriate sites for specific types of development), and

funding that encourages concentrated and intentional development patterns rather than sprawl. However, it is at the local level that smart growth policies have their greatest impact, in the form of land use planning that is designed to increase the efficiency of land and infrastructure use.

As communities' priorities shift to include quality-of-life issues such as traffic congestion, air and water quality, and the preservation of open space, many localities are responding with initiatives designed to improve livability. Atlanta, for example, as part of its Livable Centers Initiative (LCI), recently awarded grants

the region and 1.77 in the nation; 43 percent of households in the ring had no vehicle.[3] Household income was also almost 40 percent lower than that of the region as a whole—$28,678 versus $46,583.[4] Not surprisingly, residents are heavily dependent on transit, and one in eight trips made on the system starts or ends within the ring. Moreover, transit users whose trips begin or end within the ring transfer almost twice as many times as users in the rest of the metro area (an average of 1.3 transfers, versus 0.7).[5]

Because of the complexity and size of the project, the planning process for the Urban Ring has been regional. The ring will pass through six communities, all of which have agreed to cooperate in a regional planning initiative launched by the signing, in October 1995, of the Circumferential Ring Regional Planning Compact. In an area traditionally known for its localism and municipal independence, this coordination of planning efforts is unprecedented, especially since the six communities have differing goals and needs. In Chelsea, Everett, and Somerville, largely working-class localities with many industrial sites, the construction of the Urban Ring will catalyze much-needed infill

development on the acres of abandoned brownfields, and will bring economic growth without increasing congestion and pollution. Boston, Cambridge, and Brookline see the project as a way to relieve congestion in already developed employment centers.

An effective smart growth program includes more than just transit. Local planning oversight and design guidelines are needed to direct development in a pedestrian-friendly, civic-minded, and environmentally sustainable way. Through the 1995 compact, the six cities involved agreed to work together to propose, evaluate, and plan a system that will support economic development and other planning initiatives. For example, city planning boards can use zoning and other regulations to encourage transit—by requiring employers to facilitate transit ridership, allowing higher densities near transit stations, establishing transit-oriented design standards and overlay zoning districts, and placing limits on parking, among other strategies.

The development of the Urban Ring presents metropolitan Boston with an opportunity to grow in an environmentally and socially responsible way. For years, the

inner suburbs have been neglected as the region has worked on improving access to the suburbs via highways and commuter rail. Looking toward the future, Boston is now focusing its resources on a project that not only encourages development and efficiently uses existing resources, but also connects development and resources in a sustainable way. ▲

Notes

1. U.S. Department of Transportation, Federal Transit Administration, Massachusetts Bay Transportation Authority, *MIS Final Report: Major Investment Study of Circumferential Transportation Improvements in the Urban Ring Corridor.* (Washington, D.C.: U.S. Department of Transportation, Federal Transit Administration, and Massachusetts Bay Transportation Authority, July 2001), 6-2.

2. Anthony Flint, "Urban Transit Project on Track," *Boston Globe,* November 19, 2001, B1.

3. Boston data from Boston Metropolitan Planning Organization (MPO) Transportation Plan, 2000–2025. National data from Patricia Hu and Jennifer Young, "Summary of Travel Trends," in *1995 Nationwide Personal Transportation Study* (Washington, D.C.: U.S. Department of Transportation, December 1999).

4. Boston MPO Transportation Plan, 2000–2025.

5. Ibid.

to 22 communities. LCI provides communities with seed money to promote "quality growth in the region by encouraging greater mobility and livability within existing employment and town centers, thereby using the infrastructure already in place instead of building anew."[7]

Smart growth at the local level is often a way to achieve a compromise between the developer and the community. In some jurisdictions, development and zoning regulations are being rewritten to facilitate projects that contribute to the community's fiscal, environmental, and social well-being. For example, by encouraging cluster and zero-lot-line devel-

opment, planning commissions can invite a wider range of housing types into the community while creating or preserving amenities such as open space. Connecticut's general assembly recently required all municipalities to consider using clustered development in their conservation and development plans.[8]

In exchange for higher residential densities, planning commissions get a slightly higher degree of site control. And, thanks to the lower site development costs that are typical of cluster development or (nonvertical) higher-density development, developers achieve better financial returns. Expanding a developer's range of housing types and price points increases absorption by attracting a larger potential market. Moreover, the adoption of smart growth practices can speed up the local and state permitting process and decrease community resistance.

Practices That Increase Efficiency

Planners, developers, and policy makers have an expanding menu of tools and techniques to help them use land and infrastructure more efficiently and cost-effectively. Which methods will work best depends on the circumstances of each community. Nevertheless, examples of success are plentiful and can be expected to increase in number as our knowledge of these practices grows. The rest of this chapter highlights for developers some of the most successful approaches to the efficient use of land and infrastructure.

Infill Development

Development on land that has been skipped over, underused, or abandoned is known as infill development. Suburban infill development often occurs as the result of efforts to accommodate new development in an area that is largely developed; the projects are generally incremental and small in scale. For developers who take the time to understand the complexities, infill sites offer unique benefits: captive markets with limited or nonexistent competition; the chance to make use of existing infrastructure and amenities; and the opportunity to gain zoning and approval benefits in exchange for contributing to local planning and economic goals. Moreover, infill development can be a valuable public relations tool and give developers the ability to cultivate strategic relationships with local municipalities for future projects.

A national survey undertaken by the University of California's Institute of Urban and Regional Development attempted to calculate the amount of undeveloped land in the country currently zoned for high-density development (defined as 15 units per acre—37 units per hectare—or more). Approximately 1,200 communities responded to the survey, and the results confirmed that enough infill land is available to accommodate 6 million new households (assuming development at these higher densities). The study suggests that at least some of the most important conditions for infill development—the availability of land and higher-density zoning—are already present.[9]

Inner-ring suburbs, in particular, offer many vacant or underused sites suitable for residential or commercial development. Typically, the sites used for residential infill were formerly used for activities that are no longer economically viable because of rising land costs, demographic shifts, or other trends. Such sites are often large enough to offer excellent opportunities for the development of multifamily housing or housing for seniors. In some locations, they may be suitable for mixed-use projects.

Especially in aging communities with declining tax bases, commercial infill development is highly prized by local officials for its financial benefits—in particular, its role in increasing employment and property tax revenues. Where higher densities are appropriate, commercial infill is an excellent way to reuse large vacant parcels and brownfield sites. For example, many of the suburban office parks built in the 1950s and 1960s (with two to three stories, surface parking, and floor/area ratios of 0.25 to 0.30) are now functionally obsolete—and, given current land values, underused. Such prime suburban locations are being redeveloped as mixed-use campuses at higher densities and with larger building footprints (25,000 to 30,000 gross square feet—2,320 to 2,790 square meters); they also offer structured parking and on-site support services such as convenience retail, restaurants and food courts, fitness centers, daycare facilities, conference centers, hotels,

Farrcroft, an infill development in the city of Fairfax, Virginia, outside Washington, D.C., takes advantage of small lots and modified neotraditional planning concepts.

multifamily housing, and assisted-living facilities. The Princeton Forrestal Center, outside Princeton, New Jersey, is an excellent example of a site's evolution from a single-use office park to a mixed-use employment destination with a wide range of amenities.

The Redevelopment of Greyfields

A good deal of the demand created by population growth in metropolitan areas can be met through a modest increase in density, the redevelopment of abandoned and underused infill sites, and the adaptive use of existing buildings. Infill development offers tremendous potential for accommodating suburban growth without developing greenfield sites. One important emerging trend is the redevelopment of *greyfields,* which are abandoned or financially unsuccessful shopping malls. These properties, often surrounded by acres of parking, are usually in prime locations in aging suburbs.

The trend to convert these vacant and underused properties is gaining momentum—and, as more and more properties become obsolete,

greyfields will offer an ongoing opportunity for developers. In 1999, a Pricewaterhouse-Coopers study commissioned by the Congress for the New Urbanism (CNU) estimated that 7 percent of the country's 2,800 malls were "dead" or seriously underperforming, and that an additional 12 percent were headed toward extinction as single-use retail sites. According to Steven Bodzin, of CNU, the redevelopment of underperforming suburban shopping malls as mixed-use town centers and infill neighborhoods is an enormous national planning and redevelopment opportunity.

While the majority of malls will remain strong performers, new malls will continue to open, drawing business away from existing centers, meaning that these existing centers could become greyfields. National chains and other anchor tenants will continue to seek space in giant, open-air regional power centers and in new "big-box" locations, further weakening the position of some regional malls.

Some failed malls are being revitalized by being converted to town centers and infill

Redevelopment of Denver's Stapleton Airport

In 1989, with the announcement that Stapleton International Airport would close within a decade, the city of Denver embarked on an ambitious plan for a new community that would become a model of sustainable development for the nation. At 4,700 acres (1,900 hectares), Stapleton, which is located only ten minutes from downtown Denver, will be the country's largest infill project. From 1989 to 1995, elected city officials, staff, and a 42-member citizens' advisory board held hundreds of public meetings and design workshops to produce the Stapleton Development Plan, which describes a comprehensive vision for the new community. The plan integrates the city's and region's economic, social, and environmental objectives; lays a framework to guide residential, commercial, and retail development; and includes nearly 1,200 acres (486 hectares) of open space.

Since 1950, the population of metropolitan Denver has grown by 200 percent, while the city's land area has increased by 350 percent. While densities in the older urban areas are approximately 5.3 people per acre (13 per hectare), densities in newer suburban areas range from 2.6 to 3.2 people per acre (6.4 to 7.9 per hectare)—evidence that newer development has been sprawling out from the city center.[1] The sprawl has been accompanied by longer commute times, increased traffic congestion, and a loss of open space. Through compact development, Stapleton will be able to house over 30,000 residents. Residential areas will have an average density of 12 units per acre (30 per hectare), or approximately 30 people per acre (74 per hectare), sufficient to support vibrant neighborhood centers and extensive public transit systems. The density of development will also provide housing opportunities for a diverse range of household types and incomes.

Dense neighborhoods allow for the development of mixed-use town centers within walking distance of most residences, and

for the use of traditional design elements—both of which foster pedestrian-friendly environments and encourage interaction among residents. Varied lot widths within each block of the Stapleton plan create a visually diverse environment, and the use of a number of different architects, aided by design guidelines, encourages both quality and variety in the architecture and housing types.

The plan calls for the preservation of over 1,100 acres (445 hectares)—nearly 30 percent of the site—as open space. New parks, including the 80-acre (32-hectare) Central Park, will enhance existing open spaces in the area and link them via new bikeway and trail systems. The various open spaces, ranging from formal urban squares and community parks to natural wildlife corridors, will provide a framework for unifying Stapleton's mixed-use villages, which will be key to the site's development strategy.

A sustainability advisory committee has been established to aid the developers, their subcontractors, and the city in the development of a sustainability master plan. The plan will address environmental issues such as site orientation and design, energy efficiency, water management, recycling, building materials, and air quality. Much of the concrete from the runways and debris from the demolition of the terminal will be reused on site and at other local developments. Control towers and other airport-specific structures are being reused at other regional airports. Stapleton, in fact, has become the world's largest recycling program.

The city of Denver has played an active role in the redevelopment of the site, from aiding in the preparation of the master plan to encouraging commercial development (through tax incentives). While the Stapleton development plan incorporates almost every aspect of smart growth, it is not without flaws. Despite the calls for sustainable,

Hundreds of public meetings and design workshops were held over a six-year period in order to create the Stapleton Development Plan. The plan designates nearly 1,200 acres (486 hectares), or about 30 percent of the site, as open space and includes an 80-acre (32-hectare) central park. The plan's housing component calls for 12 residential units per acre (30 per hectare).

pedestrian-oriented neighborhoods and centers, a vehicle-oriented, big-box power center (euphemistically called "regional retail" in the master plan) has opened in the first phase.

But much about Stapleton's plan is taking the development in the right direction. The community-based plan has ensured that the needs of residents, businesses, and the city and region as a whole will be met. The project's location and size have attracted attention, and its mixed-use, pedestrian-oriented, neighborhood-based design will make it an example worth following. ▲

Note

1. "Stapleton Overview: Smart Growth and Stapleton" (http://www.stapletondenver.com/overview/smart_growth.asp [January 24, 2002]).

neighborhoods that use existing land and infrastructure in a highly efficient way that is profitable for both developers and municipalities. For example, Winter Park Mall, outside Orlando, and Eastgate Mall, in Chattanooga, are old regional malls that are being redeveloped into walkable, mixed-use town centers that include retail, housing, and office components. The sheer size of these properties —many malls were developed with acres of surface parking—yields enough land for public parks and other civic uses, particularly when the projects are retrofitted with structured parking.

Conversions of retail centers to residential and mixed-use development are taking place at a smaller scale as well. In Mountain View, California, a new, 18-acre (7.3-hectare) neighborhood called the Crossings offers 397 townhouses and apartments built on the foundation of the failed Old Mills Mall. In Pasadena, California, developers are building nearly 400 residences above shops at the recently opened Paseo Colorado—a high-end, three-block, mixed-use successor to a defunct mall. In San Jose, California, the Town and Country Mall has been razed and rebuilt as an upscale urban project known as Santana Row, which includes 1,300 apartments and a hotel

among shops, restaurants, and heavily landscaped plazas.

The conversion of malls to mixed-use places also represents a shift in the attitudes of Americans. According to architect Jon Jerde, a leading mall designer, enclosed malls are "slick engines for consumption and people were blurred out with this kind of thing." Now people want something more authentic and interesting, such as a main street or downtown experience.[10]

Though California has the most examples of this trend, dead malls are being reborn across the nation, in states like Colorado, Florida, New York, and Tennessee, and local governments are providing developers with hundreds of millions of dollars to transform dying malls into landmark town centers for viable, diverse suburban communities.

Transit-Oriented Development

Transit-oriented development (TOD) has many applications for improving the efficiency of suburban land use and infrastructure. Indeed, transportation is the lifeblood of a metropolitan area—or at least the circulatory system that keeps a city alive. Much has been written about the nexus between land use and

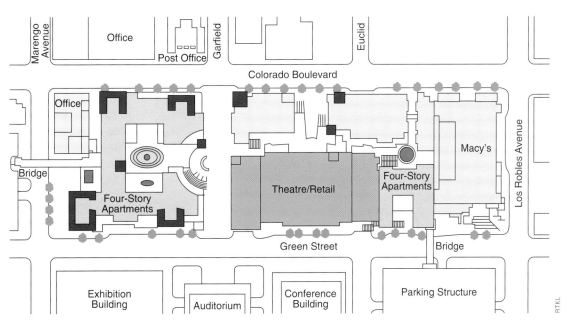

Paseo Colorado mixes retail space, restaurants, entertainment uses, and housing on a site adjacent to Old Pasadena, California. The three-square-block urban village replaces a shopping mall that had been built as part of a 1970s redevelopment effort. Paseo Colorado includes 387 rental units, a supermarket, and a 14-screen cinema.

Access to transit and other amenities has made Pentagon City, outside Washington, D.C., a desirable location for luxury high-rise apartments.

transportation in urban planning, and about the age-old question of which should come first: should development be concentrated around transit, or should transit be extended to suburban commercial centers where political will exists?

Planners have long recognized that transit use depends on density: the feasibility of transit is typically determined by the density of development within walking distance of the service.[11] Because of their low densities and auto-oriented design, suburbs have generally not been well served by public transit—and their dependence on the automobile has led, in many areas, to unacceptable traffic volumes and congestion. But as suburban residential densities increase, transit becomes a more viable option, not only in terms of cost and energy efficiency but also in terms of health and quality of life. Town centers, where suburban densities are often the highest, offer opportunities for alternative forms of transit —commuter rail and light rail connecting to nearby business districts; expanded bus systems; and bicycle commuter trails, for example. In addition, suburbs are increasingly allowing developers to build at higher densities if the developers agree to combine those densities

with strategies to manage transportation demand (e.g., reduced parking ratios, ridesharing programs, and vanpools to transit stops).

Residential density alone, however, is not enough to support transit use. To be effective in this respect, residential density must be coupled with easy access, via foot or transit, to civic, cultural, and commercial activities. Unlike the residents of the streetcar suburbs of the early 20th century, today's suburbanites are increasingly likely to work in a sprawling edge city or suburban office park, rather than in a central business district. Moreover, many land uses traditionally located in cities —such as department stores, medical centers, and educational institutions—now have a significant presence in the suburbs. Although suburb-to-suburb commutes are much more difficult to accommodate through public transit than suburb-to-downtown commutes, suburban business districts and other concentrations of commercial activity continue to form, providing good opportunities for rail and other forms of transit. Typically, for a TOD to be successful, mixed-use centers should generally extend no more than a quarter of a mile (0.40 kilometers), or a five-minute walk, from transit stations.

Because of the higher density of development and the improved access to transit, TOD and infill communities tend to be more socially, economically, and ethnically diverse than traditional suburbs. That is, they appeal to people who might not otherwise be drawn to a suburban area. From a development perspective, they are more lucrative than the homogenized, single-use suburbs of the past; proximity to transit has been shown to significantly increase property values and stimulate economic development. From an environmental perspective, TODs have a number of benefits: they reduce air pollution; and, because typical suburban park-and-ride trips can be replaced with walk-and-ride and bike-and-ride trips, more land can be devoted to open space, rather than to streets and parking. Most important, TOD gives residents and businesses more choices: it offers "alternative living and working environments that combine the suburban values and lifestyle preferences for open space, human-scale buildings, and a sense of security with the traditional urban values of walking to neighborhood shops, meeting people on the street, and being in a culturally diverse setting."[12] In the 21st century, the suburbs of regional cities can be woven together, creating more livable and sustainable suburban communities through a comprehensively managed, multimodal transit network that combines a variety of transit options such as commuter rail and light rail, buses, trolleys, bikeways, walkable streets, ridesharing, and on-demand vanpools.

In recent years, a great deal of planning has been under way for TODs that are just now beginning to be developed. Some of the best examples are in the suburbs of Portland, Oregon. One such project, Orenco Station, is located in an old village that had grown up around a historic railroad station, which is now part of Portland's new Westside light-rail system. To the north of the village are large land parcels zoned for office parks, corporate campuses, and light industry.

The design for Orenco Station integrates a range of residential and neighborhood-serving commercial development into a mixed-use plan focused along the light-rail line at the Orenco Station transit stop. Near the new station, the main street was redeveloped with a small civic park fronting the tracks. Community services are concentrated in a town center near the station. To the north, commercial development lines a major east-west arterial, while mixed-use and residential development runs along orthogonal streets connecting to the station.

Minimum-Density Zoning Codes

Even though the desired density of a suburban community may be eight to 12 units per acre (20 to 30 units per hectare), most conventional zoning ordinances do not prohibit a developer from building at a lower density. To achieve infill development in desired locations, however, some municipalities are reversing zoning codes to require *minimum* densities on sites, as opposed to the more conventional *maximum* zoning densities. For example, the metropolitan planning organization of Portland, Oregon (known as Metro), assigned population targets to each of the 24 cities and three counties within Metro's boundaries. To meet these targets, municipalities are required to rezone neighborhoods or parcels to achieve higher densities. Even more significant, local plans (which in Oregon carry the weight of law) must meet certain density targets: ten units per buildable acre (27 per hectare) in the city of Portland, and six to eight units per acre (15 to 20 units per hectare) in more suburban localities.[13]

Minimum-density zoning has pros and cons for developers. On the one hand, because residential densities are higher than those typically allowed, developers can achieve a stronger financial return in a good housing market. On the other hand, minimum densities can limit a developer's range of development options and market flexibility, which can be problematic in a weak or declining housing market. On the whole, though, minimum-density codes give the developer more, not less, choice than maximum-density codes.

Block Standards

Block standards are a flexible new technique that is continuing to gain popularity among suburban communities interested in creating a sense of place. Block standards define the essence of most great cities and towns: a system of complex blocks, a tradition of side-walk-oriented buildings, and flexibility in use and density.

Block standards identify four block types that could make up any suburban town: residential; civic; commercial; and, most important, mixed-use. Specific land uses and densities are prescribed for each block. The mixed-use block, for example, is intended to incorporate most of the significant retail in a center, along with housing and office uses. Commercial blocks are intended primarily to accommodate office and employment uses, as well as some ground-level retail. Residential blocks allow some nonresidential uses but focus on offering a range of residential densities. Civic blocks accommodate parks, public uses, and civic institutions.

Specific block standards can be developed for town centers, village centers, and neighborhood centers, with the proportion of each block type varying to suit each type of center. For example, a neighborhood center has a larger proportion of residential blocks, whereas a town center has a larger proportion of commercial and mixed-use blocks. A village center has enough mixed-use blocks to accommodate a retail center anchored by a grocery store. The standards assign each block type an approximate size that depends on its expected uses and intensities. Additionally, each type of block is assigned other simple standards: a maximum block size, building height limits, maximum parking limits, minimum floor/area ratio or residential density, and a minimum proportion of "build-to lines" (that

is, the percentage of the block that must have buildings fronting the sidewalk). Varying the densities of the blocks and the proportions of the four basic block types permits the creation of virtually any type of urban environment.

In the Southeast Orlando Specific Plan, block standards helped establish a framework for mixed-use development in a 21,000-acre (8,500-hectare) portion of the area around Orlando International Airport. (See figure 3-1.) The plan for this rapidly growing area is designed to accommodate a largely residential population of over 80,000.

First, the site's natural features, such as wetlands and wildlife habitats, were identified and designated as preserves. Greenbelts were added to the preserved land to create a continuous open-space system, drainage system, and habitat protection area. A circulation system, including rail transit, was then added to the framework. The natural and circulation networks became the foundation for a series of districts, town centers, village centers, and neighborhood centers. The urban design of each center was controlled by block standards, and each block type was assigned a maximum block size; building height; amount of parking; and, most importantly, a minimum proportion of build-to lines at the perimeter.

Land Use Regulations That Emphasize Place Making

Place making is a term used by developers, planners, designers, local officials, and community activists to describe the goal of improving the quality and experience of the built environment. As the suburbs continue to grow and mature, improving the quality of "place" is taking on increasing importance. In 1937, referring to Oakland, California, Gertrude Stein quipped, "There is no there there." The place-making movement addresses this concern about the suburbs. At ULI's first place-making conference, in 1999, Thomas Lee,

Figure 3-1
East Orlando Block Standards

	Town Center	Village Center	Neighborhood Center
Mixed-use blocks (percentage of center)	30–80	25–70	12–25
Mix of uses[1]	Retail, services, restaurants, office, cinema, grocery, hotel, residential, civic, park/plaza	Grocery, local-serving retail, restaurants, professional offices, residential, civic, park/plaza	Small retail/market,[2] restaurant/café, civic, residential, park/plaza
Maximum block size (acres/hectares)	7 /2.8	7/2.8	3/1.2
Minimum floor/area ratio	0.5	0.4	0.4
Minimum frontage (percentage of each street)	65	65	65
Parking ratio (spaces per 1,000 square feet/ 93 square meters)	3	3	3
Building height (stories)	2–10	1–3	1–2
Commercial blocks (maximum percentage of center)	55	40	12
Allowable uses	Office, retail (10% maximum)	Office, retail (10% maximum)	Office
Maximum block size (acres/hectares)	7/2.8	3/1.2	3/1.2
Minimum floor/area ratio	0.5	0.4	0.4
Minimum frontage (percentage of each street)	65	65	65
Parking ratio (spaces per 1,000 square feet/ 93 square meters)	3	3	3
Building height (stories)	2–10	1–3	1–2
Residential blocks (percentage of center)	15–70	25–65	52–78
Allowable uses	Apartments, condos, town-houses, bungalows	Apartments, condos, town-houses, bungalows, small-lot single-family	Apartments, condos, town-houses, bungalows, small-lot single-family
Maximum block size (acres/hectares)	3/1.2	3/1.2	3/1.2
Density range (dwelling units per acre/per hectare)	7–50/17.2–123.5	7–30/17.2–74.1	7–25/17.2–61.8
Minimum frontage (percentage of each street)	65	60	60
Parking ratio (spaces per 1,000 square feet/ 93 square meters)	3	3	3
Building height (stories)	2–5	1–3	1–2
Civic blocks (percentage of center)	10	10	10
Allowable uses	Parks, recreation, civic, daycare	Parks, recreation, civic, daycare	Parks, recreation, civic, daycare
Maximum block size (acres/hectares)	3/1.2	3/1.2	3/1.2

Source: Reprinted by permission of Island Press. Peter Calthorpe and William Fulton, *The Regional City: Planning for the End of Sprawl* (Washington, D.C., and Covelo, Calif.: Island Press, 2001), 213.

1. Thirty to 80 percent retail, cinema, or hotel required in each block; 20 to 70 percent other uses.
2. A maximum of 10,000 square feet (929 square meters) per block.

The Palo Alto Comprehensive Plan

The city of Palo Alto, California, has long been an example of traditional urban design. Its 1995 comprehensive plan update, the culmination of a two-and-one-half-year process headed by a 38-member advisory committee of citizens and officials, focused attention on the traditional neighborhood design principles that make its neighborhoods and commercial centers unique. The update attempted to reconcile the post–World War II suburban residential developments and strip malls with the more urban prewar neighborhoods. The goal of the process was to enrich the suburban, auto-oriented areas by creating walkable, mixed-use environments; the strategy was to borrow from design principles and vernaculars that had already been proven successful in other parts of town. Organized into six sections (Land Use and Community Design, Transportation, Housing, Natural Environment, Business and Economics, and Community Services and Facilities), the document emphasizes the relationship between land use, urban design, transportation, the environment, and economic development. To guide users making development decisions, each element contains goals (broad objectives), policies (principles and actions), and programs (specific activities and strategies developed to implement specific goals).

Palo Alto, situated in the northernmost part of Santa Clara County, has maintained close relationships with the six surrounding municipalities. Because of increasing development pressures, regional planning in the area is strong, and regional policies for controlling growth, and for conserving and preserving open space and natural resources, are already in place. Santa Clara County's general plan has discouraged sprawl by focusing development within a defined "urban service area," encouraging compact development, and directing growth toward transit corridors and existing activity centers. The updated plan takes these general policies a step further by providing more specific guidelines to maintain the balance between growth and preservation, residents and businesses, and pedestrians and autos.

Currently, over half of the city's 26 square miles (67.3 square kilometers) is designated as parks or open space (see table).[1] Of that, over one-third is designated as preserved. Large preserves extend from the southern foothills to the northeastern edge of the city (along the bay), and 29 parks, totaling 190 acres (76.8 hectares), dot the city's neighborhoods.

The plan emphasizes the need to focus future open-space purchases on parcels that will link existing habitats and create continuous regional wildlife corridors. Because many of the area's environmentally fragile areas are already protected, the environmental element of the plan concentrates on reducing solid waste and water, air, and noise pollution, and on cleaning up polluted areas by implementing policies and incentives for residents and businesses.

Palo Alto's residential areas have a relatively high average population density of 12.8 people per acre (31.6 per hectare), or 5.3 units per acre (13 per hectare).[2] About half of the city's residential areas were developed after World War II, when the city expanded southward. To serve the region's growing population, suburban shopping centers and office parks were also built. Today, there are about 35 identifiable residential

Palo Alto's Land Use Plan

Land Use	Percentage of Total
Parks, preserves, and open space	40.5
Open space, controlled development, and agriculture	15.0
Public facilities	4.5
Single-family housing	25.0
Multifamily housing	4.0
Research and development, and limited manufacturing	7.5
Commercial facilities	3.0
Vacant, developable land	0.5

Source: Palo Alto Comprehensive Plan 1998–2010, L-4.

the now-retired chief executive officer of Newhall Land, described place making as "the very essence of real estate development." Noted urban designer Dennis Pieprz says it well: "Memorable places have a physical dimension by virtue of extraordinary physical position, by being rooted in the form of the land, or through a beautiful composition of buildings and open spaces. You will personally experience the place. You will know when you are there."[14]

For their part, public officials and land use regulators are encouraging suburban place

University Park, a community of mixed housing types encompassing 8.5 acres (3.4 hectares), is one of the largest redevelopment efforts in Palo Alto's history. The development is close to Stanford University and is within walking distance of the popular shops and restaurants of University Avenue.

neighborhoods in Palo Alto, each with a distinct character; boundaries between neighborhoods are defined by patterns of land subdivision and by public perception. Districts range in character from traditional neighborhoods with narrow, tree-lined streets and on-street parking to late-20th-century subdivisions with curvilinear street patterns and homes with austere facades, oriented toward private courtyards and backyards. As a result of rising housing costs, continued low vacancy rates, and a desire for more socially and economically mixed neighborhoods, the city has instituted policies to encourage infill on small vacant lots and the development of mixed-use projects that include a diverse mix of housing types. Zoning changes have been used to convert commercial land to residential, to allow housing on smaller lots in residential

areas, and to reduce parking requirements (which increases density and lowers costs). In single-family areas, the development of new multifamily housing and accessory dwelling units will increase density, but the architecture and scale of the new structures will be designed to maintain the neighborhoods' traditional character.

In the zoning codes of many cities, the desire for more walkable, vibrant neighborhoods has spurred the development of mixed-use districts. In Palo Alto, overlay buffer zones and mixed-use zones have created opportunities for mixed-use development. To ensure that these mixed-use districts will foster pedestrian-scale neighborhoods, the city has developed design standards and performance requirements regulating scale, parking, and building set-

backs and orientation. In its already developed regional centers and four suburban employment districts, the city has encouraged the reuse of existing buildings and surface parking lots, the redevelopment of underused parcels, the introduction of support services in office parks, and the development of transit, pedestrian, and bicycle facilities to reduce automobile dependence.

Currently, 74 percent of work trips in the Stanford and Palo Alto area are by car, with the remainder divided among carpooling (9.5 percent), bicycling (8.5 percent), walking (3.5 percent), transit (3.5 percent), and other forms.[3] Because land use patterns ultimately dictate transportation choices, the updated plan employs minimum-density requirements. Requiring increased densities around transit stations, providing employers with incentives to reduce auto use, implementing parking fees and taxes to fund alternative transportation projects, and creating long-term education programs to change travel habits are other strategies that the city is considering. The plan also outlines methods of expanding and improving the existing transit, pedestrian, and bicycle facilities. ▲

Notes

1. Palo Alto Comprehensive Plan 1998–2010, L-4.

2. "Palo Alto at a Glance" (http://www.city.palo-alto.ca.us/resources/ataglance.html [June 2000]).

3. Palo Alto Comprehensive Plan, T-2.

making by modifying local zoning and land development codes to foster the creation of attractive and memorable places. In addition, they are often doing away with the more conventional zoning that dictates maximum densities and the separation of uses—regulations that preclude place making. Suburban

zoning codes need to be rewritten to create environments that focus on integrated, mixed-use development, pedestrian streets, civic plazas and open spaces, transit use, and shared parking. The codes also need to be more flexible. As A. Eugene Kohn, president of Kohn Pedersen Fox Associates, said during

ELKUS/MANFREDI ARCHITECTS LTD.

the deliberations of a recent ULI task force on place making, "Land use controls should allow projects to be modified to meet changing community needs without necessarily triggering a new entitlement process."

The overall structure of the suburbs should be based on "places" and "links" rather than "zones," through land use regulations designed to create neighborhoods, districts, corridors, centers, and open-space systems. The contrast between suburban forms based on traditional zoning categories and place-oriented standards is dramatic. Residential zones and subdivisions are transformed into walkable neighborhoods; shopping centers and office parks are reconceived as mixed-use districts with pedestrian-oriented streets; and arterials and highways become boulevards with integrated transit. Changing suburban zoning codes to emphasize place making encourages the reuse of existing buildings and the efficient siting of new development by providing a guide for the location of neighborhood centers, mixed-use districts,

employment districts, and open-space systems. The updated general plan for Palo Alto, California (see feature box), is a good example of land use policies that encourage a place-making approach.

Successful suburban place making fosters the more efficient use of land and infrastructure in a number of ways. First, attractive suburban places can draw new residents and retain current ones, increasing both the stability and diversity of the community, expanding the demand for new residential and commercial infill development, and strengthening the overall quality of life. Second, there is a direct correlation between place making and real estate values: the most memorable places tend to be the most enduring and to have the highest real estate values. Higher property values translate into greater property tax revenues for the municipality. These revenues can, in turn, be used to enhance the community's assets—for example, to preserve open space, reuse existing buildings, and rebuild aging infrastructure. Finally, improving the quality of suburban life reduces pressures to develop greenfields and extend suburban sprawl; the result is more sustainable communities and regions.

This chapter was written by Fred Merrill, principal, Sasaki Associates, Watertown, Massachusetts.

Notes

1. Peter Calthorpe and William Fulton, *The Regional City: Planning for the End of Sprawl* (Washington, D.C., and Covelo, Calif.: Island Press, 2001), 198.

2. John G. Mitchell, "Urban Sprawl," *National Geographic,* July 2001, 55.

3. John Buntin, "Dead End Revolt," *Governing,* November 2001, 18.

4. Cameron Speir and Kurt Stephenson, "Does Sprawl Cost Us All? Isolating the Effects of Housing Patterns on Public Water and Sewer Costs," *APA Journal* 68, no. 2 (winter 2002): 56–69.

5. Christina B. Farnsworth, "All Dried Up," *Builder Magazine,* March 2002, 27–28.

6. Ibid.

7. American Planning Association, *Planning for Smart Growth: 2002 State of the States* (Chicago: American Planning Association, February 2002).

8. Ibid.

9. Timothy Beatley and Kristy Manning, *The Ecology of Place: Planning for Environment, Economy, and Community* (Washington, D.C.: Island Press, 1997), 154.

10. Jim Wasserman, "Dead Malls Gain New Life as Neighborhoods," *Messenger-Inquirer,* December 23, 2001 (http://messenger-inquirer.com/features/business/3921353.htm).

11. Boris Pushkarev and Jeffrey Zupan, *Public Transportation and Land Use Policy* (Bloomington: Indiana University Press, 1977), 24.

12. Michael Bernick and Robert Cervero, *Transit Villages in the 21st Century* (New York, McGraw-Hill, 1996), 7.

13. Beatley and Manning, *Ecology of Place,* 52.

14. Geoffrey Booth et al., *Transforming Suburban Business Districts* (Washington, D.C.: ULI–the Urban Land Institute, 2001), 153.

4 Open Space as an Amenity

The efficient and effective use of open space is a key to the successful planning, design, and implementation of new communities. As high-quality construction and home features become standard at virtually every price point, competitive advantage will be driven by the quality of life that a community offers its residents. And quality of life will increasingly depend on the quality of the open spaces and amenities—and on their ability to provide for the personal fulfillment of community residents.

In the community builder's main product line—large-scale, mixed-use, planned communities—achieving quality of life and fostering personal fulfillment are typically treated as long-term propositions. Too often, however, the community builder simply provides multipurpose space within the community, in the expectation that residents will eventually create their own quality of life and personal fulfillment. This somewhat passive approach neglects the opportunity, through new and innovative uses of open space, to jump-start a sense of community.

Community builders no longer question the need to include open space, along with other physical amenities, in their projects. (An entrepreneur may occasionally feel so pressed economically that he offers only a token amen-

At the heart of Centennial Lakes, a 346-unit master-planned community in Edina, Minnesota, is a 25-acre (10-hectare) park that offers a pavilion for live entertainment and social gatherings, as well as a variety of year-round activities, including miniature golf, paddleboats, fishing, croquet, and ice-skating. The project sits on a primary commercial corridor just seven miles (11.3 kilometers) from downtown Minneapolis.

DON PITLIK, PITLIK STUDIOS 2000

ity, or none at all—but in doing so, he is well aware of the high risk to his investment.) But because many developers include open space and its associated amenities as if by rote, the final result often appears contrived, even to the untutored eye.

People today are not so much tired as they are bored. A developer's goal should be to create communities that are stimulating and that encourage and support residents' self-actualization—personal growth and fulfillment that is consistent with one's personal values. Both to discharge their responsibility as shapers of communities, and to create a selling difference, community builders must respond to the challenge of effectively using open space.

Building Value through Open Space

Although open space can fulfill an important role by preserving ecosystem components and connections, providing for the needs and wants of community residents is an equally critical role. When open space successfully fulfills this role, value is added to the community. Open space becomes an amenity in itself when it improves the experience of living in a community.

Open space can be either passive or active. Untouched, natural open space can provide psychic comfort—by creating physical separation from urbanized surroundings or just by offering a scenic view. Of course, the scale of the open space is an important factor, since

the amenity value of passive open space diminishes dramatically unless a significant land area is allocated to that purpose.

When open space offers interaction with nature, on the other hand, the use is less passive and more active; and, even if the amount of open space is nominal, it can have a higher amenity value. For example, enabling residents to interact with nature through trails, lakes, interpretive centers, and so on provides a different, higher level of amenity value than is provided by less developed forms of open space.

Developing communities means more than simply building homes. Communities should be planned in a way that creates a strong sense of place. A major element of that place should be a rich variety of leisure-time opportunities that appeal to a broad spectrum of community residents. The intent is to evoke feelings of personal enjoyment and fulfillment through a kind of "resort" atmosphere that will be recognizable to residents. The inclusion of *active* open space provides the highest amenity value and the greatest efficiency, in terms of allocating limited land resources.

Summerlin, in suburban Las Vegas, one of America's best-selling master-planned communities, fosters a sense of community through its 68 parks and extensive trail networks. The project consists of 24,000 homes and has 51,000 residents. The 22,500-acre (9,105-hectare) community is adjacent to the Red Rock Canyon National Conservation Area.

OPULENCE STUDIOS

ERIC FIGGE

Sailhouse's land-scaped walkways and boardwalks connect to the surrounding neighborhoods in Corona del Mar, California. Developers who provide residents with this type of usable open space gain a powerful marketing tool. Despite the high density (89 units on 7.4 acres—three hectares) the developer, John Laing Homes, ensured that the neighborhood would have a single-family atmosphere.

Open Space Is Good Business

There are many good reasons to use open space as a community amenity. The six sections that follow consider both financial and nonfinancial reasons for making a comprehensive open-space plan a part of any good business strategy.

Jump-Starting the Sense of Community

To a large extent, the success of a new master-planned community is determined the moment it is introduced to the marketplace. What the developer does in the first phase can establish a momentum for success —and for increasing land values—that will pay dividends through the buildout period and beyond. Yet developers often overlook the opportunity to use open space as a means

of jump-starting the most important factor in the project's long-term success: the creation of a strong sense of community.

If streets and utilities are the "bones" of a community, amenities are its heart. The successful community developer will create a strong sense of community as a means of breathing life into the development. Properly located, designed, and developed, open space can help create a sense of community, adding value to the land by creating a place that people want to come home to. In *The Great Good Place*, Ray Oldenburg writes that "Daily life, in order to be relaxed and fulfilling, must find its balance in three realms of experience. One is domestic, a second is gainful and productive, and the third is inclusively sociable, offering both the basis of community and the celebration of it."[1] It follows that community developers must strive to create physical settings, in addition to home and work, where residents can interact in their everyday lives. Especially if it is used effectively at the outset, open space can be a valuable tool in this regard.

Product Differentiation

Differentiating a community from competing ones is essential in today's highly competitive markets. Today's homebuyers are seeking the best possible investment opportunities. The community developer who can identify the targeted consumer's requirements and meet those requirements in new and different ways will have a competitive advantage.

When it comes to open space, the old real estate axiom—"location, location, location" —can take on new meaning. Using open space as a passive amenity, for example, by locating homes near a park or an open vista, can create a locational advantage. But unlocking the latent amenity potential of open space, by creating *active* recreational opportunities, can create a far better locational premium, especially when the community is considered as a whole. Also, open space can be used to differentiate product types within the community.

Incremental Profitability

Developers are constantly searching for ways to add value to the finite amount of land assets that make up the community. When determining how to allocate precious land resources, developers must pay close attention to uses that create the most "bang for the buck." While it may seem that the greatest value can be achieved by devoting every inch of property to saleable product, using surroundings and amenities to make building lots more desirable may actually be more profitable. The goal is to create perceived land value that is greater than the actual cost of the land and related improvements.

In this context, it is important for the community developer to remember that the underlying market value of a homesite may increase disproportionately each time the perceived value of the home is incrementally increased.

Open space can be used to efficiently and effectively address consumer demands, and thereby to significantly increase the perceived value of homes in a community. The effect on profitability can be dramatic.

Maintaining the Momentum for Success

Typically, the perceived value of homes in a new community, even adjusted for inflation, tends to increase well after the buildout period. This phenomenon can be attributed to a number of factors, not the least of which is the perception that the community is now mature and has a more established sense of place. The goal of the community builder should be to accelerate this process—to achieve as much increase in value as possible, as early as possible during the sales period. An increase in perceived value can speed up the pace of sales—which can lead, in turn, to increased sales prices—and can strengthen the community's momentum for success.

Again, the key is to use an open-space plan as a proactive means of accelerating the community-building process—to jump-start the creation of a sense of place and community.

Well-designed open space enhances Cherry Hill Village, in Canton, Michigan.

LOONEY RICKS KISS

Well-Satisfied Customers

Sophisticated real estate developers recognize that paying genuine attention (and not just lip service) to customer satisfaction is the key to long-term success in business. Marketing studies have confirmed that profit margins can increase when current customers become repeat customers or provide recommendations to their friends and family.

While much has been written about the importance of customer satisfaction from the standpoint of home construction, the same principles hold true for community planning as well. In community planning, the emphasis on creating happy customers needs to expand from factors such as "quality of construction" and "standard of living" to factors such as "quality of the built environment" and "quality of life." The inspired use of open space as an amenity can provide the platform for exceeding customers' expectations—and

generating happy homeowners and renters who will spread the word.

Leadership and Responsibility

In the past, governmental entities were the most common providers of community facilities and services. But in an era of increasing fiscal limitations, it is the private sector community builders who must assume a leadership role in supplying residents with many facilities and services, including recreational infrastructure and activities. This responsibility requires that available community resources—especially limited open spaces—be used in new and creative ways.

Unless community builders accept their role as primary suppliers of what have traditionally been thought of as "public" spaces, communities will suffer as suitable spaces and resources are stretched and strained. In contrast, the community builder who takes a leadership role, and ensures that open spaces

Old Elm Village, in Petaluma, California, is a mixed-use infill development consisting of 87 units of affordable housing, a community center, a preschool, and street-facing retail. By preserving the site's limited natural resources, the developer increased the project's perceived value and created a positive image for residents to identify with. The significant trees on the site were saved, including a massive elm tree that gives the project its name.

DON PITLIK, PITLIK STUDIOS 2000

A plaza in Centennial Lakes brings together residents from all over the community. The development includes nearly one million square feet (92,900 square meters) of office space; 200,000 square feet (18,580 square meters) of retail; an eight-screen movie theater; and a 100,000-square-foot (9,290-square meter) state-of-the-art medical center.

are used to draw residents together, will succeed in fostering a true sense of community that adds value to the land assets. With both the opportunity and the incentive, developers of master-planned communities are perhaps uniquely suited to play this leadership role.

Developers can make communities desirable places to live—and therefore have a responsibility to do so. The real estate industry in the United States is undergoing dramatic changes as a result of mergers and consolidations in homebuilding companies. As the remaining companies get larger, homebuilders will take on more of the characteristics of large manufacturing companies. The "commoditization" of homebuilding is, in fact, already occurring. Among publicly owned homebuilders, the quest for sales volume and related cost efficiencies will lead to an emphasis on the standardization of home designs and other "cookie cutter" initiatives. Although consumers will likely benefit from the cost savings that are passed through to them, the burden of providing unique and memorable living environments will increasingly fall to the developers of master-planned communities.

Developers have a growing responsibility to thoughtfully plan and design community assets—including open space—to create a richer experience for residents. A community is built on values and character. Governmental limitations and industry changes will require community developers to take responsibility for creating the kinds of communities that will endure long after the sales trailers and model homes are gone. This responsibility will require increased stewardship of the land and its uses.

Consumer Orientation, Not Product Orientation

An open-space plan should consider people first: it should be founded on interaction points, then the physical elements should be added. With these interaction points in mind, open space can be designed "from the inside out" to ensure a synergistic relationship with adjacent land uses. Giving some thought to how residents will use the open space allows developers to design and use the space for maximum effect early on. This approach allows open space to become a unifying element for community life.

Consumer Motivations

The effective design of open space must begin with a basic understanding of the consumer's needs and wants. A community has the same hierarchy of needs—originally identified by psychologist Abraham Maslow, in the 1950s—that are shared by all humans.[2] According to Maslow's hierarchy, the basic needs, such as food, shelter, clothing, and safety, must be met before one moves on to higher-level pursuits, which fulfill such needs as belonging, aesthetics, and self-actualization.

Figure 4-1, prepared by the EastLake Development Company, a San Diego–based developer of master-planned communities, is based on the pyramid Maslow used to depict his hierarchy of needs.

When Maslow's model is applied to community development, it becomes apparent why most new communities—which address only the bottom two levels of the pyramid—are often found lacking, from the consumer's perspective. The most successful communities address every level of the pyramid of needs. The most difficult need to provide for is, of course, the one at the very top of the pyramid: self-actualization. Communities that foster self-actualization are those that encourage personal growth, cater to residents' individual needs, and match programs to people, not people to programs. Those features that fos-

Figure 4-1
The Role of the Community Builder

Maslow's Hierarchy of Needs	Consumer Motivations	Homebuyer's Hierarchy of Needs
5. Achieving personal growth and fulfillment that is consistent with one's unique potential and values	**Achieving self-actualization**	5. A desire for a living environment that fosters and stimulates personal growth that is consistent with personal values
4. Striving to achieve a high standing relative to others; includes a desire for mastery, reputation, and prestige	**Achieving status and esteem**	4. Striving for social status and prestige as demonstrated by the desirability of location, the architectural treatments, the value of the property, and the image associated with the address
3. Striving to be accepted by intimate members of one's family or group, and to be an important person to them	**Achieving a sense of belonging and love**	3. Striving for acceptance by members of a "neighborhood" of people sharing similar values and interests; being able to make meaningful contributions to community well-being
2. Concern over physical survival in addition to satisfying hunger and thirst	**Achieving a sense of safety**	2. Concern for one's own physical safety and that of loved ones, and for the security of one's possessions
1. Fundamentals of survival (food, water, shelter, etc.)	**Meeting physiological needs**	1. Meeting fundamental needs for shelter at an affordable cost

ter self-actualization can give a new community the ultimate competitive edge.

To gain an advantage in competitive markets, a new community must evoke an image in the mind of the potential buyer, must have a recognizable "personality," and must produce a selling difference. Using open-space amenities to gain a competitive advantage is not a new notion, of course, but community developers have so far tended to fall far short of this goal. To be memorable, a community must provide fun and fulfillment. Every land use must be examined in terms of its ability to contribute to a high-quality living environment, and in relation to the community's unique selling proposition—the one thing that makes this product different from any other.

Safe Open Space

People want to pull a shell of safety around themselves. In the 1970s, lifestyle chronicler Faith Popcorn identified the trend toward "cocooning," which she defined as "a full-scale retreat into the last controllable (or sort of controllable) environment—your own digs." In her 1991 book, *The Popcorn Report,* she took the idea one step further: cocooning is about controlling one's environment, and people's environments are not limited to their homes.

Developers planning communities cannot ignore consumers' increasing need for a sense of safety and security. The challenge is to create environments that are perceived as safe so that residents will venture forth and interact. It is this interaction that creates community, with all its values and benefits. People must be able to "cocoon" within the community. For this to occur, planners must provide a strong sense of ownership, security, and belonging, extending the cocoon out past the walls of the home to embrace the neighborhood, the neighborhood park, the streets, and other public areas.

It is a given that all community open spaces must be safe. It is often up to the developer,

however, to determine how to address this requirement. Unfortunately, some solutions can create physically secure—but stark and unappealing—open spaces. A different approach, one that encourages social interaction within spaces, allows security to be achieved and adds value to the community.

Programmable versus Dedicated Spaces

Should open-space areas and related facilities be programmable or dedicated? Programmable space—general, all-purpose space—promotes flexibility by allowing multiple uses and enabling residents to determine how the space and facilities are to be used. When a developer creates dedicated space—areas that are designed to accommodate a specific activity—he or she is being proactive and anticipating residents' needs, and the appropriate elements may be in place as early as a community's grand opening.

An analogy can help explain the choices: in the 1970s and 1980s, homebuilders faced a similar dilemma regarding the effective use of space within the home. Many builders opted for something called a "bonus room,"

In Prospect New Town, an 80-acre (32-hectare) development located on the former site of a tree farm in Longmont, Colorado, nine pocket parks are all located within a two-minute walk of the neighborhood's 338 housing units. Homes facing onto the parks provide residents with a secure environment, and the parks encourage social interaction.

a programmable space that could be outfitted after purchase to suit the household's individual needs. The space was relatively inexpensive to build, and consumers tended to assign a value to it that was greater than the construction cost. The developer's role was essentially passive, and the consumer usually realized the true benefits later in time, when the bonus space was dedicated to a specific use.

Starting in the 1990s, the trend reversed: homebuilders realized that by dedicating programmed space, they could target specific market segments and capture a larger incremental value for their expenditures. In other words, the targeted consumers were willing to pay more to have the house already meet their specific needs and wants. Bonus rooms, in contrast, were blank slates that would not necessarily lend themselves to the uses that consumers had in mind (such as media rooms, housekeepers' rooms, or home offices with outside entrances). Predesigned options and design center programs allowed builders to personalize homes for the consumer. When consumers compared an additional room or space located and outfitted in a way that made the most sense for the intended use with the one-size-fits-all approach of the bonus room, they put more value on the programmed option.

Most developers today are still using the "bonus room" approach to the design, placement, and construction of open space and related amenities. Spaces and buildings are made programmable so that residents can eventually decide to employ them for the specific uses that they value. Thus, the community's realization of that value, and the developer's potential value-added benefit, is delayed well past the early development phase.

Such lost opportunities need not occur. Careful consumer research can determine the most valued types of open-space uses, and

thoughtful planning can be used to develop open-space areas in the best, most cost-effective ways to meet the demands of target markets. The front-end costs will be higher for the same amount of space, but both the real and perceived value to the consumer will also be higher. More important, the incremental added value will be achieved in the first phase, effectively raising the bar for land value in all subsequent phases.

Consumer Preference Surveys

Consumer research can be a valuable tool for answering a multitude of questions about the most efficient and effective use of open space—and for identifying the elements of a community that will elicit a "Wow!" from the consumer. However, because consumer preferences vary greatly over time and from one location to another, consumer research must be current and locationally specific. Many consulting firms specialize in such research, and some developers have in-house research departments. DMB, a community developer headquartered in Scottsdale, Arizona, conducts surveys to determine consumer preferences in a variety of categories, including the appeal of various kinds of open space. For example, a recent study showed that 70.6 percent of those surveyed preferred "small, modest parks within walking distance from home" over "larger, more elaborate parks within short driving distance from home." DMB's research also shows that consumer demands have changed over time. In the early 1990s, the company's prospective buyers wanted golf courses and other recreational amenities. But in 2000, buyers showed a strong preference for intangibles like "community, connection, and diversity." "Pedestrian access" had also become a major demand. Such valuable insights can be used to target consumer preferences and to develop strategies for the effective and efficient use of community land for open spaces.

Research can address open-space questions at both the macro and micro levels. For example, does the targeted consumer assign greater value to a community golf course or to a community greenbelt? Because a golf course is an expensive amenity, it is important to know whether consumers' interest is worth the cost to the developer. If not, the optimum solution might be a modest golf course (for recreation) that serves primarily as a visual amenity—a "greenbelt with tees." At the other end of the spectrum, consumer preferences about staffing or types of park furniture can be surveyed.

Open-ended survey questions also offer valuable clues to consumer preferences regarding open space. Responses such as the following express preferences that provide useful information to the developer:

- Open space that creates the feeling of living in the country;
- Plenty of nearby parks and open space to enjoy;
- Soccer fields close enough to allow kids and families to walk to games and practices;

- A Starbucks coffee kiosk at the recreation center on weekends;
- An outdoor stage for concerts in the park;
- Shade for summer picnics;
- A game room with someone to help organize games;
- Relocation and preservation of oak trees;
- Well-maintained greenbelt areas that include play areas with play equipment;
- Nature trails with access to natural open space;
- Common areas strategically lighted for nighttime enjoyment;
- Viewpoints that afford beautiful views to homeowners and visitors;
- Plaques throughout the community with descriptions of local culture and native vegetation;
- A water feature as a focal point for sitting and socializing;
- Walking trails with fitness stations.

In a 1998 national survey by American LIVES, Inc., a market research firm, amenities such as natural open space, walking and biking paths, and gardens with native plants were rated as very important by more than half of those surveyed. Keeping open space in a natural condition with simple improvements such as dirt trails, benches, groves of trees, and sandlot playgrounds can be a very cost-effective way of appealing to buyers. Even in relatively urban areas, the inclusion of wooded "wilderness areas," manufactured nature paths, or garden parks can allow residents to interact with the environment.

The Fields of St. Croix, outside Minneapolis, and Orange Shoals, north of Atlanta (see the case study chapter), both capitalize on the special character of their natural open space. Known as "conservation communities," they were developed with an emphasis on protecting large contiguous natural areas—St. Croix's prairies and Orange Shoals's forests and streams—that enhance the community. Both communities have been commended by environmental groups.

Programming for Residents' Needs

Open space is the hard infrastructure that is needed to launch soft infrastructure. What gives open space its value is how it fits residents' recreational goals. Traditionally, community planning has tended to reflect recreational trends and to respond to the pressures of special interest groups, rather than to provide a stimulus for residents' personal expression and growth during their leisure hours. As normally practiced, recreation has fitted people to programs, not programs to people.

Contemporary planning for open-space amenities is headed in quite a different direction. Goals for both public and private recreation focus on opening up opportunities for adventures in living. Recreation is seen as a stimulating and enriching element that is a part of—not apart from—daily life. Instead of offering only isolated leisure facilities to fill this or that hour of the day, the best communities create a total environment that is designed to meet the full range of residents' physical and emotional needs.

Open-space amenities should enhance the sensory experiences of community residents. Developers must carefully consider community spaces and facilities from the perspective of color, smell, taste, texture, and sound. Large mixed-use communities can include kiosks for food vendors in parks and along commercial streets. It does not take a very large community to support a weekend farmers' market, which will bring in the colors, smells, and tastes of local produce and flowers. Even at the smallest scale, an element such as a fountain can turn a small square into a sensory attraction. The visual interest added by a fountain, the sound of splashing water, and children's gleeful shouts as they run through the cold water all heighten the value of what might otherwise be an uninteresting, and unused, lot.

Recreational Pursuits

Community residents' basic emotional and physical needs can be broken into categories; each category of need can be met through a range of recreational pursuits.

Belonging

In the past, people depended on their neighbors for survival. Neighbors helped each other at harvest time; worked side by side battling floods, fires, and other emergencies; and managed the community's civic affairs. Today, professionals (or trained volunteers) handle emergencies, and communities are managed by elected and appointed leaders. The need for "belonging" still exists, however. The community must, therefore, be organized so as to leave a place open for those who want to contribute to the community—and thereby achieve a sense of belonging.

Relaxation

Leisure time is generally defined as residual time left over after work time. Achieving physical relaxation during leisure hours is simple. Fishing in a stocked lake, sailing, horseback riding, sailing model boats, gardening, picnicking, even people watching—all are forms of relaxation. But it is equally important that relaxation include the notion of "leisure pace" —that is, leisure that infuses the whole of life. Driving to work along a scenic parkway, walking home from school with friends, or greeting a neighbor on the way to the store bring a more relaxed pace to daily life.

Solitude

It is becoming increasingly difficult to find quiet open spaces in which to visit with nature and one's inner self. This basic need must be met within communities. Ways must be found to protect—and, if possible, heighten—feelings of oneness with nature. Vistas; greenbelts; tree groupings, even on urban streets; and natural textures, colors, and smells can be interwoven with developed components. Whether these places take the form of vista points or are simply small groves of trees in open areas, it is important to provide places in which to enjoy quiet.

Big-Muscle Activities

In new planned communities, small neighborhood parks (usually with children's play lots), and facilities such as swimming pools are becoming the norm. But facilities for "big-muscle" activities—such as football, baseball, soccer, volleyball, basketball, tennis, lap swimming, racquetball, handball, and rowing—should also be available to residents of all ages. Although this recreation category has historically been addressed by the recreation departments of municipal governments and similar public entities, fiscal constraints often prevent the public sector from providing the necessary facilities. Both public and private initiatives are important in meeting the need for big-muscle activities. Community builders must allocate the necessary resources and creative energy to ensure that this recreation category is adequately addressed.

Quiet Games

The "quiet games" category includes activities such as shuffleboard, horseshoes, croquet, and board games. Although these are often considered activities for seniors, participation is certainly not restricted to that age group. In fact, such activities provide excellent opportunities for multigenerational interaction, adding further value to the community. To foster participation in this type of activity, developers should set aside special areas in activity centers or parks and provide facilities for quiet games.

Nature Study

Developers should identify appropriate natural or naturalized areas within and adjacent to the community and plan trails for residents who are interested in nature study, bird watching, or related activities. Special areas for environmental education may be appropriate as well. Support for such activities normally comes readily from community residents and

from the local chapters of such groups as the Audubon Society, the Sierra Club, and scouting organizations.

Hand-Intellect Activities

Arts and crafts, opportunities for scientific study, vocational classes (on topics such as computers or photography), and after-school programs for children should be elements of the open-space program. Accommodations can be made within the community recreation center or in public and private parks, but creative community developers will also seek special arrangements with entities such as school districts and tenants in commercial centers. For example, a local nursery could provide hands-on gardening classes for community residents. In the case of commercial centers, the key may be to either aggressively negotiate mutually beneficial leases with tenants or to employ professional staff who will be responsible for organizing and directing such activities and matching residents' interests with activities.

Adventure and Creative Play

Adventure playgrounds, wooded areas, and specially equipped parks are all places that satisfy a child's need for adventure and excitement, and that can be made safe for creative play. Because society has become so

Mission Viejo, California, a 10,000-acre (4,000-hectare) planned community, features nearly 20,000 single-family residences; 9 million square feet (836,130 square meters) of industrial, retail, and office space; and 336 acres (136 hectares) of recreational facilities and open space. Lake Mission Viejo, ringed by extensive landscaping and walkways, serves as a recreational focal point and an emergency reservoir.

litigious, concerns about liability have all but eliminated the unstructured playgrounds that once allowed children to create their own play experiences. Nevertheless, such playgrounds, which encourage creativity (remember the imaginary worlds that you created as a child?), are important and should be provided wherever practical.

Rhythm and Music

A well-planned community should allocate spaces for performances of live music, which may be organized by the city, school districts, community associations, or a merchants' association. Facilities such as amphitheaters and bandstands should be made available for concerts, dance exhibitions, and hands-on musical participation.

Drama

The potential needs of a community theater group or similar organization should be considered during the planning stages of community development. Such activities can be facilitated, and even stimulated, if incorporated into an open-space plan. Outdoor amphitheaters and open-air plazas with staging provisions (whether permanent or as needed), can serve as stages for both professional and amateur productions.

Social Activities

Picnic shelters, town squares or quads, tot lots, meeting facilities, and places for neighborhood block parties are necessary ingredients of a community and should be programmed into the open-space plan as a means of fostering social interaction. In the case of social activities, staffing considerations (including the involvement of volunteers) are perhaps more important than for other kinds of recreation.

Community Service

For many people, participation in the life of the community—through clubs, volunteer programs, or membership on boards or committees—is a basic need and can be classified as a recreational activity. One way of satisfying this need is through the formation of common-area maintenance associations or lifestyle maintenance associations, with their attendant boards and committees. The creation of an interpretive nature center or community kiosk may encourage the participation of volunteers.

Mental Exercise

People often seek mental exercise as a form of recreation. To the extent practical, an open-space program should consider provisions for interpretive centers, lecture series, traveling exhibits, and other programs and events. Outdoor exhibit spaces and multipurpose indoor facilities can provide the locations.

Open-Space Facilities That Serve Residents' Needs

A goal of the open-space master plan should be to provide all the elements necessary to ensure a rich variety of recreational opportunities while satisfying identified recreational needs. The following seven sections identify the basic types of recreational facilities and offer some guidelines for developers undertaking an open-space plan.

Special Facilities

Special amenity areas provide for unique recreational needs not normally fulfilled by conventional public park facilities. Examples include golf courses, equestrian centers, man-made lakes, and other active-use outdoor facilities. Such facilities are often privately owned and operated through some form of community association or by a commercial entity.

Community Parks with Sports Facilities

Local recreation departments determine what types of facilities will be included in public parks. It is important to ensure that sufficient open space is allocated and that the necessary facilities are provided for big-muscle activities such as competitive soccer, base-

ball, and swimming. Often, these activities are the core of community life and are the impetus for forming community ties, particularly for families with school-age children. Developers should coordinate with local park authorities to ensure that adequate sports facilities are provided. If not, the developer may have to include such facilities as part of the project's amenities.

Neighborhood and Small-Scale Parks

Neighborhood parks or miniparks should be oriented to the projected demographics of the neighborhood in which they are located. Each neighborhood park should have a specific open-space amenity—which, when combined with other local facilities, provides a balance of recreational opportunities. Neighborhood parks should provide play courts, children's play equipment, ballfields and practice areas for informal games, and picnic facilities. Special amenities such as swimming pools, restrooms, sand volleyball courts, or community gardens may be appropriate in

certain neighborhoods. At Ladera Ranch, a large, master-planned community in Orange County, California (see the case study chapter), the amenities in neighborhood parks are tailored to the character and lifestyle of each neighborhood. Notably, the community does not have a golf course, but it has succeeded in using smaller-scale open-space amenities to appeal to buyers.

Public Schools

By coordinating the planning and design of schools and adjacent park facilities, communities can enhance recreational opportunities both for students and others in the community. Typical amenities include the ballfields and other outdoor recreation facilities usually associated with schools. Additional facilities can be included for music, drama, and nature study, and for the meetings of service organizations or for neighborhood social gatherings.

In Belle Creek, a 1,000-unit master-planned community near Denver (see the case study chapter), the focal point of daily life is a com-

A 1,273-acre (515-hectare) project that encircles one of the largest freshwater lakes in eastern China, Jinji Lake Waterfront District, designed by EDAW, Inc., features residential, recreational, and commercial components. A continuous system of pedestrian pathways and gardens wraps around the lake.

plex that includes a recreation center, daycare, and a charter school. The complex, which faces the town square, includes meeting space, a large gym, and other facilities that are available to all local area residents.

Commercial Centers

Although they are typically not viewed as offering recreational opportunities, commercial centers can be integral elements of a leisure-oriented recreational lifestyle. Commercial areas can be designed to include amenities such as libraries; sidewalk cafés and other outdoor eating areas; village common areas, perhaps with a bandstand or small amphitheater; shaded areas for quiet games and social gatherings, and so on. Bike shops can be located adjacent to a bike trail. To expand recreational opportunities, developers of commercial centers can encourage tenants to make their facilities available for learning experiences, which would create additional traffic for the business as well. Examples include photography classes in a camera shop, cake-decorating classes in a bakery, or a children's story hour in a bookstore.

In King Farm, in Rockville, Maryland (see the case study chapter), a community-oriented commercial district has been successfully integrated into the fabric of the community. Shops and restaurants are located in urban-style blocks and are oriented toward sidewalks and the village green, and restaurants include sidewalk dining. Most residents and office workers in King Farm can walk or bike to the commercial district.

Trails

Linear open space can expand recreational opportunities. The master plan should include provisions for walking, hiking, bicycling, and horseback riding; vista and picnic areas; nature study areas; fitness parcourses; and benches for simple relaxation. Most well-planned residential communities include places for walking, whether sidewalks, trails, or some combination of the two.

Civic Areas

Outdoor facilities and plazas with provisions for both live performances and cultural events are examples of civic features that help meet residents' recreational needs. Historic sites and buildings are also important, and can serve as both identifying landmarks and as venues for events. At Farrcroft, in Fairfax, Virginia (see the case study chapter), the de-

A lighted dog run, landscaped courtyards with barbecue grills, a tot lot, and a half-acre (0.2-hectare) village green all serve the various recreational needs of tenants of the Avalon at Arlington Square, a rental apartment community in Virginia. At completion, Arlington Square will feature 943 apartments, including 64 affordable units.

Figure 4-2

Recreation-Opportunity Matrix for the Planned Community of Eastlake

	Recreational Elements							
Recreational Activities	Special Amenities and Facilities	Neighborhood and Miniparks	Community or Sports Parks	Public Schools	Commercial Centers	Open Space and Trails	Civic Areas	Facility Types for Each Activity
Big-muscle activities	■	■	■	■		■		5
Quiet games	■	■			■		■	4
Nature study	■	■				■		3
Hand-intellect activities	■			■	■			3
Adventure and creative play		■				■		2
Relaxation	■	■	■		■	■	■	6
Rhythm and music	■			■	■		■	4
Drama				■			■	2
Social activities	■	■	■	■	■		■	6
Community service	■			■			■	3
Mental exercise	■			■	■		■	4
Activities addressed by each facility type	9	6	3	7	6	4	7	

■ = A strong recreational opportunity.

veloper preserved a historic mansion on the site for public and private special events—demonstrating that, even in a relatively small project, amenities can be created that bring people together and build a sense of community.

An open-space amenity program should help residents meet as many of their emotional and physical needs as possible. While recreational *activities* provide the means of fulfilling some of these physical and emotional needs, open-space *amenities* are a vehicle through which those needs can be satisfied.

The opportunity matrix shown in figure 4-2, which illustrates the interrelationship between physical elements and recreational activities in a community, is a handy tool for planning a community's open space. While somewhat subjective, the matrix does offer an example of how to develop an open-space master plan.

It should be noted that the number of opportunities shown under an amenity category is not necessarily indicative of the need for, or relative value of, that amenity in the overall open-space program. It does, however, indicate the degree of design flexibility and creativity essential to a comprehensive and balanced open-space master plan.

Planning and Design Considerations

The following planning principles should be used when designing an open-space plan for a community:

■ Every open-space element has to contribute to the overall goal of establishing

Through innovative uses of pond and waterfall features, Colonial Grand at Town Park, in Lake Mary, Florida, maintains a 100-year flood retention plain. Designed to make apartment living more like resort living, Colonial Grand consists of 456 units on 59 acres (24 hectares) and includes a clubhouse and pool area. Almost every apartment has a view of woods or water.

and maintaining a special *place,* and a special *quality.*

- Nature must predominate over manmade improvements. The natural environment should appear to have been there first. To create the impression that each amenity is part of an ecosystem, all parks should be linked by open spaces.
- Homes should have direct access to open-space amenities.
- Open-space amenities should help residents meet as many of their basic emotional and physical needs as possible.

In designing open-space amenities, developers should look to nature for direction. Often developers have failed to understand that a natural amenity is always part of a larger ecosystem—and, as such, cannot emerge full-blown out of nothing. Recognizing the natural birth process of a lake, for example, not only lends credibility to the look of the place, but holds the key to ensuring the low-

est possible costs per acre of amenity produced. For example, the ecosystem for a lake includes

- Tributaries: dry, ragged, linear open space, scoured by the sudden and infrequent force of flash flooding.
- A "maximum high pool": the maximum possible flood contour of the water body. A scour line and a gradually sloping grassy edge define this zone.
- The permanent pool: the lowest contour line maintained by the water in the course of a year.
- The discharge channels: a system similar in appearance to the tributaries, through which water flows out of the permanent pool.

The development team must recognize important aspects of such an amenity. First, the physical feature itself is static. Second, the implied scope of the physical feature should be dynamic. The trick is to *produce* as little as possible and *imply* as much as possible, with the end result being a complete, believable, open-space environment for minimum dollars.

Conclusion

Recreation has taken on increased importance in people's lives—and, because of a variety of factors (increased stress in the workplace, the expanding number of two-worker households, and the value placed on leisure time), will continue to remain important. When planning new communities, developers should make easy, safe access to a full range of recreational experiences a primary goal.

For builders and developers, providing creative, high-quality amenities will be a key to continuing success. It will require the innovative use of open-space resources. Developers must proactively use open space as a value-added amenity, thereby creating competitive marketing advantages, demonstrating leadership in creating livable communities, and enhancing profitability by jump-starting a strong sense of community.

To accomplish these goals, developers need to understand consumers' needs and expectations. Armed with such information, they can effectively turn open spaces into investments that achieve a "big bang for the buck" for everyone involved. Community builders have a responsibility to use precious open spaces wisely. In addition, doing so is just plain good business.

This chapter was written by Robert Santos, division president, Lennar Communities, Mission Viejo, California; and Pam Engebretson, president, Interra Strategies, Inc., San Diego.

Notes

1. Ray Oldenburg, *The Great Good Place* (New York: Marlowe & Co.), 1989.

2. Abraham Maslow, *Motivation and Personality* (New York: Harper), 1954.

5 Mixing Housing Types for Greater Value

Older cities and towns can teach developers a great deal about creating value in new communities. Throughout much of history, cities and towns were founded and expanded according to well-established principles of town making that had been handed down through the centuries. As a result, many older cities and towns offer streets and public spaces that are truly memorable—places where the details of the architecture and landscape ring true, where all the activities of daily life occur, and where great communities thrive. These streets and public places provide a ready balance among all aspects of a healthy community where people can live, work, shop, play, worship, and learn. They foster a living continuum that delivers to a community's residents the ability to grow up and grow old in place. Each of these aspects reinforces the others, creating a self-renewing dynamic that promotes continued growth and prosperity.

A lively scene in a traditional neighborhood: Capitol Hill, in Washington, D.C. Townhouses, apartments over retail, and small apartment buildings all coexist on the same block.

TORTI GALLAS AND PARTNERS

INTERFACE MULTIMEDIA

In these vibrant and robust communities, economic value grows in direct proportion to the quality of the built environment, which is itself linked directly to the residents' lifestyles. Charleston, South Carolina; Capitol Hill, in Washington, D.C.; Forest Hills and Bronxville, in New York; and Shaker Heights, outside Cleveland, Ohio, are but a few examples of how quality of place creates value. People love to live in such places, and pay extraordinary prices for that privilege. For developers of large, long-term projects, the implications are obvious. Such communities will increase in value as development progresses and the community takes shape. Developers of smaller projects can readily achieve similar results through the synergies that are created when a development fits into its context and is integrated into a full-life community.

What are the principles on which these kinds of communities are built? A close examination of successful models like those listed above reveals five common, interdependent components of high-value communities:

- A strong public realm;
- A mix of uses;
- Good connections (local and regional);
- Pedestrian-oriented streets and public spaces;
- A mix of housing types (single-family detached houses; townhouses; and multi-family housing units).

The principal focus of this chapter, mixed housing types, is often neglected in discussions of community planning because its

relation to the other components of high-value communities is not always understood. This chapter describes a number of important considerations that developers need to take into account in planning and implementing communities that will have a mix of housing types. It also discusses the relationship between mixing housing types and other aspects of good community-building, and shows how the decision to mix housing types can add value to a development.

Why Mix Housing Types?

Why mix housing types within a single community? The short answer is increased value. On the same piece of land ordinarily allotted for a single housing type—say, detached single-family houses—a neighborhood that offers a balanced mix of housing types and prices will return more value to the community, to the residents, and to the developer. A variety of building types, plans, and prices enhances value by broadening the market for the development, while careful design and planning ensure no loss of control over quality, project phasing, or economies of scale. This manifold approach to the market will increase absorption while creating an attractive, aesthetically diverse neighborhood that avoids the "cookie cutter" syndrome that so

Bethesda Row, in suburban Bethesda, Maryland, is a successful mix of retail and office uses. The next phase will add mid-rise apartments over retail.

The historic Georgetown neighborhood in Washington, D.C., sets a precedent for a mix of housing types, often on the same block.

many buyers resist. As in communities of the past, the public realm will be more likely to become a pleasurable and memorable pedestrian environment, further adding to the community's desirability and marketability.

In addition to broadening the market potential by diversifying the housing stock, such a strategy increases the value of the homes: many consumers will pay a premium for a home in a diverse community. This observation has been borne out in many new urbanist communities, where prices escalated rapidly because of pent-up demand for such neighborhoods. Research cited in ULI's *Valuing the New Urbanism* showed that prices for homes in five diverse new urbanist communities across the country were between 4 and 25 percent higher than the prices of comparable homes in more conventional suburban subdivisions.[1]

Demographics are one reason that broader housing choice adds value today. As discussed in chapter 1, traditional families now represent 27 percent of all suburban households —a figure that, according to U.S. Census projections, is expected to decline to 20 percent by 2010. Instead, households once considered "alternative" are now mainstream. Such households continue to locate in new communities in large numbers, bringing a taste for smaller homes, greater diversity, and urban-style amenities. Impatient with traffic congestion, these new households—which include singles living alone, married couples with no children, gay couples, empty nesters, and single parents—are searching for fine-

grained neighborhoods that offer housing flexibility and choice. Many are also searching for the excitement and the sense of community that they enjoyed earlier in their lives, when they lived on college campuses, in shared housing, or in diverse urban neighborhoods.

Also, multiple generations are choosing to live near each other. Instead of being isolated in retirement communities, many older people prefer to live in the same area as their children and grandchildren, creating further demand for multifamily housing, accessory units, and small-lot single-family homes.

What's Old Is New Again

Mixed uses and mixed housing types are time-tested ideas that have worked for centuries, both in this country and abroad. For example, in the Georgetown neighborhood of Washington, D.C., almost any block includes a broad mix of residences that can house the full spectrum of income groups. Elegant mansions are home to some of the wealthiest families in America. The townhouses and the smaller detached houses that are mingled in with the mansions house another demographic layer. And most blocks include small apartment or condominium buildings that house young single people and couples. In some cases, apartments that have been carved out of larger homes house students and others of lesser means. The buildings of Georgetown are of different sizes, types, and values, but of equal character; the result is a community where residents with different income levels can find suitable homes. Shopping and employment are never more than a few blocks away, making this neighborhood not only one of mixed housing and mixed incomes, but also of mixed uses.

A drive along any pre-1940 residential corridor—upper Connecticut Avenue in Washington, D.C., for example—reveals an orderly progression of densities, tapering from high to low: mid-rise elevator apartment buildings are located directly on the avenue; on the portions of the side streets closest to the avenue are walk-up apartments and townhouses; farthest from the avenue are duplexes and single-family homes. Behind the eight-story apartment buildings that line the avenue, merchant builders routinely turned out large and small freestanding houses, semidetached houses, fourplexes, townhouses, and small garage apartments—all on the same block, and all sharing the same stick-built technology. Then as now, such a repertoire offered a way of increasing absorption and meeting a range of different needs, incomes, and tastes.

Then along came sprawling, suburban-style development, with its single-use zoning and its separated subdivisions—each offering a single housing type with a narrow range of values, and each inhabited by residents from a single income bracket. The American suburb—which was highly successful for the second half of the 20th century and helped to generate the greatest prosperity that the world has ever seen—has created an entirely new set of problems. The combination of single-use zoning and the hierarchical roadway system created widely separated clusters of development, so that when residents travel from home to work, from work to shopping, from home to shopping, or from home to school, each trip must be made by personal vehicle on road systems that are increasingly clogged. As suburban densities decreased even further, the separation among uses, housing types, and people only worsened. Now the $250,000 single-family houses are located in one land bay and the $150,000 townhouses in another. In many developments, walls and gates separate each housing type from the others, reinforcing separation.

Today, new development models offer alternatives to sprawl and its shortcomings. The new urbanism, for example, uses proven neighborhood-making principles to address current social, environmental, and economic issues. The new urbanist model—when combined with the skills of a successful suburban real estate developer who understands large-tract entitlements, production building, financing, market analysis, marketing, and management—can create communities that win faster approvals, gain greater market acceptance, and make a positive contribution to the built environment.

Understanding the Context

History has proven again and again that it is important to understand the interdependency between neighborhoods and the public realm, and the relationship between region, neighborhood, and neighbor, and to build on these connections. These relationships create the context that developers must con-

Along Connecticut Avenue, in Washington, D.C., large apartment and condominium buildings line the busy avenue, while lower-density housing types are set back on the side streets.

sider when formulating a housing mix. The following six sections explore a set of interrelated elements that are pertinent to housing mix and that must work together if a development is to achieve success. Taken together, these elements create a matrix of rules for mixing housing types:

- Place;
- Entitlements;
- Demographics and lifestyles;
- Cost of land, parking, and buildings;
- Building types;
- Absorption.

Place

The parameters of place include where the neighborhood is located relative to the center city, how large the city is, and the amount and type of competition, from both new and existing housing stock. While a neighborhood of mixed housing types can be created in any area, the specific approach will vary with the location. An appropriate mix of housing for a downtown location, for example, will not transfer to a midtown location, an inner-ring

suburb, or a new greenfield suburb. Furthermore, the same approach will work in different ways in different cities. New York, Baltimore, Charleston, and Orlando each require unique strategies to create a successful housing mix. The type of housing and the appropriate mix will be determined by the scale of the city, town, or village, and by the project's proximity to the center.

When a project is proposed for an infill location, one basic rule predominates: the new housing must reflect residents' vision of the existing community. No longer can developers, builders, and architects design housing from the kitchen sink out; they must design it from the curb in. Designing homes that are in keeping with the way that current residents see the community will help to maintain the sense of place while fostering the cooperation of existing residents, who will see the new development as furthering their vision. When residents' perceptions clash with reality, however, and they expect the community to continue to consist of low-density suburban pods when the economics of the area are

At Santana Row, in San Jose, California, the shops and restaurants that line the main street have townhouses on the upper floors. Parking is located both underground and in above-grade structures.

forcing higher densities, developers and designers may need to engage in neighborhood education and consensus building (see chapter 8).

The most successful infill developers understand the goals of the existing community and translate those goals into a financially feasible and marketable product. Often, success depends on providing a denser product that is compatible in scale and form with the existing buildings in the neighborhood and that reflects the style and quality of the architectural context. In some ways, it is easier to design a community on an infill site than on a greenfield site because the surroundings provide a template. There are, of course, neighborhoods that do not provide an acceptable template; in those cases, the designer must come up with a new, but still compatible, kind of development.

If the proposed project is a new community on a greenfield site, the decisions about housing mix are more complex. The old formula of suburban development was simply to provide a unit in an acceptable location. In today's live-work-play communities, developers need to provide a complete lifestyle—including, ideally, a transit-friendly location; walkable streets; amenities; and close proximity to work, services, the community core, and neighborhood open spaces. In addition, the developer should strive to create neighborly blocks, and to offer a dignified and well-integrated mix of housing choices.

Sense of place in the suburbs has evolved considerably since the 1980s, and consumers now demand more from builders and developers. Nearly all suburban homebuyers and renters are more concerned about the quality of the places where they live, and some are even willing to accept measures—such as localized density and diversity—to bring about the kinds of changes that they want. Developments such as Celebration, Florida, and Kentlands and King Farm, in Maryland,

TORTI GALLAS AND PARTNERS

are communities that meet these higher expectations.

The mixed-use component of development has come a long way, too. No longer a mini-mall tacked onto a subdivision, today's town center is likely to be the real thing: the geographic center of several walkable neighborhoods, offering goods, services, and a community core within a five-minute walk of most residences. From both a design and a marketing perspective, the idea of mixed housing types is intimately connected to current notions about place making.

Entitlements

During the entitlement process, two conflicting points of view begin to form—that of the municipality and that of the developer. The municipality wants to know exactly what is being proposed, even if it is ten or 20 years in the future, and the developer wants to maintain maximum flexibility so that he or she can adjust the plans to respond to a constantly evolving market.

Celebration, Florida, is made up of a broad mix of housing types —including, in the town center, residences above shops.

The housing types at King Farm, in Rockville, Maryland. From left to right: apartments over retail space, Charleston-style apartments, townhouses and single-family detached houses, apartment buildings, manor house apartments, and single-family detached houses.

Normally this schism is bridged by means of a good design plan and a set of quantitative and qualitative guidelines, or regulating codes. The quantitative guidelines set the parameters for how much is to be built, including the total number of units and the square footage of nonresidential buildings. The qualitative guidelines describe the design of both the site and the buildings, and set parameters for height, bulk, setback, and parking. The regulating plan offers the municipality the assurance that it will get a place of a certain quality; thus, the implementation guidelines go far beyond simple zoning ("The 7,000-square-foot lots go here, and the 5,000-square-foot lots go there.") In the best of situations, the regulating plan allows the developer the latitude to fine-tune where, when, and how large.

The development team that created King Farm, in Rockville, Maryland (see the case study chapter), worked closely with the municipality to instill confidence that the project would meet the city's objectives; the city responded by allowing the developers the flexibility that they needed. For example, the approved plan specifies a maximum of 3,200 residential units and describes the types of units, but it does not prescribe the number of units of each type, which leaves room for adjustments as buildout proceeds. The plan also includes a provision permitting the developer to increase the number of units to 3,600 at an unspecified time, if the increase is approved by the mayor and city council. Such flexibility would not be possible if the city did not have confidence in the overall plan. This kind of flexible, holistic approach to planning and development goes a long

way toward defusing resistance on the part of both the market and the financial community, and toward overcoming the political and regulatory objections often faced by projects that incorporate mixed housing types. Further, securing entitlements for a large development all at one time, rather than phase by phase, insulates the developer from changes in the political climate that may, in the future, be less favorable toward new development.

A now familiar argument for building a conceptually integrated, mixed-use, mixed-housing-type neighborhood—rather than rows of identical units in a subdivision—is that it makes "growth" a good word. Often, residents of an existing neighborhood will fight any proposed development because, in their experience, a vacant lot is better than the development that will replace it. Having one's neighborhood surrounded by unbuilt lots is considered ideal; having a handful of neighboring houses is less ideal; and seeing a lower-priced house go up next door is a cause for alarm. In contrast, when current homeowners are shown plans for a genuinely mixed-used, mixed-unit development that will add value and amenities to their community, they may be more likely to accept the proposal.

The goals of nonprofit sponsors, socially conscious developers, or local governments may also be part of the equation. In Colorado's Belle Creek, for example (see the case study chapter), a socially conscious developer teamed up with a nonprofit sponsor to create a community with a mix of housing types to serve a broad range of renters and owners.

For those who believe that diversity of age, income, and occupation is part of what defines a good place to live, a variety of unit types is essential. Moreover, projects that offer a mix of housing types can help jurisdictions achieve a range of social goals—from meeting the required minimums for affordable or ADA-accessible units to providing places for seniors and students, and providing service workers with reasonably priced housing that is close to their jobs. Of course, addressing social goals can also yield non-altruistic benefits. For example, the community goodwill generated can translate into faster approvals for the development.

In the end, local jurisdictions, lenders, home-buyers, and neighboring property owners all benefit from including a mix of housing types in a community.

- By allowing a mix of housing types, a community can help satisfy a wide range of local housing needs while reducing the impact on traffic, infrastructure, and open space.
- When the overall development employs a mix of unit types, all of which are similar

in the quality of their design and materials, affordable units can be blended seamlessly into the community.

- A broad mix of housing—and household types—is better able to support urban-style public amenities and retail activity, which benefit the community as a whole.
- A mix of housing types at a full range of prices helps make it possible for local employees to live near their jobs.

Demographics and Lifestyles

To create a successful project, the developer must understand what part of the geographic spectrum each market segment will be drawn to, from the urban core to greenfield suburbs. Many different types of people, forming many different types of households, find it locationally desirable to live in a particular village, town, or neighborhood, but have different requirements for the type of home that suits them best, and for the rent or purchase price they can afford. Generation-Xers, married couples without children, single-person households, and empty nesters, for example, want and need different unit types. In addition, their needs will be best met within a range of price points that, depending on the income diversity of the market, might be wide or narrow.

Among younger and older home-seekers alike, convenience, low maintenance, and time for themselves and their own pursuits are increasingly likely to be the principal factors influencing housing choice. (This trend also points to the potential for younger and older people to live on the same block, in the same neighborhood, and even in the same building.) Moreover, among today's households, the proportion of older singles is larger than ever, and many people in this group are choosing lifestyles that depend on a live-work-play environment in either a center-city or sub-urban location. Whether the residence is a loft apartment with easy access to entertainment and work, or an apartment with direct access to the garage, convenience is often central to the choice of location.

Located next to an 80-year-old apartment building turned condominium, the Victoria Townhomes in Seattle takes its design cues from the original building and the surrounding neighborhood. Intended as a solution to the parking problem at the condominiums, the ten Victoria Townhomes were constructed atop a partially submerged garage that serves both buildings.

How can developers emulate these examples? Experience suggests that size matters: clearly, the larger the neighborhood, the more diverse the opportunities. Communities of at least 200 units can offer diversity in housing choices. In smaller developments, the key is to become part of the surrounding built environment, and to provide unit types that enhance the existing mix. In addition, a high-quality public realm—whether existing or proposed—can make new neighborhoods, with high densities and a mix of housing types, more feasible, improving their marketability and the likelihood that they will be approved.

For a neighborhood of mixed housing types to succeed, an appropriate market must exist to respond to what is being offered. Although determining the market potential for such neighborhoods can be more challenging than determining the potential for subdivisions offering a single housing type, a growing number of market research firms understand the complexities of examining markets for these kinds of developments.

Cost of Land, Parking, and Buildings

Regardless of the type of project, every successful developer must bring all cost factors

Living with Affordable Housing

In the early 1960s, middle-class Montgomery County, Maryland, consisted of subdivisions of identical-looking dwellings, in the same price range, housing people of similar incomes. When a proposal to build a nursing home near one of these subdivisions was brought to the county planning board, the neighbors hired an attorney who argued that different land uses would change the character of the neighborhood and lower property values. The facility was built nevertheless, and neither prediction came to pass. The neighborhood remained a one-class (and, until 1967 fair-housing legislation, an all-white) community. Any attempts to develop lower-priced housing there or anywhere in the county were met with community outrage. "Not in my backyard"—"NIMBY"—became the rallying cry.

But things changed rapidly in the mid-1960s. The county became an employment center, the population increased rapidly, and the lack of adequate public facilities and infrastructure led to growth controls. As a combination of factors drove housing prices up, builders found it more profitable to develop high-end housing—and home prices soared even further, putting pressure on the aging population, on entry-level workers, and on

young families. Housing that moderate- and low-income households could afford was in severely short supply.

After six years of negotiations between housing advocates and elected officials, Montgomery County responded, in 1974, by passing a zoning ordinance that is believed to be the country's first mandatory inclusionary zoning law. Under the Moderately Priced Dwelling Unit (MPDU) ordinance, between 12.5 and 15 percent of dwellings must be affordable in most new subdivisions of 50 units or more. Since the modestly priced homes are built at the same time as the market-priced homes and families with different incomes move into the same community at the same time, the law effectively removed NIMBYism from the agenda.

Though two-thirds of the MPDUs were reserved (mainly for purchase) by moderate-income families, whose incomes are 65 percent of the area median income, the county also used the ordinance to address the desperate needs of its low-income residents by requiring that one-third of the MPDUs be offered to the county's public housing agency, the Housing Opportunities

Commission (HOC). In addition, the county required the affordable units to be of the same tenure type as the market-rate units (that is, the MPDUs had to be either owned or renter-occupied—whichever the market-rate units were).

Though some local governments have voluntary inclusionary zoning programs, such programs have produced few units. Montgomery County, in contrast, by 2002, had produced more than 10,100 MPDUs in more than 250 different subdivisions; 1,600 of those units were under the HOC's control. (Even so, the production of MPDUs is clearly tied to overall housing production, so the number of units being developed at any given time will vary with the strength of the housing market.)

In some townhouse communities, the income disparity between the market-rate and MPDU owners or renters is minimal. However, higher-end communities have their share of MPDUs as well. Even in neighborhoods where the houses cost several hundred thousand dollars (in one case, more than $1 million), a visitor to Montgomery County can find MPDUs, some of which are public housing.

into balance. The economics of the market usually dictate the expenditures on land, building, and parking. To maximize value and market appeal, these three elements must be considered simultaneously. As densities increase, land value increases. The more costly the land, the more efficiently it must be used. Thus, the cost of structured (or even underground) parking can be justified when densities are high and land is expensive. It follows that in areas where density is highest, the market should be capable of supporting the highest sales prices per square foot. In contrast, it would not be cost-effective to pay for structured parking in less dense, outlying areas, where land is inexpensive. The quality of the buildings usually follows land prices as well. When land is expensive, as in the heart of a major city, a high sales price is needed to make the project financially feasible, so the quality of the buildings tends to be high also.

Building Types

For a developer or homebuilder deciding whether to tackle a residential project with a mix of housing types, ease of construction and continuous access to the site are always issues. Standard industry techniques used to build rowhouses, duplexes, or garden apart-

The county's success can be attributed to many factors that other jurisdictions should consider if they attempt a similar program. First, proponents need to form a strong coalition to get mandatory inclusionary zoning legislation on the books. Second, the interests of builders, environmentalists, homeowners, and other interested parties must be respected. Third, it is important to realize that inclusionary zoning complements economic development efforts: economically healthy communities feature a range of businesses and services, staffed by employees at all income levels. At one time, Montgomery County employers had to charter buses and bring in lower-level employees from other jurisdictions. That is no longer the case.

Builders need to get a fair deal. To address the constitutional issue of taking property without just compensation, Montgomery County's law provides builders with a density bonus of up to 22 percent, depending on the number of MPDUs. The bonus allows developers to offset the cost of building the MPDUs and protects them from losing opportunities to develop market-rate housing. The ordinance also allows builders to use different housing types to achieve the density bonus.

The legislation applies to all subdivisions of 50 units or more on property zoned for one-half-acre (0.2 hectares) or less, with a density increase of up to 22 percent of what would normally be permitted in that zone—in effect, discounting the lot cost enough to compensate for the lower-priced units. The MPDUs vary in type, from garden apartments and duplexes to single-family detached homes. Although the prices for the MPDUs are set by the county's Office of Housing and Community Affairs and are pegged to annual cost-of-living adjustments, builders are allowed to construct slightly higher-priced units to achieve compatibility with the market-rate units. For some developers, the MPDUs are the most profitable units because of the density bonus and the ease of sale; others say that constructing the MPDUs is basically a break-even deal. The resale prices of MPDUs are controlled for ten years; rents are controlled for 20 years.

Required inclusionary zoning is appropriate in areas where there is a strong and growing housing market, where the local govern-

ment has legislative and zoning powers, and where advocates can sustain the necessary political will. Advocates in Montgomery County included a fair-housing organization, the League of Women Voters, and some politicians.

The MPDUs now represent about 3 percent of Montgomery County's housing stock, and almost one-third are rented to low-income households through a variety of programs. The county's MPDU law could serve as a model for other areas of the country that are undergoing rapid growth and facing affordability problems. Moderate-income housing is now distributed throughout developed areas of the entire county, and residents have accepted the concept because it has been universally applied. Property values of market-rate homes have not been affected by their proximity to MPDUs; land is being used efficiently; and, as housing production remains in the hands of the private sector, the cost to the local government of providing affordable housing is minimal. ▲

Source: Joyce B. Siegel, "Living with Affordable Housing," *Urban Land,* May 1999.

Hearthstone Mews, in Alexandria, Virginia, is a development of fee-simple townhouses at 32 units per acre (79 per hectare). Garages are accessed from attractively designed rear alleyways.

ments can be easily used to create a sophisticated, low-rise neighborhood offering 12 different unit plans. Although it might seem more efficient, in theory, for a small builder to construct the same house on individual sites throughout a large new town, in practice it can be both easier and more profitable for a single builder to build a mix of apartments, fourplexes, rowhouses, and detached houses on a single land parcel, or even to include a few less conventional housing types, such as live/work lofts or residences above separately leased retail space.

Although mixed residential construction rarely strays from conventional, stick-built methods, the architecture and urban design can be quite complex; for example, the developer must decide which unit types can and should be adjacent to each other, how buildings will fit into the site and in relation to each other, and how to vary elevations to give each neighborhood and street a distinctive character and curb appeal. The following are some useful design rules:

- Building heights should be incrementally changed—that is, variations in height should occur in small steps, generally of one or two stories.
- Architectural design elements used on the taller buildings should be used on the smaller buildings as well, to ensure that the buildings relate to each other.
- Changes in building types should occur back-to-back, along the center of the block, not facing each other across a street.

- Rear elevations should be of good design quality, especially for the higher-density units.
- Like tenures should face each other across streets: owner facing owner, renter facing renter.
- High-density building types should be in the busiest areas and should surround the major public spaces, where their mass can help define the space. Lower-density units are more appropriate for the quieter secondary streets.
- Mixed-use portions of the development should be located on busier streets, where traffic can support retail activity; the quieter residential areas should be somewhat insulated from the bustle of commercial activity.
- All public buildings, such as courthouses, libraries, and town halls, should be designed as landmarks and assigned prominent sites in the plan.

There are three basic categories of tenure: fee-simple ownership, condominium ownership, and renter occupied. At ten dwelling units per acre (25 per hectare) or fewer, fee-simple ownership predominates, but at the highest densities, units tend to be either renter occupied or under condominium ownership. Many developers would rather develop a fee-simple product because it is easier to regulate, finance, and sell and because they wish to reduce the risk of potential claims from condominium associations. On a site of just under one acre (0.40 hectares), Hearthstone Mews, in the historic district of Alexandria,

Virginia, achieved a density of 32 dwelling units per acre (79 per hectare), and is an example of a high-density project in which fee-simple ownership worked well. The project succeeded on two levels: it was accepted as a part of the existing neighborhood because, even though it was twice as dense as the surrounding neighborhood, it had the same scale and architectural character. It was also accepted by the market, because the higher density enabled buyers to purchase in a great location at prices that were below those for existing neighborhood dwellings.

Mixing housing types within a single block challenges both the developer and the architect to give each household a secure sense of "turf" and identity. When directly adjacent or facing units are of different price or tenure—for example, when owner-occupied single-family homes face renter-occupied apartments—such arrangements can be problematic even in locations where people are comfortable with social diversity. Neighborhoods that offer a successful mix of housing types are not arranged at random, but with subtle, comfortable hierarchies and carefully planned adjacencies.

A Matrix of Housing Types

Figure 5-1 shows how, with a few construction changes, the once-standard categories of single-family house, townhouse, duplex, fourplex, and garden apartment have been segmented into many more unit types to respond to more finely targeted market niches, and to reflect the greater range of urban design concepts in use today. An example is the "mansion house," a variation on early-19th-century terrace houses. In a mansion house, small units are grouped in a single building that has the presence and formality of a mansion and provides the larger scale required for a proper town square—or for a development adjacent to real mansions.

Figure 5-1 illustrates an important point: namely, that similar construction techniques can be used to achieve a wide variety of housing types and densities and meet the needs of a wide variety of lifestyles. Since the early 1990s, major advances in the construction industry have made it possible to create higher-density, low-rise, wood-frame buildings that incorporate some type of structured parking. These advances allow builders to spend less per unit than they would for steel or concrete construction, while still achieving a density of 50 to 60 units per acre (124 to 148 per hectare). In some cases, as many as 80 or 90 units per acre (198 to 222 per hectare) can be achieved if the net size of the site is used as the basis for calculating density and if the unit sizes are small. Such configurations offer several advantages: they allow developers to achieve very high densities; the structured parking makes the cars disappear from view; and the four-story height is an excellent scale for a neighborhood. The community, the developer, and the new residents all win.

Figure 5-1 shows that as communities have become more complex and marketing has focused on more specific niches, the industry has responded by developing a larger variety of unit types, each of which correlates to a demographic and lifestyle niche. For example, loft apartments—offering two-story volumes and an open floor plan—are popular among childless couples in their 30s but are unlikely to fit the requirements of seniors, who may prefer a mid-rise or high-rise building with an elevator, or a townhouse with a first-floor master bedroom. These variations in lifestyle requirements drive product differentiation—and, over the past decade, developers have increasingly come to recognize the market opportunities that these variations create.

Three basic types of construction are typically used in residential development: wood frame; wood/steel hybrid; or steel and/or concrete. Each construction type is associated with certain limitations on density and height, and with implications for construction cost. Wood-frame construction is the cheap-

Figure 5-1
A Matrix of Housing Types

Building Type	Tenure			Construction Type			Parking				
	Fee-Simple	Condominium	Renter Occupied	Wood	Wood/Steel	Steel/Concrete	Underground	Podium	Structured	Internal	Surface
High-rise building		■	■			■	■				
(8 stories and up)		■	■			■		■			
		■	■			■			■		
		■	■			■					■
Mid-rise building		■	■		■	■	■				
(5–7 stories)		■	■		■	■		■			
		■	■		■	■			■		
		■	■		■	■					■
Low-rise building		■	■	■			■				
(2–4 stories)		■	■	■					■		
		■	■	■						■	
		■	■	■							■
Lofts and live/work units		■	■	■					■		
		■	■	■						■	
		■	■	■							■
Courtyard building		■	■	■						■	
		■	■	■							■
Manor- or mansion-style building		■	■	■							■
		■	■	■						■	
Charleston-style house		■	■	■						■	■
Carriage house		■		■							
Townhouse with yard	■		■	■						■	
Townhouse without yard	■		■	■						■	
Townhouse with first-floor master bedroom	■		■	■						■	
Duplex	■			■						■	
Cottage: small lot	■			■						■	
Single-family dwelling: medium lot	■			■						■	
Single-family dwelling: large lot	■			■						■	
Villa	■			■						■	

	Potential for Mixed-Use Development		Scenario*					
	Yes	No	1	2	3	4	5	6
High-rise building	■							■
(8 stories and up)	■						■	
	■							■
	■							■
Mid-rise building	■							
(5–7 stories)	■							
	■							
	■							
Low-rise building	■				■			■
(2–4 stories)	■			■		■	■	
	■		■		■			■
	■		■		■			■
Lofts and live/work units	■							
	■							
	■							
Courtyard building		■			■	■		
		■			■	■		
Manor- or mansion-style building		■		■		■		
		■		■		■		
Charleston-style house		■				■		
Carriage house		■			■	■		
Townhouse with yard		■	■	■	■	■		
Townhouse without yard		■	■	■	■	■		
Townhouse with first-floor master bedroom		■	■	■	■	■		
Duplex		■	■	■	■	■		
Cottage: small lot		■	■	■				
Single-family dwelling: medium lot		■	■					
Single-family dwelling: large lot		■	■					
Villa		■						

*See figure 5-5.

est, but it has height limitations—usually four stories. At the midrange is wood/steel hybrid construction, which can be used for projects that are up to eight stories in height. Beyond eight stories, steel and/or concrete, the most expensive alternative, must be used. Figure 5-2 offers a rough summary of the characteristics of each construction type.

Similarly, different types of parking have a significant impact on density and project cost. The following table shows a rough approximation of parking costs.

Type	Cost per Space ($)
Surface lot	2,500
Wood-frame garage	5,000
Above-grade parking structure	8,500
Podium parking supporting residential units above	15,000
Underground garage	20,000

Mixing Architectural Styles

When building types are mixed in a development it is often appropriate to mix architectural styles as well. If the project is large enough—typically, 300 to 400 units—a mix of architectural styles adds visual interest and expands the market potential by broadening the perceived product type. A good strategy is to develop several building types, then create a matrix with several compatible architectural styles. For example, in a section of Celebration, in Orlando, Florida, designers created a set of five styles to use as the basis for six

building types; each style is appropriate for one or more building types.

The advantages of this technique are immediately apparent. As shown in figure 5-3, a combination of five architectural styles and six building types allowed the builder to achieve 14 building alternatives. And, because each building includes two- and three-bedroom models, the 14 building types offer the market a total of 28 different products. The addition of three alternative color schemes means that, in a neighborhood of 300 units, a total of 84 options have been created. This strategy produces a wonderfully idiosyncratic neighborhood—one that pleases buyers who have a wide range of needs and tastes.

Same Building, Multiple Housing Types

Multiple housing types can also be created within a single building. Large buildings, in particular, can be good candidates for this approach, especially when the developer is trying to ensure that new development is compatible with the surrounding neighborhood. Mixing product types within a single building accomplishes the same goal as it does in a neighborhood or larger community: it allows for the development of multiple unit types at multiple price points.

The Hudson, in Arlington, Virginia, is a single building with the character and market segmentation of an entire neighborhood. Built

Figure 5-2

Construction Type, Cost, Density, and Height

	Wood Frame	Wood and Light Steel	Steel or Concrete	Cost per Square Foot/ Square Meter	Dwelling Units per Acre/ per Hectare
1–4 stories	▪			$50–$75/$538–$807	4–50/10–124
5–7 stories		▪		$70–$100/$753–$1,076	50–90/124–222
8 stories and up			▪	$95–$150/$1,023–$1,615	90+/222+

Figure 5-3

The Mix of Architectural Styles and Building Types in Celebration, Florida

	Classical	Colonial Revival	Mediterranean	French	St. Augustine
Garden apartments	■	■	■		
Courtyard apartments			■	■	
Carriage houses			■		■
Corner houses	■	■			
Three-story townhouses	■	■			
Two-story townhouses	■	■	■		

with a combination of wood framing and post-tension concrete construction and designed for an established, mixed-use, inner-ring suburb, the building marks the transition from an adjacent single-family neighborhood to high-density commercial neighbors. The Hudson includes a section of 142 units that resemble four-level townhouses and a 12-story structure that houses 151 units. Included in the mix are lofts, flats, live/work units, and a penthouse. (See figure 5-4.) Two levels of underground parking, which would not be economically feasible with low-rise development alone, serve the entire project. The underground garage keeps the cars out of sight and makes the higher density possible. Renters, in turn, can choose between the high-rise and the walk-up portions of the building and select from a range of unit types, sizes, and prices.

Figure 5-5 depicts six scenarios, each of which illustrates the kinds of buildings that can be mixed within a single project or neighborhood to accommodate a range of densities, from 12 to 150 dwelling units per acre (30 to 370 per hectare). These groupings are only a few examples of an infinite number of possibilities. In fact, mixing is possible even at lower densities than are shown here. Implicit within each scenario are further distinguishing characteristics—such as tenure, construction type, and parking arrangements—that can be used to generate even more alternatives.

Decisions about construction, tenure, and parking type will depend on the relationship between the value of the land, the cost of construction, and achievable sales price. The goal is to develop multiple unit types for a more diverse and aesthetically attractive neighborhood, which will achieve faster absorption by offering multiple price points and meeting the needs of a range of lifestyles.

Mixed Uses

Many neighborhoods are enhanced, both in terms of aesthetics and market potential, by the inclusion of a mixed-use center. A good public space plan for the surrounding areas can even help to defuse the objections of lenders, regulators, and neighbors.

The best examples of mixed-use town centers usually consist of buildings lining streets, with

Figure 5-4

Unit Types in the Hudson

	Penthouse	Lofts	Live/Work	Flats
Tower	■	■		■
Four-story live/work		■	■	
Townhouse				■
Manor house		■		■

street-level stores and office space or residential units above. As greater numbers of mixed-use projects are completed, the industry is acquiring more knowledge about what kinds of commercial activity work best with a residential component. For example, developers generally agree that restaurants do not work well below housing because of odors that drift up to the residences. And while many people would be pleased to live in an apartment above a stylish boutique or art gallery, few would welcome an auto parts store adjacent to their dwelling. In general, the quality, style, and scale of retail establishments should add a positive note to the residents' experience, rather than being considered a nuisance or a burden.

Another question is whether to mix vertically or horizontally. In most town centers, a vertical mix adds to the impression of density and to the vibrancy of the center. But the entire center need not be vertically mixed. At Baldwin Park, for example, a mixed-used town center located in the former Orlando Naval Training Center, several design strategies were used. Restaurants and a supermarket are housed in single-use buildings, and the remaining re-tail is on the ground floors of buildings that have offices or apartments above. The town center as a whole has 75 percent of its housing in buildings that are residential-only. By including vertical mixing where needed, the developers achieved the desired "main street" character and preserved a strong overall mix without actually including a high percentage of mixed-use buildings.

Absorption

Developers who carefully target the most appropriate market niches for their site and offer a desirable, pedestrian-oriented neighborhood that is more diverse, better looking, and available at more price points than its competitors will reach many market segments at once. The result will be faster absorption.

Because there is almost always more demand for affordable units but more profit in higher-priced units, a mixed development plan can be balanced to maximize absorption, keeping building and sales at a steady pace. A mixed plan can also build in a certain amount of flexibility to accommodate market changes. For example, a hot-selling rowhouse can be sub-

Figure 5-5
A Range of Density Scenarios

Scenario 1
12 dwelling units per acre (30 per hectare)

- Single-family detached, large-lot houses
- Single-family detached houses (small cottages)
- Duplexes
- Townhouses

Scenario 2
15 dwelling units per acre (37 per hectare)

- Single-family detached cottages on small lots
- Duplexes
- Townhouses
- Manor houses

Scenario 3
20 dwelling units per acre (49 per hectare)

- Duplexes
- Townhouses
- Carriage houses
- Courtyard apartments
- Garden apartments

Scenario 4
30 dwelling units per acre (74 per hectare)

- Townhouses
- Plexes/Charleston-style houses
- Manor houses
- Garden apartments with structured parking

Scenario 5
60 dwelling units per acre (148 per hectare)

- Low-rise multifamily housing with aboveground structured parking

Scenario 6
150 dwelling units per acre (370 per hectare)

- High-rise multifamily housing with aboveground structured parking
- Low-rise multifamily housing with aboveground structured parking

stituted for a slow-moving duplex without extensive redesign or repricing. Similarly, a mixed plan can accommodate changes in phasing. During an economic downturn, for instance, the developer can build the smaller, less expensive apartments first, delaying construction of the more expensive units until the economy improves. With this type of flexibility built into the approvals, a builder can continue to maximize profits while creating a community that builds on its own increasing value.

In large mixed-housing developments—such as Stapleton, in Denver, Colorado—the land developer can use several techniques to keep alive the mixed-type goals.

- To ensure steady production and a range of price points and character in the community, employ a variety of national, regional, and local homebuilding companies.
- Always have the next neighborhood ready for development when a builder sells out in the current phase.
- When assigning land parcels to builders, make sure that the parcels are large enough to allow the builders the production efficiency they need, but small enough to ensure overall diversity in the development.

Conclusion

Ultimately, the developers of communities that offer a mix of housing types depend on the same factors that determine the success of most kinds of development: a good location, market demand, good transportation and access, and reasonable land and infrastructure costs. The mix of housing types will be further enhanced by a strong and viable public realm, an appropriate balance of uses and building types, and strong regional connections. Good management and careful architectural and community design will gain the support of lenders, regulators, and neighbors, and help to produce a marketable product. The additional technical capability, cost, and risk involved in offering a mix of housing prices and types are relatively small, and the payoff can be large and cumulative: steady absorption, a flexible hedge against changes in consumer tastes and incomes, a bankable track record for future phases, and a social and environmental contribution to the overall community. By responding to the evolving makeup and demands of today's—and tomorrow's—households, a development that offers a mix of housing types can create value in more ways than one.

This chapter was written by John Torti, president, Torti Gallas and Partners.

Note

1. Mark J. Eppli and Charles C. Tu, *Valuing the New Urbanism: The Impact of the New Urbanism on Prices of Single-Family Homes* (Washington, D.C.: ULI–the Urban Land Institute, 1999).

The Hudson, in Arlington, Virginia, combines four-story walkups with a mid-rise component served by elevators. The range of units includes lofts, flats, live/work spaces, and a penthouse, all served by underground parking.

6 Opportunities in Neighborhood Revitalization

At the Block, in Richardson, Texas, a higher-density component is integrated into a single-family neighborhood. The Block features a mix of for-sale and rental housing and includes neighborhood-oriented retail space.

As suburban residential development becomes increasingly challenging and complex, developers are discovering a robust and growing alternative right in their own backyards. Older, inner-ring suburban infill locations are ripe for redevelopment and revitalization, often with ready market acceptance, and are capable of commanding premium sales prices. Infill properties are located within a developed area but have either been bypassed for development altogether or are not currently at their highest and best use.

Because of political resistance to new development, most suburban developers have encountered entitlement processes that are expensive, time-consuming, and often adversarial. Some developers, however, are looking to previously passed over or underused sites in closer-in suburban locations and are willing to overcome the obstacles and challenges involved, including tight sites and potential contamination. In the process, they, the community, and consumers are reaping big rewards.

JAMES, HARWICK + PARTNERS, INC.

This chapter examines approaches, opportunities, and pitfalls associated with developing residential infill sites. The issues that will be explored include the market, site selection and market research, successful product types, securing entitlements, construction challenges, and sales and marketing.

The Market for Suburban Infill Locations: Deep and Broad

In suburban markets, there is extensive and increasing housing demand from empty nesters, childless couples, single-person households, single parents, and other non-traditional households for products other than conventional, single-family homes in subdivisions—demand that is often under-served and overlooked.

For today's consumers, time is at a premium. The typical suburban purchaser has been willing to endure a longer commute in exchange for greater housing value, better schools, and the opportunity to raise a family in suburban surroundings. However, a sizable segment of the market seeks convenient transportation to work, a pedestrian-friendly environment, and proximity to entertainment, restaurants, and other amenities. These consumers' motivations are distinctly different from those of family-oriented suburban homebuyers.

Many Generation X professionals, for example, seek one-of-a-kind housing choices in unique locations. Because they value being able to walk to nightlife and transportation,

they will tolerate more rugged, transitional surroundings and will even pay a premium for the unconventional, both in for-sale and for-rent spaces. Similar forces motivate the baby boomers who are "pre-retirement but post-children." This new life stage—which did not even exist for prior generations—presents growing opportunities for the development of distinctive new kinds of living spaces.

Because of the unique nature of infill sites and the scarcity of products to choose from, the market has shown a willingness to pay significant price premiums for housing in such locations. Also, infill consumers are more likely to accept innovative products at higher densities and in pioneering locations. Close-in locations even appeal to a segment of the single-family market. When larger sites are assembled in such locations, allowing the development of single-family detached houses, sales are typically brisk—and conventional single-family detached housing has reportedly sold for prices 20 to 50 percent higher than comparable houses farther out.

Whether multifamily, attached, or single-family; rental or for-sale; small, one-of-a-kind projects or larger, more conventional single-family communities, infill development appeals to a broad and deep market characterized by a wide range of lifestyles and demographic profiles.

Spotting the Opportunities

Infill sites come in all shapes, sizes, and conditions. Since undeveloped sites were

Brownfields: A Golden Opportunity for Suburban Infill Development

According to the National Association of Home Builders, there are over 500,000 potential residential sites in desirable, close-in areas where expansion or redevelopment is complicated by real or perceived environmental contamination. Until recently, the redevelopment of these abandoned or underused industrial or commercial sites has been hindered not only by the high costs of cleanup but also by potential liability, under federal law, for any party in the chain of title. Recent changes in federal and state laws, along with an exciting array of public programs and environmental insurance, have opened up many more possibilities for brownfield development.

Brownfield development is a winning proposition for all involved. It revitalizes blighted communities by transforming previously unavailable land into suitable sites for new homes and businesses—and, in so doing, attracts new development and increases property values and tax revenues. Like other forms of infill, brownfield development addresses housing demand while channeling housing development into areas that are already built up, thereby reducing sprawl and protecting open lands from development. Developers benefit because they can tap into premium markets, receive positive media attention, and solidify relationships with local governments, which may make it

possible to secure future entitlements more readily. Businesses benefit from the investment and from new residents' purchasing power. And, of course, consumers benefit because they gain conveniently located new homes close to business districts, shopping, universities, and mass transit.

Liability Problems and Solutions

Until recently, residential developers who sought to purchase contaminated property faced significant obstacles. Standards for residential cleanup are high—and, in the case of certain contaminants, not even established. The Environmental Protection Agency (EPA) has held owners responsible for cleanup of contamination that occurred during prior ownership, even in cases in which contaminated groundwater has migrated underground from unrelated sites held by other owners. Many states have their own, equally rigorous environmental laws. Recognizing that such laws were having an unintended chilling effect, however, approximately 40 states have implemented initiatives protecting innocent landowners who successfully complete a state-regulated voluntary cleanup program. Under such initiatives, developers know precisely what is expected of them and are protected from future state action. As a practical matter, the EPA has in most cases accepted state-regulated voluntary cleanup

efforts, although without any formal waiver of federal enforcement. Moreover, where safe public drinking water is available but the underground aquifer is contaminated, the EPA has also issued prospective purchasers nonbinding "comfort letters" to signal lack of intent to enforce liability, as long as certain conditions are met. To give further comfort to lenders, developers can purchase environmental insurance to underwrite unforeseen cleanup costs, should an enforcement action be taken in the future.

New Legislation

In an effort to provide greater certainty to developers and lenders, Congress passed the Small Business Liability Relief and Brownfields Revitalization Act in early 2002, which amends the Comprehensive Environmental Response, Compensation and Liability Act (CERCLA) of 1980. Under the new law, prospective purchasers of contaminated sites and innocent owners of property that is contiguous to sites on the CERCLA National Priorities List are protected from liability if they meet certain conditions, such as performing due diligence and achieving compliance with a state-regulated cleanup program. Although it is a good first step, the law has a number of problematic provisions. For example, it does not address liability under the Resource Conservation and Recovery Act (RCRA), under which owners of properties contaminated by common pollutants—

typically passed over for a reason, well-located sites may be blemished by proximity to expressways, high-tension wires, or active railroads. Others may be environmentally contaminated (see feature box) or difficult to assemble because of complex ownership issues. Occasionally, pristine, undeveloped land—such as farmland, an orchard, or a nursery—has stayed in a family for generations, allowing development to bypass it

completely; however, the zoning for such land often lags behind current highest and best use for the site. Some suburban developers, such as Taylor Morley Homes, in St. Louis, have painstakingly assembled small parcels of land, some of which include older individual residences, over a period of several years, in order to create larger, well-located sites that permitted the development of sizable communities of new, single-family

such as petroleum, lead-based paint, and asbestos—are subject to continued liability under federal law. Also, the language describing the circumstances under which the EPA could reopen a case is somewhat vague, and will need to be interpreted in the future. With luck, future legislation will provide innocent landowners who successfully complete a state brownfields or voluntary cleanup program with complete protection against federal liability under RCRA.

In the meantime, developers and lenders can take some comfort in the availability of environmental pollution insurance, and in the knowledge that, as a practical matter, state voluntary cleanup programs are very rarely overruled by the EPA.

Funding Available for Cleanup

Besides attempting to clarify liability standards, the Small Business Liability Relief and Brownfields Revitalization Act also provides $1 billion in federal funding over five years to states and government entities to accomplish the following:

- Assess the level and type of contamination at targeted sites;
- Inventory brownfield properties in a given area;
- Plan and design cleanup programs;
- Undertake cleanup at the targeted sites;

- Streamline the revolving loan fund that is currently used for brownfield cleanup;
- Assist colleges and universities and non-profit organizations with training in site assessments, remediation, and community involvement.

These funds can be combined with those available through various state and local programs, as well as with those available through other federal programs, such as the grants and low-interest loans provided under the Section 108 Brownfields and Economic Development Initiative program of the Department of Housing and Urban Development. In some cases, funds can be used for site preparation, including grading, demolition, and construction of infrastructure—costs that would be incurred even in the case of greenfield development. Grants are generally highly competitive and are often awarded according to the community's level of financial distress or the project's potential to create jobs or spur economic development. If a site is located in a state enterprise zone, the developer may be eligible for further benefits, in the form of loans and tax credits. Other state assistance includes grants, low-interest bonds, revolving loans, tax abatements, and tax incentives to offset cleanup costs. Developers can obtain more information by contacting the relevant department of the state in which the project is located.

Testing and Remediation

Remediation standards for residential development are higher than for industrial or commercial properties, and cleanup costs are proportionately higher. Most commonly, contaminated materials are removed from the site and replaced with clean soil. In some cases, contaminated soil can be used for deeper fill areas, to create berms, or to terrace lots. Other creative solutions involve capping and covering the bad soil, or mixing bad soil with good soil until contaminants have been diluted to acceptable levels.

Marketing

The market is demonstrating surprisingly broad acceptance of new housing on reclaimed brownfield sites—particularly in the case of convenient, well-located properties, which are otherwise hard to come by. Although some developers have been concerned that even when there is no demonstrable health hazard, there might be a stigma attached to new homes on reclaimed brownfields, these concerns have generally been unfounded. As long as there are, in fact, no health hazards, consumers seem surprisingly accepting of housing on these sites. Marketing campaigns that promote brownfield projects as progressive alternatives to suburban sprawl have been particularly effective. ▲

---

detached homes. In fast-growing cities like Atlanta and Houston, it is common, and cost-effective, for developers to assemble whole blocks of old, obsolete homes and tear them down to create a large site for higher-density housing.

Often, sites have outgrown their former uses, which were typically industrial. In Brighton, outside Detroit, Crosswinds Communities

has transformed a former lumberyard into a development consisting of 44 townhouses and flats, including seven live/work lofts. In Kenosha, Wisconsin, a 69-acre (28-hectare) lakefront industrial site was transformed to HarborPark Townhomes and Condominiums. In older neighborhoods throughout the country, former machinery plants, electrical transmission stations, railroad yards, lumberyards, shopping centers, elementary schools, and

Built on a reclaimed lakefront brownfield, HarborPark, in Kenosha, Wisconsin, is just a few blocks from a Metra station, easing the commute to Chicago.

churches are some of the many kinds of suburban infill sites being developed as new housing.

Because municipalities with land to revitalize often choose to sell the land to established suburban developers with good reputations, some developers make a point of being visible and politically active in a community as a way of building relationships and gaining credibility. Municipalities will often work with a developer partner to rezone a site for a preferred use, or will offer concessions in order to get the project financed or constructed. Tax increment financing is one technique that local governments often use to spur private sector interest in infill sites. Tax abatement schemes are also common.

What is true of any real estate acquisition is especially true of infill: it is best to focus on a particular area, and to learn as much as possible about it. Developers should become experts on the political climate and acquire detailed—and constantly updated—knowledge of the market. Municipal planning offices are good sources of leads and information. Many maintain GIS (geographic information system)

data banks on properties, including sites that are owned by the public and that are available for sale.

The appropriate size for a suburban infill site varies tremendously. It depends, in large part, on the management structure of the developer's organization and on how well equipped the company is to oversee unique projects. An optimum size for a project or phase is probably 50 units, with 25 being the minimum efficient number.

In return for a convenient location, the market will usually forgive negative aspects of the area surrounding a suburban infill development. For example, residents often reach their new community by driving through an older residential area where resale prices are significantly lower than housing prices in the new community. This situation has not, however, affected the success of new projects in suburban Detroit, Philadelphia, St. Louis, or Washington, D.C., to name but a few of many examples. Similarly, the market easily accepts conveniently located sites that are near deteriorated or abandoned structures, blighted industrial properties, and the like. Surprisingly, even single women—a large buyer segment—do not appear to be deterred by questionable surroundings, as long as garage parking and home security alarms are provided. Some successful marketing consultants have learned that when it comes to infill projects, the market is bolder than many developers.

When no established market has yet been identified for a project, deals can often be structured very creatively. Many sellers, including public entities, will share some of the land risk with the developer, either as a means of selling the property or in exchange for some of the profits if the project is successful. Such partnerships, in turn, can help developers to secure project financing and can allow them to be more creative with the proposed product. Once a site has been secured, it is advisable to purchase or obtain options on adjacent or nearby sites as well. Typically, prices escalate dramatically after the first successful project. The developer should also try to anticipate the next "hot" area, and to obtain, if possible, options on sites in that area.

Market Research

Gauging the level of market demand and the likely response to a unique product is a big challenge in infill development. It is difficult to identify the depth and breadth of the market when there are usually no comparables to analyze and when each site features unique characteristics.

Qualitative Factors

In the absence of any direct comparables to study, it is best to begin with a hypothesis. "Follow the kids," advises marketing consultant David Mayhood, of the Mayhood Companies, in McLean, Virginia. As a starting point to determine where infill may be viable, Mayhood recommends that developers identify areas where Generation Xers frequent restaurants and bars. For this market segment, access to work is less important than access to fun; being within walking distance of business dis-

tricts, shopping, mass transit, and universities is also important. The next step, for the developer, is to "live there" for a while—to spend time in the restaurants, bars, and stores in the immediate area to learn more about the characteristics of the potential market.

Sites within walking distance of transit stations naturally appeal to commuters to downtown who seek a hassle-free lifestyle. The success of many recent infill projects can be traced to the presence of rapid-transit stops, or to other publicly sponsored redevelopment initiatives. Commercial activity in former residential structures is a further signal that a neighborhood is in transition, which often opens up new infill opportunities.

Developers can also learn a great deal by studying comparable suburban markets in other parts of the country, to identify target markets and product ideas that might be used at the subject location.

Some developers begin by mailing teaser communications to targeted demographic sectors within a certain geographic radius of the site. In addition to generating phone inquiries, such efforts yield returned questionnaires, which include valuable market information, and also create a list of potential candidates for focus groups. Once a site is under control and some product sketches have been created, developers find that focus groups are great sources of feedback, not to mention future sales.

Quantitative Factors

Like any other kind of real estate investment, infill projects require a study of quantitative factors. This means identifying the target group by age, education, marital status, employment, and income. It is also important to summarize general trends—past, present, and future—related to the target group.

Naturally, any competition that might illuminate the preferences of the target market should be analyzed. To gauge purchasing power, the developer should study the resale prices and rental rates for existing products. He or she should also evaluate the size, value, features, and amenities of competing products. It is important to understand why the competition is succeeding or not succeeding.

Once the developer has accurately defined the market needs, it is time to formulate the parameters for the envisioned development, including the product type, the design char-acteristics, and the price range. On the basis of the quantitative and qualitative data that have been gathered, a developer can gauge the number of buyers in the identified niche, at various price points. The developer should understand how many units can be sold per year, and what the likely short- and long-term costs are of a wrong decision.

Land Planning and Product Design: Keys to Success

Daring products can entice buyers or renters to a marginal neighborhood. A unique product can capture the imagination of local government officials and enlist them as partners in implementing the project. Exciting products can galvanize consumers and create buyers who would not otherwise be in the market. And, to the extent that a new product blends attractively into the existing community, it can win neighbors' support. The opportunities to be creative are endless because, by definition, each site is unique.

Determining how to deal with automobiles is one of the key issues in designing for infill in existing communities. Infill development is well suited to the creation of new urbanist neighborhoods, with their grid street patterns and rear alleys. In older suburban areas, particularly those that grew up around train stops, alleys often already exist. Extending an existing alley system can help a new development blend in with its surroundings.

Condominium or Rental Alternatives

Stacked townhouses over flats, or stacked townhouses, each with a private entry and a rear-loaded individual garage, are a creative way to build street-oriented, pedestrian-friendly communities while achieving densities of over 30 units per acre (74 per hectare). Garages are accessed from alleys or motor courts. In order to accommodate rear garage entries and to minimize the massing of the buildings, the front grades are artificially

At Woodward Place at Brush Park, in Detroit, Crosswinds Communities developed stacked townhouses over flats with garages, achieving densities of over 30 units per acre (74 per hectare). The same product was also successfully developed in the close-in suburb of Royal Oak, Michigan. Architects: Hobbs and Black, Progressive Associates, and Barton Associates.

raised, and a half-flight of stairs leads to the front entry. Crosswinds Communities introduced a product in Royal Oak, Michigan, outside Detroit, consisting of four-story buildings that contain 22-foot- (6.7-meter-) wide units: a 1,300-square-foot (120-square-meter), two bedroom/two bath flat on one level, and a two-story, 1,600-square-foot (150-square-meter), two bedroom/two bath townhouse above. Two garage bays at grade level serve each unit: one is a one-car garage and the other is a two-car tandem garage. Pedestrian access for each unit is on the street side of the buildings, and is either at grade or by way of a raised front porch. Units are for sale as condominiums.

Another parking arrangement that may be practical for a condominium project is a common garage that is accessed at grade and faced with materials that are consistent with those of the units above. A creative example is the Gates at Westfalls, in Falls Church, Virginia, where seven- and 14-unit buildings offer two garage spaces per unit. The community of 98 units is close to the West Falls Church Metro station and appeals to Washington, D.C., commuters.

Fee-Simple Ownership

As long as there is adequate depth and acreage, zero-lot-line urban-style plans can work well in the suburbs. Footprints can be as narrow as 26 feet (eight meters) in width, with depths of up to 80 feet (24.4 meters), including the front porch and rear garage. While the resulting densities are often greater than those in the existing community, the market shows a surprising tolerance for higher densities in exchange for a convenient location, a new product, or greater affordability. Moreover, municipalities are increasingly willing to provide zoning for traditional neighborhood developments (TNDs) in suburban locations. Taking into account the strengths of a given location, the developer needs to research the potential for market acceptance. At Farrcroft, in Fairfax, Virginia (see the case study chapter), the developers built a modified TND project at a higher density—and with much higher sales prices—than those of the surrounding older neighborhoods.

Conventional three-story townhouses can take on a pedestrian-friendly, courtyard orientation with densities of over ten units per acre (25 per hectare) and rear-loaded garage access

Main Street Crossing, in Brighton, Michigan, is a live/work product developed by Crosswinds Communities and designed by the firm of Hobbs and Black. The units are 22 feet (6.7 meters) wide and include two alley-loaded garages per unit. On the first floor is a work space and on the second a residential flat. The third floor is a separately owned residence.

at grade. They can be sold as fee-simple properties, with a homeowners' association owning the alleys and courtyards.

Back-to-back townhouses can yield densities of 14 to 15 units per acre (35 to 37 per hectare) while taking advantage of existing streets for access. One configuration anticipated for Brambleton, a Miller and Smith project in northern Virginia, consists of wide and shallow attached units, back-to-back, bookended by narrow and deep units on either end. Each unit has an attached one- or two-car garage. Typically, a building consists of eight units and is 138 feet (42 meters) wide and 48 feet (14.6 meters) deep. Such products can be configured as conventional townhouses or as loft-style units.

At Malden Court, in Seattle, Washington, developed by Threshold Housing, architects Marcia Gamble Hadley and Stickney Murphy incorporated ten two-story condominium units into two structures resembling old houses, which blend seamlessly into the surrounding neighborhood.

Live/work lofts, often used as visual gateways to the larger project, are a recent innovation taking hold in suburban infill locations. Because this product type is appealing to municipalities that are exploring more progressive planning concepts, developers who include a small number of live/work lofts in a development may, in some cases, be allowed to increase density elsewhere in the project. The design generally involves a modest work space on the ground floor and a two-story living unit above, which is owned or rented by the same party. Alternatively, the live/work unit

can be the first two floors, with a separate flat unit on the third floor. Rear access and a rear attached garage provide one or two parking spaces for the unit. In some jurisdictions a separate business or occupational use license is required, which can hinder or delay marketing. Also, this product type works best in a relatively high-density location with urban-style amenities, so the location-specific nature of the product may limit demand. However, with the increasing prevalence of working at home, and consumers' growing emphasis on protecting their personal time, the live/work unit can be an appealing lifestyle choice.

Integrating Infill into Its Surroundings

The uniqueness of infill sites affords a myriad of product possibilities. A good architect who has experience in designing infill products is the best place to start. Often, developers can obtain design clues by studying the existing neighborhood patterns and going from there.

In Seattle, for example, one nonprofit developer figured out a way to make ten condominium townhouses look like two large old houses. To comply with the 35-foot (10.7-meter) height limitation, the first floor and the parking are depressed a half-level below grade. Surface parking below a first-floor deck

provides 1.4 spaces per unit. Each unit, ranging from 800 to 1,100 square feet (70 to 100 square meters), has its own private entry. Eaves and dormers on the fourth floor create space for a fifth unit to fit into each of the structures.

New townhouses can be styled to resemble stately old buildings in upscale, historic urban neighborhoods. Careful massing, arched windows, wrought-iron railings, and precast concrete detailing can make new construction look old. Roof decks on the top floor and rear balconies are attractive amenities that capitalize on the space and appeal to this market niche.

Entitlements and Zoning Considerations: A Manageable Challenge

In some respects, the entitlement process for infill projects is no different from that for other real estate projects: local interest groups that may feel threatened by change are often engaged in the process. Neighbors' concerns often focus on traffic, building heights, potential tax increases, and the potential loss of views; they may also be concerned about lights at night (from surface parking). Sometimes reactions are based on general "NIMBYism." Neighbors are often well organized, and may be surprisingly entrenched. The key is to turn these groups around and to make them allies—and even buyers.

One of the recurring challenges of infill developments is that archaic zoning laws often prohibit the higher densities that are necessary to make the project feasible. In addition, building heights are often capped at 35 feet (10.7 meters)—the same height that is typical for single-family zoning. Ideally, a local government would partner with a developer, contributing as its share of the bargain the necessary zoning changes. In cases where municipalities seek partnerships with devel-

BOB NAROD

opers, concessions on zoning laws should be a standard part of the equation.

Sometimes, where rezoning is not possible, the architecture and land planning will require extra creativity. Developers of the Gates at Westfalls, for example, actually raised the surrounding grade in order to meet the 35-foot (10.7-meter) building height limitation. The architects of Malden Court, in Seattle, used another creative solution: in order to fit four floors of living space into a 35-foot (10.7-meter) roof height, they recessed the buildings and parking one half-level. As part of initial due diligence, developers should carefully examine the language of the codes. Terms such as "roof height," for example, can be more favorably defined as average height—as opposed to the more restrictive

At Park Place at West Market, a Miller and Smith development in Reston, Virginia, architect Pappageorge/ Haymes, Ltd., gave new construction the appearance of a fine old neighborhood. The 122-unit project on 9.8 acres (four hectares) averages 12.5 dwellings per acre (31 per hectare).

definition, which considers only the height at the roof's highest point.

Jurisdictions increasingly want a mix of uses, often with ground-floor retail development. This requirement makes the project more complex, and more difficult to market and finance. Buyers and renters do not always want to live in the midst of the noise, odors, and strangers (not to mention rodents) that are associated with retail activity. It may be preferable to put the retail space adjacent to the residential project rather than in the same buildings.

When the local government is not a partner in the process, the developer, more often than not, will have to persuade the jurisdiction to create a new zoning category or to overlay an existing category in order to accomplish what is desired. The sales pitch is usually made first to the neighbors and to citizens' groups, who can then help persuade the local government. To avoid a lengthy and expensive process later, it is essential to build consensus for the project by winning over the neighbors first.

If a new development can mitigate existing problems in a neighborhood, this factor can work in its favor. A developer in suburban Philadelphia, for example, used a new, 35-unit townhouse community on the site of a former nursery to correct a serious storm-water problem that had caused flooding in the basements of the surrounding houses. In other cases, a site might be zoned for an industrial or other use that neighbors regard as incompatible, and neighbors will view the proposed development as a more desirable alternative. A developer's willingness to fix existing traffic or other problems, as part of the plan, can turn neighborhood naysayers into enthusiasts who will help to get a project approved. Generally, a developer can identify a single "hot-button" issue to focus on in selling the project to the community. Concessions do add to costs, so they need to be factored into the pro forma upfront.

Sometimes neighbors are won over by a progressive planning argument. The developer might, for example, make the case for the environment, pointing out that the new development will mitigate suburban sprawl and increase mass-transit ridership. In other instances, making the case that the development will achieve a mix of ages, ethnic and racial backgrounds, and income levels may appeal to community groups. In areas that are failing to attract new investment, a developer can make the case that rental housing will lay the groundwork for further investment. If and when current neighbors begin to envision themselves—or their children—as buyers or renters in the new project, the tide of support turns dramatically.

Successful developers who specialize in infill are usually able to identify upfront someone in the community who has knowledge of all the issues and parties. Such people are typically those who speak up at public meetings. As a starting point, developers organizing initial "kitchen" meetings and presentations to neighbors should approach these leaders. Some developers even end up adding knowledgeable and well-connected community members to their payroll as project consultants.

Businesses can be valuable allies in efforts to bring new development to older suburban locations. A new project can offer a range of advantages to local businesses, from bringing in new purchasing power for a retail district to correcting failing infrastructure. Inviting business owners to express their support to neighbors and municipal leaders taps a ready-made source of support.

Finally, some developers actually find that the entitlement process for infill development is easier than for other proposals in the suburbs. This is particularly likely when a site has been zoned for a use that neighbors do not want, or where there is little or no residential development surrounding the site. (Chapter 8

Iron Horse Lofts is the for-sale component of a multifamily development in Walnut Creek, California. The development also includes an affordable rental-apartment component. The project achieved a density of 35 units per acre (86 per hectare) without height or bulk variances.

provides further details on dealing with NIMBY issues.)

Construction and Cost

Infill construction poses extremely difficult obstacles. The tightness of the sites makes planning and staging especially challenging, and ultimately more expensive.

What might be a simple task on a greenfield site, such as storing excavated earth or dirt brought to the site, can be tremendously complicated on an infill site. Developers should carefully map out plans for earth storage as part of the upfront construction design. It may be necessary to plan and budget to move dirt several times within a site. Some developers rent adjacent land for earth storage when possible.

The higher density of infill development creates additional constraints. With as little as five feet (1.5 meters) separating single-family units, it is often necessary to undertake grading and construction of whole sections of

homes at once, which entails preselecting model types and options; this limits consumers' choices and may create some marketing constraints.

When a site has limited storage capacity, the manufacturing concept of "just-in-time" delivery may be a practical necessity. Because there is little room for error, thinking through what equipment will be needed at what times becomes paramount. It may require changes in scheduling practices, and perhaps even the addition of staff with more logistics experience. Sometimes the construction or sales office will have to move from place to place to accommodate construction, as in a game of checkers.

Stormwater drainage poses particular challenges for developers of infill sites. Often, stormwater is retained underground, in concrete cisterns or underground basins. In some cases, the only place to store stormwater is under paved surfaces. Where infrastructure is ancient and deteriorating, developers will have to rebuild existing piping.

Because it is often old or inadequate, existing infrastructure can be another expensive challenge for infill developers. Ironically, even though infrastructure is already in place, it may be inadequate or so old that it must be augmented. In many cases, water and sewer lines—some over 100 years old—have to be replaced outright. Relocating streets and burying overhead utility lines add to the expense. Costs such as these should be anticipated and built into the pro forma.

Due diligence at the initial planning stage is essential. Older sites are often filled with underground debris or have soil-related problems that will affect excavation and building foundations. Developers should pay careful attention to the planning, design, and construction of foundations to avoid expensive surprises.

Multifamily products must meet stricter building codes than single-family housing. It is therefore critical that designers be familiar with local fire codes and fair-housing laws, as well as with local and federal requirements related to the ADA (Americans with Disabilities Act). The design of high-density housing often calls for rooftops to be used as outdoor living space. But one of the most common problems in construction is water infiltration through flat roofs and decks; if the development will feature these elements, the developer should retain experts in commercial construction to ensure that they are properly designed and constructed.

Because infill projects are often built in close proximity to existing neighbors, the development team must be adept at managing issues such as construction dust and noise. It is best for developers to address these issues head on, keeping neighbors apprised, accurately and forthrightly, of the progress being made. In marginal neighborhoods, where theft can be a problem, developers may have to hire security guards for after-hours oversight. Because infill development can be so different from greenfield development, some developers establish a separate division to handle all aspects of the infill project—one that recognizes the need for additional patience, creativity, and sensitivity to the concerns of the existing community.

Inevitably, infill construction means greater costs. Moving dirt several times, undertaking demolition, rebuilding infrastructure, adding landscaping to hide eyesores, coping with unexpected environmental contamination, and implementing one-of-a kind designs all drive up the costs—and, ultimately, the prices that must be obtained for the product. Some developers have encountered development costs as much as 100 percent higher than those required for comparable greenfield development. However, the robust market demand for conveniently located housing typically accommodates sales prices that are high enough to offset these greater costs.

Marketing Infill Projects

Often, infill projects are located where there is no competition and no recent development activity. The downside is that the market may be unprepared to consider such a location for a new home purchase. The upside is that such locations often come with a built-in market: residents who already live nearby and are excited about the prospect of buying a new home while remaining in the neighborhood they know and love. Typically, the majority of buyers of infill housing come from within a small radius of the project. It is important to create a local "buzz" about the development; grand openings, sales trailers, and lavishly decorated models can help to do so.

The marketing campaign for infill properties should focus on lifestyle: closer-in living, greater convenience, better amenities, and the rich diversity of activities offered by the location. The marketing program for Park Place at West Market, in Reston, Virginia, capitalized on all these features. Print ads promoted the project's location in Reston Town Center and alluded to a lively, "Upper-West-Side lifestyle," similar to that of New York's neighborhood of that name. Models (with names like "London," "Paris," and "New York") were furnished in sophisticated urban styles, to appeal to buyers seeking that particular lifestyle.

Conclusion

Inner-ring suburbs offer great opportunities for developers willing to learn the intricacies of infill development. But there are difficulties. Land tends to be expensive and may come with environmental hazards. Sites may have to be assembled. NIMBY forces may delay a project or cause it to be altered significantly. Design and planning must reflect the character of the surroundings, which can sometimes pose limitations, but may also spur creative solutions.

Despite the greater difficulty, some developers actually prefer infill projects over greenfield ones. Precisely because development is more difficult, competition for market share is limited and may even be nonexistent. The market potential for new housing in older suburbs is substantial; and, typically, sales prices can compensate for the more difficult and expensive development process.

The case studies in chapter 9 feature several projects in older suburbs. Belle Creek, outside Denver, has brought high-quality development and new households from a broad range of incomes into what was once a largely industrial suburb. Farrcroft, in Fairfax, Virginia, created a walkable link to a historic commercial district. King Farm, a large infill project in Rockville, Maryland, took advantage of transit access and brought mixed-use living to the suburbs. At the smallest scale, Winslow Mews, on Bainbridge Island, Washington,

added 22 homes to a bedroom community outside Seattle.

This chapter was written by Sarah E. Peck, principal, Progressive Housing Ventures, Malvern, Pennsylvania.

Sources Consulted

Carter, Donald. "Density by Design." Paper presented at the ULI symposium "Developing Infill Housing: Successful Strategies for Market-Rate Projects," Atlanta, Ga., June 6, 2001.

Everett, Carl. "Navigating the Changes in the Brownfields Revitalization Act" (http://www.saul.com/publications.htm).

Glieberman, Bernie, chief executive officer, Crosswinds Communities, Detroit, Mich. Interview by author.

Lochery, Rob, Keystone Heritage Group, Lebanon, Penn. Interview by author.

Lurz, Bill. "Interesting Infill." *Professional Builder*, July 1999.

Manko, Gold and Katcher, LLP. *Brownfields Law and Practice* (http://www.mgkbrownfields.com).

Mayhood, David. "Understanding the Market for Infill Development." Paper presented at the ULI symposium "Developing Infill Housing: Successful Strategies for Market-Rate Projects," Atlanta, Ga., June 6, 2001.

Morley, Harry, chairman emeritus, Taylor Morley Homes, St. Louis, Mo. Interview by author.

Murphy, Bill, Murphy Architectural, West Chester, Penn. Interview by author.

National Association of Home Builders. *Building Greener, Building Better*. Washington, D.C.: NAHB Research Center, March 2002.

Rombouts, Christine. "Banking on Brownfields." *Urban Land,* May 2002.

Stouffer, Spence, marketing director, Miller and Smith, McLean, Va. Interview by author.

Terwilliger, J. Ronald. "Infill Housing Trends and Opportunities." Paper presented at the ULI symposium "Developing Infill Housing: Successful Strategies for Market-Rate Projects," Atlanta, Ga., June 6, 2001.

7 Sustainable Development and Green Building

Many changes are taking place in the homebuilding and development industries today. In response to increasing concern and debate about growth, environmental health, and quality of life, some sectors of the development industries are listening, learning, and changing. In fact, what is now referred to as "green building" has become one of the most interesting movements in residential development in recent years.

Several forces are driving these changes, including population growth and an accompanying increase in resource use; concern about climatic changes; increasing energy costs; and technological advances. Some green building programs began as emergency responses to local environmental crises, such as threats to local species or the impact of construction on local landfills. Others emerged from the recognition that the time was right for such

initiatives. The further evolution of green building programs, accompanied by a deepening global dialogue on sustainability and intergenerational equity, led to the development of guidelines for the wiser use of energy and natural resources and for improved indoor air quality in the residential building sector. The building science community, including the Energy and Environmental Building Association (EEBA) and the joint Department of Energy/Environmental Protection Agency (DOE/EPA) Building America Program, has added the language of physics and "integrated design," or "systems thinking," to the green building vocabulary. Most recently, the furor in the liability insurance industry concerning construction defects has spurred intense interest in housing durability and performance.

There is growing awareness that the world needs "smarter," more fulfilling communities in which people can live, work, and play, as well as communities that are less demanding of, and more connected to, the natural environment. The efficient use of energy resources is also a growing concern. Perhaps most important, many residential developers are realizing that the market itself is demanding both higher quality and greater environmental responsibility: increasingly, the rewards will go to those who can create value with minimal environmental costs *and* cost-effectively provide that value to their customers.

Sustainable Development

In its 2001 document *Our Built and Natural Environments,* the EPA reported that the

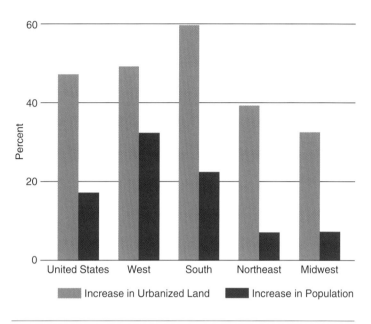

Figure 7-1
Population Growth and Land Development
1982–1997

Legend: Increase in Urbanized Land ∎ Increase in Population

Source: William Fulton et al., *Who Sprawls Most? How Growth Patterns Differ across the U.S.,* Brookings Institution Survey Series (Washington, D.C: July 2001).

amount of urbanized land area in the United States had quadrupled since 1954. Between 1950 and 1990, urbanized land area in most large metropolitan regions grew more than twice as fast as population did.[1] A 2001 study by the Brookings Institution revealed that between 1982 and 1997, the U.S. population increased by 17 percent, while the amount of urbanized land increased by 47 percent.[2] Moreover, the Natural Resources Inventory conducted by the U.S. Department of Agriculture Natural Resources Conservation Service shows an increase of 11.2 million acres (4.5 million hectares) of developed land for the period from 1992 to 1997—an average of over 2.2 million acres (0.89 million hectares) per year.[3]

The expansion of the urbanized portion of Colorado's Front Range typifies the experi-

Facing page: In the latest phase of Las Campanas, in Santa Fe, New Mexico, neighborhoods are designed around the site's existing grades. As part of the water management strategy, drought-resistant natural vegetation has been preserved.

ence of many areas of the country that are growing in population, diversity, and economic vitality. According to U.S. Census data from 2000, over 2,290,000 people live in the Denver metropolitan area, an increase of over 450,000 since 1990. During the same time period, the urbanized portion of the metropolitan area grew by 79 square miles (205 square kilometers); during the previous decade, the urbanized area had increased by 88 square miles (228 square kilometers). By 2020, an estimated 700,000 to 800,000 additional residents will live in the metropolitan area.[4] Such figures, accompanied by concerns about traffic congestion, air and water quality, sprawl, loss of open space, and diminished quality of life, led to the development of a November 2000 ballot initiative for a statewide constitutional amendment on growth management. Though the initiative was eventually defeated, the concerns that gave rise to it are likely to influence all future planning and development. Nevertheless, most land use decision makers continue to operate within the tradition of local, municipally based planning—a model that typically encourages sprawl, undermines regional cultural identity, and fragments natural habitats because self-interest within a locality tends to prevail over a more comprehensive and regional approach.

The conservation community has developed scientifically based ecoregional planning models to identify potential conservation areas for targeted species and natural communities. The Nature Conservancy, for example, in conjunction with the Colorado Natural Heritage Program, successfully employs such a model. Future land planning might be improved by learning from such efforts.[5]

The private sector has also stepped in. For example, EDAW, an international design and planning firm, has developed a program called Green Communities to help its clients develop more ecologically responsible projects. EDAW's program lays out specific goals, and strategies to achieve each goal; the goals and

strategies are based on the recognition that the program must be tailored to each community, taking into account economic factors, the location and type of development, existing natural resources, and the political climate.

The following six sections describe some guiding principles of green development for the residential development industry.

Compact Development

Compact development consolidates growth and diminishes sprawl. As less and less undeveloped land is available to accommodate the needs of more and more people, the issue of *where to build* becomes increasingly important. The green developer looks for the best site for a concentration of housing and services, and considers the site's proximity to existing infrastructure (e.g., sewers, utilities, roads, and public amenities). This approach minimizes random development, helps protect sensitive habitats, and lessens pollution by decreasing the need for vehicle travel.

Mixed-Use Development

Mixed-use development refers to the integration of residential, commercial, retail, employment, civic, recreational, and educational uses; the integration is accomplished in such a way as to reduce traffic congestion and contain urban sprawl. The mix of land uses within a compact area not only supports and enhances each element within the development but also gives residents a rich and diverse environment in which to live, work, shop, play, and learn.

Transit-Oriented Development

Transit-oriented development minimizes vehicle travel by concentrating development near rail stations and other modes of public transportation. In support of such efforts, Fannie Mae is currently testing its Smart Commute mortgage program in various cities across the United States; the program encourages homeownership near rail and bus stops by offering more flexible qualifying

MCSTAIN ENTERPRISES

guidelines. Over the long term, such initiatives may help generate demand for higher-density housing near public transportation.

Ecological Stewardship

Sustainable development is founded on the belief that every place has its own unique ecology. Ecologically based land planning, design, and development, therefore, consider the *type of land* where development is to occur, and preserve sensitive natural areas such as shorelines, wetlands, streams, floodplains, steep slopes, critical habitat, and prime agricultural areas.

Innovative developers can create a competitive advantage by leaving significant natural areas undeveloped and using them as open-space amenities. As discussed in chapter 4, the open space can be visual (e.g., protected wetlands, bird and wildlife habitat), or it can be a passive recreational area with trails for walkers, joggers, and bikers. Studies have shown that open space provides a value-added feature in new communities and that home-buyers will pay a premium for lots adjacent to protected open space.[6]

Colorado-based developer and homebuilder McStain Enterprises has attempted to capitalize on this advantage by working with the natural systems and land features of its High Plains Village community to create value from the unique identity of place. High Plains Village

is the primary residential component of Centerra, a master-planned community in Loveland, Colorado. A large portion of the community's land is designated as open space, and all homes are within a five-minute walk of the central park or one of the pocket parks. Centerra features approximately eight miles (13 kilometers) of walking and biking trails, including five miles (eight kilometers) through natural areas. The community's crown jewel is the High Plains Environmental Center (HPEC), which is staffed by a full-time environmental director. The HPEC is overseeing the restoration and enhancement of 275 acres (111 hectares) of lakes and wetland areas that are central to the Centerra master plan. It also acts as an educational outreach center for residents of Centerra and the larger Loveland community, offering instruction about the unique ecosystems found at the intersection of the Rocky Mountain foothills and high plains.

Improved Stormwater Management

The runoff volume produced by a one-acre (0.4-hectare) parking lot is almost 16 times larger than that produced by an undeveloped meadow of the same size.[7] While that figure may vary with the intensity of the rainfall, the reality is that impervious surfaces (areas such as sidewalks, rooftops, roads, and parking lots, which cannot effectively absorb rainfall) prevent stormwater from slowly filtering through the soil and recharging streams, rivers, lakes, reservoirs, coastal waters, and aquifers. These same receiving waters are vulnerable to the pollutant loads that typically originate from exposed soils, from the oil and rubber from cars, and from lawn fertilizers and pesticides; these and other pollutants are carried by runoff volume through conventional and costly stormwater conveyance systems.

Low-impact development (LID) has emerged as an alternative strategy for controlling runoff volume and protecting receiving waters from polluted stormwater. LID practices, originally pioneered by the Prince George's County

At Village Green at Indian Peaks, in Lafayette, Colorado, the neighborhood park is easily accessible to all residents. The development includes a mix of townhouses, cottage-style homes, and larger residences, all of which meet numerous green standards and offer green features.

Wattle Grove, a brownfield redevelopment in Sydney, Australia, set a national standard for environmentally responsible land development. The 2,800-unit development features innovative systems for water quality and stormwater management.

Department of Environmental Resources, in Maryland, reduce the need for conventional stormwater conveyance mechanisms, including curbs, gutters, storm sewers, and pipes. Instead, LID manages stormwater by replicating predevelopment hydrology patterns. LID commonly involves the creation of infiltration basins—including bioretention areas, grass swales, and permeable pavements—to capture stormwater as close to the source as possible and to allow pollutants to be filtered through the soil.

While LID is still a relatively new practice, preliminary findings indicate that it can offer both economic benefits (by reducing the need for conventional stormwater infrastructure) and environmental benefits (by conserving natural features). Whether LID is appropriate will depend, however, on site conditions, including slope, the depth of the water table, and the permeability of the soil. Local planning and zoning regulations may present additional obstacles to innovative stormwater management practices.[8]

Building Connections between People and the Environment

The best green development practices foster the creation of sustainable, livable communities and neighborhoods where people feel connected to each other, to their environment, and to the world in which they live. Connections begin with roots. If the best places are firmly grounded in the rich texture of their history, then sustainable community building must allow a community's historical and cultural traditions to guide its land use decisions. Sustainable communities must also include a mix of housing types and densities to accommodate the needs of a diverse population and to reflect the demographic mosaic of our changing world. Such diversity allows for both stability and constant renewal, as the young learn from the old—and, growing old themselves, turn yet again to teach the young. Community support systems, including educational opportunities, high-quality child care, and accessible public transportation and recreational facilities, support and enhance community building. The result is a healthy and vibrant mix of people, architecture, and amenities.

Sustainable communities feature design on a human scale—design for people, not cars. Visually appealing sidewalks lined with planting strips (also called tree lawns) and street trees make for highly walkable neighborhoods. Parks, gathering areas, and bike and pedestrian trail systems provide spaces for visits with friends and family. Front porches, once an icon of American housing, have once again come to symbolize a sense of welcome and connection to the outside world. It is this strong focus on design that makes a house a home, and a subdivision a community.

Getting Started

As with any project, a developer should begin by assembling a team of experts—in this case including ecologists, hydrologists, land planners, market consultants, and other professionals with expertise in green development. The developer should also establish realistic goals based on the unique characteristics of the project. These goals can be broken into two categories: altruistic and economic. Altruistic goals include protecting natural resources, providing a healthier environment, and reducing energy consumption; economic goals include speeding up the approvals process, increasing market potential, increasing value, and reducing maintenance costs. Some of the altruistic goals will translate to economic results. It is important to evaluate and understand the costs and benefits of the various components of green development. Some initiatives pay for themselves immediately, others require several years for payback to

occur, and others never pay but may offer significant nonfinancial rewards.

A number of organizations can help developers to evaluate their projects in relation to green standards; of these, some offer certification, which can be useful as a marketing tool. LEED (Leadership in Energy and Environmental Design), a rating system devised by the U.S. Green Building Council, rates developments in terms of numerous criteria, including site selection, erosion control, stormwater management, and waste management. SPeAR (Sustainable Project Appraisal Routine) rates developments in four categories: economic, societal, natural resources, and environmental. The Audubon Signature Program provides environmental planning assistance and offers bronze, silver, and gold designations based on the complexity of the project and the stage at which the developer applies for membership in the program. Web sites for these and other programs are listed in the feature box on the following page.

The Long Term

The success of a green development depends, in large part, on longer-term management strategies, including educating residents to become stewards of the community. EDAW's

Jinji Lake Waterfront District, just east of Suzhou, China, is an environmentally responsible development built around one of the largest freshwater lakes in eastern China. The new masterplanned community will eventually be home to 600,000 residents. Plans include a series of active and passive public spaces and an environmental education center with wetland gardens.

EDAW, INC.; © 2001; PHOTO BY DIXI CARRILLO

Green Communities program, for example, lays out a long-term plan tailored to the needs and circumstances of the specific development. Typically, the plan includes an environmental management strategy that

- Sets maintenance and management practices, including acceptable levels of use for sensitive areas;

Green Building Resources

There are more than 20 green building programs in the country, and more state, local, and home builder association–affiliated programs are being developed all the time. The following organizations' Web sites can help anyone get started:

- Austin Green Building Program, Austin, Texas: www.ci.austin.tx.us/greenbuilder.
- Built Green Colorado, Denver, Colorado: www.builtgreen.org/.
- Build a Better Kitsap Program, Kitsap County, Washington: www.kitsaphba.com/.
- EarthCraft House, Atlanta, Georgia: www.atlantahomebuilders.com/earthcraft/.
- Florida Green Building Coalition, Naples, Florida: www.floridagreenbuilding.org/.
- Wisconsin Green-Built Home, Madison, Wisconsin: www.wi-ei.org/GBH/index.htm.
- Energy and Environmental Building Association (EEBA): www.eeba.org. See also the EEBA's Criteria for Energy and Resource Efficient Buildings, at www.eeba.org/technology/criteria.htm.
- Building America Program: www.eere.energy.gov/buildings/building_america/whoweare.shtml. Performance targets for new home construction can be found at www.buildingscience.com/buildingamerica/targets.htm.
- American Lung Association Health House: www.lungusa.org/air/healthhouse_index.html or www.lungusa.org.
- U.S. Green Building Council's Leadership in Energy and Environmental Design–Residential (LEED-R): www.usgbc.org and www.usgbc.org/LEED/LEED_main.asp.
- National Association of Home Builders Research Center: www.nahbrc.org. For additional information on green building from the research center, see www.toolbase.org/secondary.asp?CategoryID=1&TrackID=.
- Sustainable Buildings Industry Council: www.sbicouncil.org/home/index.html.
- Environmental Building News: www.buildinggreen.com.
- SPeAR, a toolkit for assessing sustainability: www.arup.com/environmental/html/whatwedo/spear.htm.
- Audubon Signature Cooperative Sanctuary Program: www.audubon intl.org/programs/signature/. ▲

- Specifies monitoring procedures;
- Establishes an environmental education program for residents, workers, and visitors that addresses communication methods, staffing levels, and facilities.

Even a relatively small development can create an instructional manual and a Web site or newsletter to keep residents informed and up-to-date. A larger development might have the resources to establish a staffed facility with a comprehensive environmental education program.

Green Building

Sustainable development is supported by green building; that is, energy-efficient building practices that rely on environmentally safe materials and methods. Because increasing numbers of homebuyers consider green building practices important, builders who implement such practices can use them as a marketing tool to gain an edge over competitors.

Energy Efficiency and Renewable-Energy Alternatives

Energy efficiency is critical to the philosophy of green building; and, in survey after survey, homebuyers overwhelmingly select energy efficiency as the most important green feature in their new homes. Green builders—such as Ideal Homes, in Oklahoma City; Artistic Homes, in Albuquerque; and Medallion Homes, in Austin, not only share a commitment to environmental sustainability but have also developed residential energy-guarantee programs as a means of creating additional value for their homebuyers. And, recognizing that the reduced operating costs of an energy-efficient home make more dollars available for the mortgage and create the potential for higher resale value, the lending community has developed both energy-efficient mortgages (EEMs) and energy-improvement mortgages (EIMs).[9] If the home to be purchased or refinanced is energy-efficient, a homeowner can use an EEM to qualify for

a larger loan. An EIM can be used to finance energy-efficiency-related improvements in an existing home, giving homeowners the advantages that a mortgage has over other kinds of loans.

The standards for energy efficiency established by the EPA's Energy Star Program are among the highest such standards for production homebuilders today. Energy Star, a voluntary climate-protection program, was begun in the mid-1990s with the goal of reducing carbon emissions.[10] Homes built to the Energy Star standard are estimated to perform 30 percent more efficiently than those that meet the requirements of the International Code Council's Model Energy Code, a standard since 1983. While the Energy Star Program is just one of many such programs, some homebuilders find that this program offers a particularly useful framework for their energy-efficiency programs; moreover, because the program has a wide reputation and strong credibility, it is also valuable as a marketing tool. Testing protocol for the Energy Star Program requires third-party energy ratings on 15 percent of the homes in a given community to ensure compliance with performance standards. Although the ratings add about $300 to the cost of a home, they provide a quantitative measurement of home energy performance that has translated into a highly cost-effective communication and quality-control tool for sales and marketing professionals, construction firms, and subcontractors.

McStain Enterprises, a homebuilder that is committed to the Energy Star program, uses a number of practices to improve the performance of the building envelope and thereby increase the energy efficiency of new homes: improved methods of assembling and insulating exterior walls; improved air-sealing strategies (to reduce air infiltration and heat loss); high-performance, low-emissivity (low-E) windows; and energy-efficient mechanical systems. (Along with an improved building envelope, it is imperative to use engineering analysis to determine the appropriate size, design, and sealing methods for mechanical heating and cooling systems. The alternative—formula-based calculations—is less likely to reflect rapid changes in heating, ventilation, and air-conditioning systems and design.)

The city of Santa Monica is using Colorado Court—a 44-unit affordable-housing project built on an infill site—as a model for its Green Building Design Guidelines. The project, which includes numerous solar-powered design features, is 100 percent energy-neutral, meaning that it actually returns unused power back to the energy grid.

A number of other strategies can help reduce heating and cooling loads within the home. For example, homes designed according to the principles of passive solar design take advantage of the sun's energy and other microclimatic patterns. Although the site design and orientation required for classic solar design pose challenges to conventional lot development and production homebuilding, even architectural shading elements—such as awnings, overhangs, trellises, and covered decks and porches—can be highly effective in reducing solar heat gain.

Properly placed landscaping elements can also help reduce utility bills. Deciduous trees planted on the west and south sides of the house, for example, provide shade during the summer's peak heat-gain times but allow the warmth of the winter sun to enter the home. Once solar heat gain has been reduced by means of architectural and landscape elements, whole-house fans and energy-efficient ceiling fans can offer effective, low-energy alternatives to traditional compressor cooling.[11]

Finally, many household items, including appliances and lighting, are now more energy-efficient than ever before. In 1975, the average North American refrigerator used 1,800 kilowatt-hours of energy per year. Many of today's refrigerators use about 75 percent less energy, without a decrease in performance or a significant increase in price. Fluorescent lighting and other advanced lighting technologies continue to evolve and to offer viable alternatives to the standard type-A incandescent lights, which produce electricity at an *inefficiency* level of 90 percent.

Renewable-energy markets saw huge growth in the 1990s. Between 1992 and 2002, wind power generation increased from 2,170 megawatts to 24,800 megawatts—more than a tenfold increase. Between 1987 and 2002, the cost of electricity from wind energy dropped from $.35 per kilowatt-hour to about $.04. Between 1991 and 2001, annual solar-cell production grew from 55 megawatts to 391 megawatts, a sevenfold increase. And since the mid-1980s, the cost of electricity from photovoltaic panels has plummeted from $15 per kilowatt-hour to about $.20.[12] Given the costs of energy and the volatility of the West Coast electricity markets, some California homebuilders are capitalizing on the growth in the renewable-energy market by offering buyers alternative energy choices. At Scripps Ranch, in San Diego County, northern-California-based Shea Homes offers both solar electric (photovoltaic) and solar hot-water systems as standard features in their Shea High Performance Homes. By coupling energy efficiency with renewable-energy features, Shea has built a competitive advantage and successfully positioned itself as an innovative production homebuilder.

While rebates, incentive programs, and state-mandated initiatives offer California homebuilders support for renewable-energy features, homebuilders in many other areas of the country lack similar advantages. In the absence of such programs, the high upfront costs for renewable-energy features continue to discourage both consumers and builders in the production-home marketplace. Builders interested in incorporating such features may find more opportunities on the land development side, where solar-powered community lighting, for example, may provide some cost savings by eliminating the need for utility-line extensions.

Indoor Air Quality

The American Lung Association (ALA) reports that Americans spend more than 90 percent of their time indoors, and that an estimated 36 million Americans suffer from allergies or asthma. The EPA lists poor indoor air quality (IAQ) as the fourth-largest environmental threat to the country's health. In 1993, the Minnesota chapter of the ALA developed the "Health House" to teach people what they could do to improve their indoor living environments.[13]

With the advent of nearly airtight, energy-efficient homes, IAQ has become an increasing concern. Because tightly sealed homes reduce the intake of fresh air, occupants of new housing are potentially exposed to higher levels of pollutants, including radon, formaldehyde, particulate matter, biological pollutants, and carbon monoxide and other byproducts of combustion.

In the case of biological pollutants, much current concern—and litigation—is centered on mold toxins, which can harm occupants' health. Mold growth depends on three factors: temperature, moisture, and the availability of a food source. Food sources include wood; cardboard boxes; ceiling tiles; the paper facing on gypsum board; the starches in wallpaper

paste; and even organic matter, such as the dead skin cells and pet dander found in household dust. Because it is impractical to eliminate such food sources, the homebuilding industry is focusing on controlling the entry, accumulation, and removal of moisture.[14]

A number of measures, all of which are designed to prevent moisture from entering and being retained in the foundation and building, have succeeded in reducing the number of customers' complaints about mold. These measures include door and window sealing; the installation of foundation waterproofing, roof flashing and guttering, and perimeter drain systems; and lot-specific grading plans to improve drainage. Because homeowner-installed plantings or irrigation within five feet (1.5 meters) of the foundation may negate the effects of such measures, builders should stipulate that homeowners who make such changes risk voiding the structural warranties on their homes. To ensure that homebuyers understand their responsibilities, McStain Enterprises provides extensive education through its homeowners' manual and orientation process.

Preventing excessive mold growth also involves dealing with moisture generated inside the home. A variety of activities—including showering, cooking, clothes washing, and the respiration and perspiration of occupants—generate water vapor. The only way to control these indoor sources of moisture is to exhaust inside air and to replace it with (typically) drier outside air. In older, less energy-efficient houses, air exchange was a function of random air leaks. But in newer houses, mechanical ventilation strategies are used to give occupants control over IAQ. Although the homebuilding industry continues to debate the merits of mechanical versus natural ventilation, both the homebuilding industry and the building science community—including the DOE's Building America Program and the American Society of Heating, Refrigeration and Air Conditioning Engineers (ASHRAE)—

Har-Ber Meadows, a 425-acre (172-hectare) master-planned community in Springdale, Arkansas, is designed to encourage pedestrian activity and includes single- and multifamily housing as well as housing for seniors. To shield the development from nearby highway traffic and to supply the residences with trees for landscaping, a 20-acre (eight-hectare) tree farm was planted on the site before construction began.

strongly agree on the need for ventilation that provides a controlled amount of outside air, both to dilute or remove indoor pollutants and to provide for the occupants' comfort.

One way to improve air quality inside the home is to use low-VOC (volatile organic compounds) paints, adhesives, and finishes, and to ensure that combustion appliances—including fireplaces, furnaces, and hot-water heaters—are sealed. Sealing combustion appliances insulates the combustion process from the indoor environment and prevents combustion byproducts from mixing with the air in the home.

Efficient Use of Material Resources

Data from the 2000 U.S. Census indicate that the typical home built in 1950 was about 1,000 square feet (93 square meters) in size. By 2000, the typical home was about 2,265 square feet (210 square meters)—an increase of more than 100 percent during a time of steady decline in the average number of household members. With an average of 1.5 million housing starts since 1996, not only is housing a key element in the nation's economy, but it is also an enormous consumer of materials and resources. A June 2001 study by the National Association of Home Builders (NAHB) entitled *Housing: Facts, Figures, and Trends,* lists the primary materials used to build a 2,082-square-foot (190-square-meter) house:

- 13,837 board feet (32.5 cubic meters) of framing lumber
- 11,550 square feet (1,070 square meters) of sheathing;
- 3,011 square feet (280 square meters) of exterior siding material;
- 3,061 square feet (285 square meters) of insulation;
- 5,550 square feet (520 square meters) of interior wall material;
- 2,117 square feet (200 square meters) of interior ceiling material;

MCSTAIN ENTERPRISES

- 2,841 square feet (260 square meters) of roofing material;
- 2,082 square feet (190 square meters) of flooring material;
- 226 linear feet (69 meters) of ducting;
- 16.92 tons (15.3 metric tons) of concrete;
- 18 windows.

It is precisely because of the staggering volume of materials used in new home construction that green building programs and environmental organizations advocate the use of recycled, reusable, renewable, and more durable building materials.

Lumber, for example, is by far the largest material component in a new stick-built home. According to the Montana-based Center for Resourceful Building Technology, over 400 studs are used in framing an average house, meaning that up to half a billion studs are required annually for residential construction, a quantity that puts a strain on forests and forest ecosystems alike.[15] Although alternative building materials such as structural insulated panels, insulated concrete forms, steel, and even straw bales have made some inroads in the industry, the vast majority of homes—more than 80 percent—are still framed in wood.

The purpose of wood certification programs is to direct purchasers to lumber products that originate in sustainably managed forests. The Forest Stewardship Council (FSC) and the Sustainable Forestry Initiative, both of which are international nonprofits, are prominent among the many certification programs in the United States. Both organizations provide a "seal of approval" to forestry operations, and to companies that process and sell products made of wood, if the firms adopt socially and environmentally responsible practices. Such efforts have affected the way that timber companies and large suppliers of lumber products do business: two of the nation's largest homebuilding operations have agreed to stop buying products from endangered forests, and Home Depot now carries FSC-certified lumber.

Certified wood poses challenges because it is more expensive, less available, and less familiar to consumers; however, other strategies also promote the efficient use of lumber. Engineered framing components, for example, consist of laminated chips or strands of recycled or reconstituted wood. Such products typically come from wood that is harvested from faster-growing trees in intensively managed timber stands. Engineered structural products allow each log that enters the lumber mill to be used more efficiently; the downside is that the manufacturing process requires more energy and greater use of adhesives. Traditional, solid-sawn lumber uses only about 50 percent of each log, while engineered lumber uses as much as 80 percent. In addition, framing components such as glue-laminated beams, headers, joists, roof trusses, and finger-jointed studs offer more durable alternatives that do not warp, split, or shrink the way that solid-sawn dimensional lumber does. Indeed, the market share of more environmentally friendly floor trusses and I-joists went from 2 percent in 1978 to 29.2 percent in 1999; during the same period, the use of dimensional lumber for floor framing dropped by more than 20 percent, in part because the engineered products were more durable.[16] Nevertheless, the U.S. continues to be a net

importer of lumber, and to have a level of foreign dependence that, given the rate of growth in demand, may pose future challenges and risks.

Optimum value engineering (OVE) refers to a variety of design and construction techniques that help to reduce the amount of lumber used in residential construction. Proponents of OVE place a strong emphasis on the simplicity of form and the minimization of volume. Examples of OVE practices include placing framing studs every 24 inches (61 centimeters) on center rather than every 16 inches (41 centimeters); aligning door and window openings with the spacing of studs; at all partition wall connections, aligning framing and using a single top plate and ladder-backed framing; and sizing headers for actual load conditions. OVE, as the name suggests, requires engineering analysis to ensure that structural load-bearing requirements are met and that the specifications meet local building codes.

Significant environmental benefits can be gained when materials recovered from the waste stream, rather than obtained from virgin resources, are used as raw materials in manufacturing. In the case of aluminum production, for example, manufacture from virgin raw materials requires between 150 and 220 gigajoules per ton (between 136 and 200 gigajoules per metric ton), whereas manufacture from recycled materials requires between 10 and 15 gigajoules per ton (between 10 and 13.6 gigajoules per metric ton).[17] Consumers benefit as well. Recycled-content decking—a composite of wood fibers, plastic grocery bags, and milk jugs—provides builders and homebuyers with a maintenance-free alternative to traditional wood decking. Cellulose insulation—made from recycled newspapers, cardboard fibers, and computer papers—is not only more dense than traditional insulation, which improves the energy efficiency of the building envelope, but also seals cavities better, preventing drafts and increasing comfort. Recycled-content "pop bottle" carpet, manufactured with yarn spun from the polyester resins of recycled soda bottles, consistently demonstrates better stain resistance than many other types of carpet fibers.

On a final note, a variety of resource-efficient flooring materials made from either rapidly renewable nontimber materials or reclaimed timber products have appeared (or reappeared) in the marketplace over the past few years. Bamboo flooring, for example, is manufactured from timber bamboo that grows to a height of 40 feet (12 meters) and matures in less than five years. The production of cork from the living bark of the cork oak has expanded significantly in recent years, leading to the greater availability of cork flooring products. With the rise of the "deconstruction" industry, the use of reclaimed timber flooring has made small strides in niche markets.

Playa Vista is a major brownfield redevelopment on the site of the former Hughes Aircraft plant in Los Angeles. The developer is restoring wetlands and coastal areas and recycling much of the material from the aircraft plant. Buildings will be energy-efficient, taking maximum advantage of natural light, air ventilation, and solar power.

Construction Waste Management

According to *Residential Construction Waste Management: A Builder's Field Guide,* a publication of the NAHB, a typical new home creates anywhere from 3.0 to 5.2 pounds of waste per square foot (15 to 25.4 kilograms per square meter), and roughly 80 percent of a homebuilder's waste stream is recyclable. The primary components of this waste stream are wood, drywall, cardboard, and metals. Both builders and solid-waste management agencies can realize significant cost savings through strategies that prevent the generation of waste at its source— examples include reducing packaging (primarily cardboard and plastics from plumbing, appliance, and cabinet vendors) and obtaining more accurate lumber estimates that assume a lower level of waste. Turnkey framing operations can also significantly reduce lumber waste.

Effective construction-waste management requires careful planning and directives from the onset of the project, as well as ongoing efforts to develop innovative strategies to meet recycling goals. For example, the strategic placement, sizing, and marking of recycling bins facilitates compliance. Recycling efforts can also be reinforced through incremental changes—such as the use of two-sided copies—that can make a big difference and send strong messages throughout the organization. Most important, a construction waste policy must not only be supported by top management but also implemented at every level of the organization. To influence behavior at the field level and ensure that all staff members are held accountable, it is also critical to include the policy in all contract documents and subcontractor training.

Some innovative builders have succeeded in developing construction waste management strategies that reduce both the financial and environmental costs of waste disposal. With the purchase of two site-based grinding systems, Artistic Homes, in Albuquerque, has reduced the number of hauls to the landfill by 70 percent, in a minimal amount of time. Construction waste is ground daily on site and picked up by a landscaping company that converts it to mulch. The operation was also cost-effective: the two grinders paid for themselves within one year.

Water Conservation

Even without severe drought conditions, there are strong environmental and economic advantages to developing water conservation standards for new home construction. Green building programs around the country promote conservation for both indoor water use and outdoor landscaping.

Water efficiency standards included in the Energy Policy Act of 1992 dictate maximum water usage levels for plumbing fixtures used in all new home construction; toilets are required to use no more than 1.6 gallons (six

liters) per flush, and maximum flow for showerheads and faucets is 2.5 gallons (9.5 liters) per minute. Showerheads are available with flow rates as low as 1.5 gallons (5.7 liters) per minute, and dual-flush toilets (which offer a choice of two flushing powers) and aerators for kitchen and bath faucets reduce flow rates even further. Many leading green homebuilders use dishwashers and washing machines that perform in the top one-third of the DOE's Energy Guide rating scale and provide considerable savings on both water and energy use. On-demand and recirculation devices for hot water also provide additional water savings. Time has shown that water-efficient plumbing can substantially reduce water consumption and consumer and municipal water costs, including the costs of associated environmental damage and the construction and maintenance of wastewater infrastructure.

Unfortunately, significant savings in indoor water use are often difficult to obtain because use depends on homeowners' purchasing decisions and behavior and is not susceptible to enforcement, except perhaps through rate structures designed to encourage water conservation. The greatest opportunity for water conservation is in the wiser and more strategic use of water in the installation of landscapes. The following are examples of strategies that support water conservation:

- The use of nonpotable water, whenever possible, for landscape irrigation systems;
- The installation of drought-tolerant or habitat-appropriate plants;
- "Hydro-zoning"—grouping plants according to their water needs;
- Soil amendment and mulching, to conserve moisture;
- A landscape management plan that protects the integrity of the landscaping while adhering to an established water budget;
- Design guidelines and homeowner covenants that limit the area of irrigated

turf and encourage the use of water-wise landscaping practices;

- Using the landscaping around model homes as demonstration gardens that highlight water-wise landscaping and efficient irrigation methods;
- Training and education for homeowners' associations.

Conclusion

For a developer or builder, a strong environmental ethic can be fundamental to brand identity and to the creation of value. At the same time, building practices that protect and support the environment are not, in themselves, enough to compel consumers to buy a green home or live in a green community. Consumers rightfully look for value in their purchases, and environmental advocacy doesn't necessarily translate into homebuyer action. For this reason, builders and developers should look to incorporate "premium" building practices that provide homeowners with significant, tangible benefits; such benefits include savings from lower fuel use, and the opportunity to own a healthier, more comfortable, and more durable home in a community that enhances the well-being of its residents. Through a green focus and an unqualified commitment to quality workmanship, outstanding customer service, operational excellence, and stewardship of the community, a company can develop lasting and profitable relationships with employees, customers, subcontractors, and local jurisdictions.

This chapter was written by Kristin Shewfelt, director, Environmental Programs, McStain Neighborhoods, Boulder, Colorado.

Notes

1. U.S. Environmental Protection Agency, *Our Built and Natural Environments,* EPA Document 231-R-01-002 (Washington, D.C.: EPA, January 2001).

2. William Fulton, Rolf Pendall, Mai Nguyen, and Alicia Harrison, "Who Sprawls Most? How Growth Patterns Differ across the U.S.," Brookings Institution Survey Series, July 2001 (http://www.brook.edu/es/urban/publications/fulton.pdf).

3. Natural Resources Conservation Service, U.S. Department of Agriculture, *Summary Report 1997 National Resources Inventory* (Washington, D.C.: U.S. Department of Agriculture; revised December 2000), 1.

4. Home Builders Association of Metropolitan Denver and Wirth Chair in Environmental and Community Development Policy, *Growth Management: Problems, Challenges, and Opportunities* (Denver: Home Builders Association of Metropolitan Denver, 1999), 2–3.

5. For information on the work of the Colorado Natural Heritage Program, see http://www.cnhp.colostate.edu/index.html.

6. There are many examples, but see in particular the case study on the Garnet Oaks community, which consists of 80 single-family homesites on 58 acres (23 hectares) in Bethel Township, Delaware County, Pennsylvania, at http://www.natlands.org/planning/growgreen5.

7. EPA, *Our Built and Natural Environments.*

8. There is a growing body of literature on low-impact development strategies. See U.S. Environmental Protection Agency, *Low-Impact Development (LID): A Literature Review,* EPA Document 841-B-00-005 (Washington, D.C.: EPA, October 2000). Additional information can be obtained at the following Web sites: http://www.lowimpactdevelopment.org; http://www.nrdc.org/water/pollution/storm/chap12.asp; and http://www.stormwatercenter.net.

9. For additional information on energy-efficient mortgages, see http://www.pueblo.gsa.gov/cic_text/housing/energy_mort/energy-mortgage.htm.

10. For further information on this program, see http://www.energystar.gov.

11. The Davis Energy Group (http://www.davisenergy.com), in California, is currently working on the Alternatives to Compressor Cooling Project. Davis's research has yielded both energy-efficient home designs and innovative ventilation cooling technologies.

12. Craig Cox, Executive Director, Colorado Coalition for New Energy Technologies; see http://www.newenergytechnologies.org.

13. For more information, see http://www.healthhouse.org.

14. Duncan Prahl, construction manager, Integrated Building and Construction Solutions (IBACOS); see http://www.ibacos.com. For a more detailed analysis of strategies to manage mold and moisture, see Joseph Lstiburek, "Moisture Control for Buildings," *ASHRAE Journal* (February 2002).

15. See Daniel Imhoff, *Building with Vision: Optimizing and Finding Alternatives to Wood* (White River Junction, Vt.: Watershed Media, 2001).

16. National Association of Home Builders, *Housing Facts, Figures and Trends 2001* (Washington, D.C.: NAHB Public Affairs, June 2001), 45.

17. David Malin Roodman and Nicholas Lenssen, *A Building Revolution: How Ecology and Health Concerns Are Transforming Construction,* Worldwatch Institute Paper 124 (Washington, D.C.: Worldwatch Institute, March 1995), 27.

8 Gaining Community Support: A Strategic Approach

Community opposition to growth can be one of the most difficult challenges facing developers of suburban projects. Today, neighboring residents have more opportunities than ever to engage in local land use politics. Flexible work schedules and telecommuting make it easier for local residents to attend meetings and testify at hearings. Web sites such as www.sprawl-busters.com and www.sprawlwatch.org offer activists instant access to strategic advice and technical guid-ance. Books such as *Up against the Wal-Marts* and *The Hometown Advantage* provide detailed campaign plans for resisting chain stores, and e-mail offers an easy and impersonal way for citizens to inundate public officials with cries of "Not in my back yard!"

Throughout America, lengthening life spans, expanding wealth, shrinking household size, and increasing demand for new product types are creating more and more pressure for new

housing, especially in desirable suburban locales. But citizens who already live in these areas do so because they like it; they are not looking for changes to the status quo. Indeed, local residents are often prepared to invest significant amounts of time and money to prevent the construction of any new suburban project in their backyard.

This chapter looks at some community relations issues unique to suburban development, discusses when to "go public" with a land use proposal, and outlines the fundamental components of a community outreach program that is designed to minimize opposition to, and mobilize community support for, new suburban development.

Community Relations Issues

Much community opposition is based on the desire to maintain the status quo. Current residents are satisfied with the surrounding land uses, with their quality of life, and with the demographics of their neighborhood. New development will forever change these elements, and developers should be prepared to understand and alleviate community concerns.

Existing Use

Suburban land use debates often begin with the fundamental question of whether or how the land is currently being used. Some builders look at rippling hillsides or litter-choked weeds and see prime opportunities for first-time development. Neighbors, however, see the open space as already in active use: the land is *their*

recreational area, *their* dog-walking park, *their* view corridor. Failing to acknowledge the presence of these existing uses—albeit very low-intensity uses—can make it difficult for a developer to reach consensus with neighbors about future use of the land.

The situation is different when the land is already being used so intensively that there is no longer a question of leaving it in its current state. In this case, instead of debating a "yes versus no" question ("Should the land be kept in its existing state?"), citizens and the developer must explore the more complex question of whether the proposed use is more or less desirable than the existing use.

Quality of Life

While urban dwellers are sometimes eager for the reinvention of their deteriorating neighborhoods, suburban residents tend to be significantly more resistant to change. People living near proposed new subdivisions are often "lifestyle refugees"—immigrants from the urban center who have decided that the quality of life in the suburbs is better than that in the city. But what, exactly, constitutes quality of life in the suburbs? What leads people to move from the urban core to the suburban edge?

It is important to understand that suburban homebuyers are both running *away* from perceived urban problems and running *toward* anticipated suburban benefits. Poor schools, the high cost of housing, and fear of urban crime drive citizens out of the cities, as do dissatisfaction with traffic, noise, competition

Facing page: One of the major factors in California's housing shortage is resistance to development on the part of NIMBY groups. The developers of Playa Vista, on the west side of Los Angeles, spent more than 20 years navigating the approval process before finally breaking ground for the 3,200-unit development.

for parking, and other problems that come with residential density. People moving to the suburbs are lured not only by the promise of better schools, more affordable housing, and greater safety, but by more subjective hopes for a quieter lifestyle, a stronger sense of community, friendlier neighbors, and a rural—even bucolic—environment.

This vision of idyllic nonurban living is often, however, quite different from the reality. Although parents may believe that they moved to a less urban community so that their children could, in theory, raise chickens and goats in the backyard, the reality is that chickens are noisy and goats smell: in other words, quality of life is principally an emotional issue, not a rational one. Thus, for many suburbanites, Wal-Marts and Home Depots are more than mere retail outlets; they are the manifestation of the soulless sprawl so contrary to their idealized vision of a small-town utopia. Nevertheless, citizens' commitment to a nonurban lifestyle should not be dismissed simply because it is emotionally based; indeed, their perspective is a legitimate part of the suburban planning process.

Views, for example, are an extremely important aspect of community character. One of the principal ways that suburban adults experience their community is as a sequence of views observed as they drive to and from work each day. Because what they see along the drive materially defines their perception of the area's quality of life, even minimal changes in views along commuter routes can have a huge impact on community opinion about a project. From a community relations standpoint, therefore, protecting view corridors along well-traversed roads can be more persuasive than providing setbacks and open-space reserves that few neighbors will ever see.

Developers often insist that a proposed project will "fit in" with the community, but the developer is not a particularly credible expert —nor does a professional planner or techni-cal land use analyst provide the best assurance that a project will be compatible with the surrounding neighborhood. Whom, then, do residents believe? They believe people who share their suburban lifestyle and values: people who live and work near similar existing projects. Although it is important to have technical experts rationally evaluate consistency with community character, citizens themselves are the best source of nontechnical evaluations of what is, and is not, consistent with community character.

Affordable Housing

Increasingly, master-planned communities include a range of housing types and housing prices. Too often, however, affordable housing runs headfirst into a belief that moral worth is linked to material wealth: "If you don't earn what I earn and live the way I live, it must be because you're lazy or irresponsible." Many Americans unconsciously assume that socially responsible conduct originates in wealth, and that lower-income residents will therefore engage in such unneighborly behavior as failing to maintain their properties, dealing drugs, blasting loud music, or hanging laundry on the front porch.

Proposals for monolithic apartment buildings usually trigger the most serious community opposition, and it is usually worth investing in top-quality architectural renderings and photomontages to demonstrate that affordable housing units will be visually compatible with surrounding single-family homes. Neighbors also worry about whether a faceless property management company can be trusted to protect community interests, which is why the company's track record is very important: people like to know they've got an experienced team that knows how to maintain the property and properly select and supervise tenants.

Homeowners typically prefer inclusionary units to be scattered anonymously throughout the neighborhood, especially when those below-

Both local residents and the city council supported the development of Nava Adé, a community of affordable homes in Santa Fe, New Mexico. The developers preserved the natural landscape and ensured that the project design was compatible with the character of local historic structures.

market units are made available only to home-buyers and not to renters. Secondary units, such as granny flats that are controlled by the owners of market-rate homes, can also provide a sense of security, particularly when the principal homeowner lives on site and is able to monitor the activities of the lower-income tenant or buyer.

Mixed Uses

In conventional suburban communities, different uses are typically isolated from each other by means of exclusive zoning districts that are linked only by automobile. Many of today's more innovative master-planned communities, on the other hand, are mixed-use projects that blend single- and multifamily housing with commercial, retail, and community uses. While many buyers and renters are attracted to the pedestrian-friendly intensity and social diversity of new urbanist proposals, some homeowners living in conventional suburban communities worry that a mixed-use project will be incompatible with the lifestyle they are used to. They fear a loss of control over their environment, when pedestrians and nonresidential land uses become part of it. The challenge for developers is to reassure suburbanites that walkable, mixed-use development is not some weird, untested fad that they have never seen, but is part of the

traditional American fabric, and blends well with more conventional suburban developments.

Density

When it comes to density, neighbors often demand that new homes be isolated on ranch- or estate-sized parcels. Suburbanites believe that large lots are necessary for several reasons. First, larger lots logically mean fewer homes, fewer homes mean fewer people, and fewer people mean less traffic, less school crowding, and less demand for public services. Second, to minimize competition for parking, protect views, and maintain privacy, existing residents want a buffer between themselves and new development. Third, burdening a new home with costly land is an effective way to discourage lower-income residents from moving into the neighborhood, a goal that is important to some existing residents. Finally, and probably most importantly, residents often insist that the only way to preserve the nonurban character of the community is to prohibit the high-density housing and population that they associate with urban development patterns.

Regardless of the relative size of the property or the overall density, neighbors are often shocked by the raw number of proposed rooftops. The resident of a cul-de-sac lined

Perimeter Summit, in Atlanta, is being converted from an office park into a mixed-use development that will include a hotel, 3.5 million square feet (325,160 square meters) of office space, and Summer Villas, a 400-unit apartment complex. A new bridge that will connect the development to Perimeter Mall will, in effect, add a retail component to the project.

with five other homes who hears figures like "50 new homes" or "5,000 new units" can be quite frightened. Thus, when developers discuss density or the number of new homes to be built, it is often more effective to relate the proposal to a well-known example than to cite abstract figures: "This project will have the same density as the Maple Grove project," or "This project will have about the same number of housing units as the Pinehurst Development over in Pleasantville." If a project will be phased, it can also help to break down the number of units on a yearly basis ("an average of 25 new homes per year") rather than to describe the project at total buildout ("500 homes over 20 years").

Use versus Siting

As the analysis of citizen opposition to development proposals has spawned its own vocabulary, terms like NIMBY (not in my back yard) and LULU (locally unwanted land use) are often used interchangeably. It is helpful, however, to recognize the difference between conflicts that center on a proposed *use* and those that center on the *siting* of that use.

True NIMBY disputes are almost entirely about location: that is, citizens recognize the inherent value of the proposed use but believe that the site is inappropriate. Suburban uses likely to provoke NIMBY resistance include airports, gas stations, low-income housing, schools, houses of worship, and social service facilities (such as hospitals or drug rehabilitation centers).

Opponents in NIMBY disputes may argue, directly or indirectly, that unique features make the surroundings unusually sensitive to project impacts. Opponents of a new retail project, for example, may agree that a new grocery store is desirable but assert that the proposed site is inappropriate because it contains wetlands. In a conscious effort to avoid the selfishness often ascribed to NIMBY activists, sophisticated opponents will often criticize a proposal for its alleged failure to meet basic development goals. People who object to a new subdivision, for example, might argue that homebuyers will not be attracted to houses so close to an earthquake fault, or that home prices will be too high for the project to be successful.

While NIMBYs are acknowledged to be desirable land uses as long as they are properly sited, no one wants a LULU *anywhere*. People who oppose LULUs often argue that the proposal should be rejected because there is simply no real need for the use. Recreational projects, such as theme parks, and convenience-related uses, such as drive-through restaurants, are classic examples of LULUs that fall into this category. Opponents of LULUs may also argue that better alternatives are available: the county should implement a crime prevention program instead of building a new jail, for instance, or modify an existing arena rather than construct a new one. Developers facing this type of opposition must fight a battle on several fronts: demonstrating the need for the proposed use, proving that the project meets that need, and showing that no other type of use can meet the need as well as the proposed use.

Timing Outreach Efforts

At what point should a developer let neighbors know that a large suburban project is planned for their backyard? Before filing the application? When the story hits the newspaper? Only after a public hearing is scheduled and a public notice has been mailed out? A more important strategic question, however, is *whom* to involve first. Developers typically reach out to neighbors first—those

living or working closest to the project site. Unfortunately, those citizens are likely to experience more than their fair share of negative impacts and are therefore most likely to oppose the project. As the first people brought to the table, neighbors often try to define themselves as the only "real" stakeholders and to restrict community debate to the discussion of adverse impacts and the need to preserve the status quo. A better starting point is to identify the community's recognized leaders and begin to educate them about the project.

It is thus crucial for the developer to line up some supporters before reaching out to likely opponents. Specifically, the developer should get allies on board *before* the proposal explodes into a high-profile, highly divisive issue. The community is filled with people who will benefit from development of the new project, and the developer needs to find them, educate them, and get them involved in the land use discussion. Encouraging these supporters to be actively involved in the entitlement process will lead still others to step forward in support of the project and will ultimately help to create a critical mass of citizens who are interested in working cooperatively with the developer. Getting supporters involved in the project before opponents set the agenda can also expand the civic debate to include consideration of larger issues such as economic stability, tax base growth, job creation, and the creation of affordable housing.

Avoiding Opposition

Even more desirable than successful handling of opposition is avoiding it altogether. Developers who do their homework can sometimes see that opposition to a project never surfaces. Providing accurate information upfront, avoiding misperceptions, and treating the community with respect can go a long way toward building community support rather than resistance.

Get the Facts Right

A significant amount of opposition to development proposals is based on misperceptions, lack of information, or exaggerated fears of project impacts. A neighbor might say, "Whaddaya mean you're building 40 luxury homes . . . I heard you were building 400 low-income apartments!" Areas where misinformation is likely to crop up include consistency with zoning and general plan criteria; effects on property values, views, traffic, and community character; and the types of residents or commercial tenants expected in the new project.

The developer can minimize opposition that is based on lack of information by providing clear, credible data about the proposal. High-quality public information materials can effectively educate citizens and can also help to convey the sophistication, excitement, and lifestyle values of the project. Such information, however, typically flows *from* the developer *to* the public—via direct mail, newsletters, advertisements, and read-only Web pages—and, although one-way information is certainly an important part of community relations, developers must also ensure that citizens have an opportunity to engage with them interactively, and to make their voices heard. It is important for citizens to feel that they have had an impact on the shape of a new development, not just that the development has had an impact on *them*.

Although many developers believe that the most efficient way to communicate with the public is to host a massive community meeting, these events are rarely the best way *either* to convey information or to provide a comfortable forum for community response and interaction. A large audience usually brings up so many issues than none can be addressed in depth. Many people, particularly those who are unaccustomed to public speaking, feel uncomfortable revealing their ignorance or confusion in front of a crowd, and those who actually favor the project may re-

press their opinions for fear of triggering condemnation from skeptical peers in attendance. A developer who wants to both convey a great deal of information to a large number of people, and to address their concerns, is better off hosting smaller, invitation-only events, serial meetings, or open houses stretching out over several hours or several days.

It is important to realize, however, that public information is not a magic cure for all types of NIMBY opposition: it can only reduce opposition that is based on lack of information. Simply disgorging data without regard for the real origins of community resistance is both insensitive and inefficient. Moreover, one-way public information runs the risk of appearing condescending. A developer, for example, who invites neighbors to come to a meeting "so we can tell you what we're doing" gives the impression that he or she feels entitled to make unilateral decisions—and then to inform neighbors about plans after the fact. A better way to encourage neighbors to attend a meeting is to tell them you would like to know what they think about your proposal, and ask them to attend a meeting so *you* can listen to *them*.

Saving Face

The intensity of a neighbor's anger about a proposed project is often directly related to how insulted, ignored, or humiliated that individual feels. Indeed, 64 percent of participants in a study on anger reported that the reason they behaved aggressively was to redeem a damaged self-image or to repair a social image. Although it is always important to treat citizens with respect, it is crucial to do so when a controversial proposal is under consideration.

Respect for neighbors can be demonstrated in many ways. The top tactic: listening without interrupting. Making good eye contact and inclining one's body slightly toward the speaker also communicates respectful listening; covering one's lips while listening sends strong signals of rejection. When speaking, the developer should refer to citizens by name and comment on the unique concerns of each individual.

Acknowledging the legitimate role of neighbors in the planning process can help defuse community anger. Neighbors need to feel they are respected as stakeholders, that their concerns are understood, and that their input will actually affect how a proposal evolves. Large community meetings or public workshops, after the groundwork has been laid with the community leadership, should therefore be recognized as opportunities to meet neighbors' emotional needs, not merely their informational needs.

Right and Wrong

When a proposal involves converting raw, environmentally desirable land into an intensely developed project, some citizens are going to perceive the situation as a conflict between good and evil. For traditional economic moralists, progress and change are good, additional jobs and tax revenues are good, and any environmental impacts are strictly incidental to the pursuit of material gain. Environmental moralists, in contrast, believe that preservation of the environment takes priority over any other public good, such as exploiting the land for human gain. Even where no genuine ethical conflict exists, parties in a dispute may try to characterize each other as morally corrupt in order to justify behavior, on their own part, that would otherwise be considered inappropriate—or even unethical.

So what should a developer do when the land use debate starts sounding like a battle between good and evil? First, there may not be a conflict of values at all: the developer

In Bellevue, Washington, the developers of Avalon Bellevue and city government staff worked as a team, expediting the permitting process.

may share citizens' commitment to protect the environment. If that is the case, the developer should affirm the shared viewpoint that protection of the environment is an important goal. If citizens respond by challenging the developer's credibility, the business rationale should be explained; for example, "Saving the old oak trees will increase the value of the new homes," or "We're preserving this wetland in order to comply with federal regulations." Such explanations may be more believable than a more altruistic one, even if the latter is true.

When opponents characterize conflict over a suburban project as a battle of "right versus wrong," it can often be shown that, at worst, it is a case of "right versus right." Yes, preservation of the environment is important, but how does that principle rank in comparison to other values—such as those associated with property rights, or fairness, or tolerance, or compassion? The developer does not have to challenge the validity of a neighbor's ethics: merely getting opponents to recognize that they hold other values, besides those that they are focused on at the moment, can help broaden their view of the project.

What does a developer do if he or she holds vastly different views than those held by citizen opponents? Do differing values always lead to irresolvable conflict? No, of course not. Developers deal every day deal with people who hold different values than they do, and they still manage to solve common problems. When land use controversies appear to be grounded in ideological conflict, the key is to focus the parties on their mutual interests, not on their nonmutual beliefs.

Persuasion and Negotiation

Citizens have a *positive* interest in gaining new benefits that they do not currently enjoy: additional tax revenues, new jobs, more housing, new parks, and an improved civic image. Most people who support proposals for new suburban communities do so because they're excited about the new benefits that can come from responsible development. By comparison, most project opponents are motivated by their *negative* interest in protecting the status quo. Project opponents like their community the way it is, and are not willing to suffer more traffic, impaired views, or loss of the community's rural character. The perception that a proposed project will conflict with these interests gives rise to significant opposition and controversy.

Not surprisingly, a bird in the hand is worth two in the bush: people are much more likely to defend what they already have than to risk their current quality of life for some vague future benefit. That is why it may be useful to emphasize how the project will protect existing benefits ("This proposal ensures that the old barn isn't demolished") rather than to describe how it will create new benefits ("The old barn will be turned into a new community center").

It is also important to make future benefits as credible and as certain as possible. For example, the proposal should be presented through detailed renderings that demonstrate its quality and its compatibility with the neighborhood. And, instead of offering vague promises that retail tenants will cooperate with a community-based job training and referral agency to maximize local hiring, the developer should ensure that the tenants are contractually required to send hiring information to local agencies.

Conflicts of interest are usually resolved by a political body that arbitrates between two opposing positions and selects the more politically acceptable option. Political arbitration is usually seen as a zero-sum scenario, because the only way for one party to win is if the other party loses. And, since citizens who lose the first round do not necessarily give up, such arbitration can be very risky for developers, particularly if it leads to appeals, litigation, or ballot-box land use planning.

Coggins Square Apartments, an affordable housing complex that adjoins the Pleasant Hill Bay Area Rapid Transit station, replaced a surface parking lot.

The most successful conflict resolution strategies for land use debates are persuasion and negotiation. Persuasion involves presenting arguments in order to change neighbors' beliefs, opinions, and intentions. When developers engage in persuasion, they are trying to get residents to feel more favorably toward development in general or to believe that the specific project is desirable. Once citizens regard a project more favorably, the developer then focuses on persuading them to take action consistent with those beliefs, such as testifying in favor of the project at a public hearing or writing a letter of support.

Developers often focus on rational persuasion, offering facts and logical arguments that they hope neighbors will evaluate and accept. In the face of potential information overload, however, many citizens rely largely on peripheral cues, focusing on the external context rather than on the internal content of the developer's statement. "Is the developer likable? Then the presentation must be believable." "If the project sponsor paid for this, it must be a bunch of hogwash." "Since everyone seems to hate this proposal, it must be a bad project."

In addition to using rational and peripheral persuasion, both project opponents and proponents typically engage in emotional persuasion. A builder who plants red, white, and blue flowers around the entrance to a new project, for example, is trying to trigger feelings of patriotism and to link those emotions with the project. Appeals to pity ("This will kill the baby birds!"), appeals to fear ("We'll sue!"), and guilt trips ("How can you do this to us?") are intended to persuade the developer to change his or her plans. Personal attacks ("You're a liar!") are intended to discredit the developer in the eyes of an audience. A builder on the receiving end of emotional attacks should focus on not overreacting to these obvious strategic ploys.

Unlike persuasion, negotiation is not about convincing neighbors that a development project is consistent with their personal interests. Negotiation focuses on the external outcome of the interaction, not on the internal attitudes of the parties. When people engage in confrontational negotiation, each party fights for the best outcome for itself, even if that means the other party "loses." In the consensual approach to negotiations, all stakeholders attempt to reach a "win-win" solution in which no party suffers unreasonable harm.

Compromise, one of the most common outcomes of negotiation, comes into play when different parties make different demands about the same thing, and the parties respond by giving up roughly comparable expectations or making comparable sacrifices. For example, if a developer wants to build 1,000 new homes and neighbors insist that only 200 homes should be built, the parties might meet in the middle and agree to 600 homes. Conflicts that involve numbers—square footage, acreage, housing units, building height, and so on—are the most likely candidates for middle-ground solutions that neither fully satisfy nor seriously injure any party.

Rivermark, an infill project in Santa Clara, California, combines market rate and affordable housing and features a new city library.

DAHLIN GROUP

Not all outcomes, however, are ready subjects for compromise. If the conflict is about whether a piece of land should remain as undisturbed open space, there is simply no middle ground: the land either will be developed or it will not. Moreover, it is very difficult to quantify—and compromise on—intangible outcomes such as dignity or justice. Conflicts that do not lend themselves to compromise are usually resolved by an exchange of concessions, in which the developer and the residents concede on issues that they do not really care about in order to gain something that is important to them. Three types of concessions are considered during negotiation:

- The proposal can be modified to eliminate the real or perceived threat to the neighbors' interests. The height of the apartment buildings can be reduced, for example, or single-family homes can be built instead of townhouses.
- If negative impacts cannot be avoided, they can be mitigated. For example, while construction of a new development may indeed affect the views of nearby neighbors, attractive landscaping or berms can be used to make the effect acceptable. Mitigation measures, like project modifications, are aimed primarily at preserving the status quo.
- If negative impacts cannot be addressed through modification or mitigation, developers may offer counterbalancing benefits: some new feature, amenity, or program so desirable that it offsets the negative impacts of the project. Benefits commonly touted by developers include public open space; recreational facilities; job creation; and community facilities, such as fire stations or senior centers.

Concessions can cost millions of dollars, so it is important not to make a significant concession for community relations purposes unless there is clear evidence that it will have a real impact on project acceptance. Public opinion research can help evaluate the entitlement value of different concessions to different target audiences, and, more importantly, can distinguish between concessions that are merely *popular* and those that are actually *persuasive*. Here is a simplistic example of the difference between a popular and a persuasive concession: in America, just about everyone likes the color blue. But painting a project blue will not necessarily increase citizen support for the proposal. Similarly, only a small proportion of citizens may believe that a new turn lane will solve the anticipated traffic problems created by a new project, but the turn lane could be the "silver bullet" that has a huge impact on the opinions of key target audiences, such as seniors, renters, or high-frequency voters.

Building Support

A comprehensive community relations program actually involves two separate outreach campaigns: one aimed at likely opponents, the other at supporters. Each of these audiences is composed of different types of people, and each will respond to different messages. While it may be enough to merely discourage opponents from taking action against the project, developers usually need community allies to provide a public expression of support for the proposed project.

Identifying Potential Supporters
There are five distinct groups of potential supporters, and the first step in any program to develop support is to identify people who can be most effectively tapped for assistance:

- *Direct beneficiaries* are those who will immediately and materially benefit from development of the project: investors, construction contractors, construction workers, and so on.
- *Indirect beneficiaries* are those who will benefit when the project leads to general improvements in the local economy. Local merchants, for example, can benefit if new residents increase pedestrian activ-

ity, while tax base proponents (such as the "Friends of the Public Library" and the local firefighters' union) will benefit from the increase in tax revenues generated by the project.
- *Project users*—whether potential buyers of new housing units or tenants of future commercial or retail space—make highly credible witnesses.
- *Special interest groups* tend either to support most kinds of development (e.g., the local chamber of commerce, the builders' association) or to support one particular component of the proposal (e.g., child care advocates, the soccer league). Religious groups, for example, often support affordable housing and social justice programs, while members of Ducks Unlimited are avid supporters of wetland restoration programs.
- Finally, support can be drawn from people who will suffer *relational consequences* if they don't help: the developer's friends, employees, relatives, vendors, and contractors, whose future relationship with the developer depends on the support they give today.

Recruiting Supporters
Before asking potential supporters to agree to a big request, such as testifying at a public hearing, the developer should start with a much smaller request. If a citizen agrees to some minor, painless request—such as signing a support petition—then when demands are later escalated, the neighbor will feel both internal and external pressure to comply with the request or else look shamefully inconsistent. Once a supporter agrees to an initial request, she will start seeing herself as a cooperative, helpful, and compliant person—and as someone who cares about the project and takes action to influence local community decisions.

A sociological study conducted in the 1960s offered a stunning example of this "foot-in-the-door" technique. Sociologists went door to door asking homeowners to comply with a seemingly trivial request: to place a three-inch-square card in their front windows reading "Be a Safe Driver." Two weeks later, the researchers went back to those homes seeking permission to erect an enormous and hideous billboard in the front yard reading, "Drive Carefully." Just 17 percent of those who had refused to post the tiny card in their windows agreed to the request for the larger billboard. Of those who had made the initial commitment by posting the card, however, a whopping *76 percent* agreed to allow the billboards to be installed on their lawns. Within a development context, it is obvious that someone who signs a petition, fills out an endorsement card, or even attends a neighborhood coffee is substantially more likely to testify in favor of the project than someone who never makes that initial commitment.

Mobilizing for the Hearing

As the hearing approaches, the developer must turn to those in the community who have previously committed their support. The way to approach these initial supporters is to begin with a large request that is likely to be rejected, such as, "Will you attend the hearing on Tuesday and testify in favor of the project?" If the large request is accepted, so much the better. If it is refused, then a smaller favor should be requested, such as, "Will you call the mayor and let him know you support the project?" The developer, by lowering her expectations, will appear to the supporter to have made a significant concession—triggering a sense of obligation, on the part of the supporter, to repay that concession by complying with the second request. In other words, the second request will seem so small and reasonable in comparison to the first that the supporter will feel compelled to comply.

Successful public hearings require more than just getting supporters to city hall and hoping everything works out. Citizens' testimony in favor of the proposed development should be carefully coordinated to ensure that the vocal minority opposing the project does not overwhelm supporters' political strength. By monitoring and managing all facets of the public hearing process, the developer can make certain that decision makers truly appreciate the level of community support for a project. A number of steps can be taken to ensure that the public hearing process has maximum positive impact:

- Learn the rules: The developer should become familiar with how the commission, council, or board conducts its hearings. Are they "cattle calls," where citizens wait in the aisles for their turn at the microphone? Are witnesses called up in the order in which they sign up? Do opponents testify before supporters have an opportunity to make their case? Does the chairperson alternate advocates and adversaries, or call witnesses in some other order? The developer should speak with the chairperson or the appropriate staff person well in advance of the hearing to know what procedures to expect.

- Sign up supporters: If developers are permitted to submit speaker cards or to sign up supporters before the public hearing begins, they should certainly do so. However, it is better not to register all supporters to speak one right after the other. Some should be reserved to testify later in the hearings, both to rebut attacks and to ensure that speakers who oppose the project are intermittently balanced by positive messages about the project.

- Get the good seats: By occupying front-row seats, supporters can ensure that decision makers can see them—and that they will be aware of the level of audience support for the proposal. A few supporters might sit scattered among the audience members to monitor the tone of the opposition, and possibly even to voice disagreement with opposing views.

- Make sure visual aids are visible: Charts, projection screens, or other visual aids

The Parks of Austin Ranch, a multifamily rental community in suburban Dallas, overcame community resistance through careful planning and design.

should be visible to both decision makers and the public. An audience excluded from the presentation may feel offended, and decision makers could start treating the development team harshly simply to prove to the audience that no one has the advantage. Keeping visual aids on display can also help to maintain a civil atmosphere by focusing attention on facts rather than on emotions. If it is not feasible to set up easels or projection screens so that both the public and the politicians have a clear view of them, handouts might be an appropriate way to permit the audience to follow along with the presentation.

■ Provide talking points: A one-page fact sheet or list of bulleted talking points can help ensure that speakers who like the project emphasize the key messages for decision makers to focus on.

■ Encourage supporters to look supportive: Project allies, including the developer's own team members, can express enthusiasm for the project even when sitting still. Supporters should be encouraged to raise their hands or to wear buttons that identify them as project advocates.

■ Try to speak last: The developer should be the last voice the decision makers hear before they cast their votes. By speaking last, a developer can rebut attacks made by earlier speakers and make certain that key messages are fresh in officials' minds when it comes time to make a decision. The project sponsor should request a brief rebuttal period or hold at least one persuasive supporter in reserve to summarize key points at the end of the hearing.

Community opposition can be one of the most difficult challenges facing suburban developers, but a proactive, strategic approach can make a difference. By recognizing citizens' legitimate concerns about proposed development, respecting the public's role in the decision-making process, and separately targeting and mobilizing community support for a proposed project, developers can effectively respond to the community relations challenges of building suburban projects.

This chapter was written by Debra Stein, president of GCA Strategies, in San Francisco.

Case Studies

Winslow Mews

Bainbridge Island, Washington

Winslow Mews is a small-scale residential infill development sited on 1.5 acres (0.60 hectares) in the town of Winslow, on Bainbridge Island, Washington. This pedestrian-oriented community of 22 single-family houses and duplexes features a densely urban design that highlights Pacific Northwest architectural influences. The development is within walking distance of Winslow Way (the town's main street) and the ferry to Seattle.

Bainbridge Island, with a population of 20,000, is a 35-minute ferry ride from Seattle. The town of Winslow, located at the ferry terminus, is a waterfront community with a friendly, small-town atmosphere. Bainbridge Island is quickly becoming attractive as a bedroom community, drawing 350 to 500 new residents per year. The island is planning to meet the needs of incoming residents by directing 50 percent of the new growth to Winslow. However, these new residents are quickly driving up home prices in the community. With single-family homes averaging $435,000, affordable housing is at a premium. By developing Winslow Mews, Rod McKenzie, who moved to Winslow in semiretirement, was able to create an interesting, small-scale project on an infill site, with relatively affordable housing. As the lowest-priced new housing on Bainbridge Island, Winslow Mews is a good fit for the town; it also met the developer's needs by allowing him to continue his relaxed lifestyle.

According to architect Greg Hackworth, the goal of the project was to design an architec-

The 22 units at Winslow Mews are a mix of single-family houses and duplexes. The houses enclose a central courtyard that contains a common green and an interior driveway. The homeowners' association sponsors social events in the space.

turally integrated neighborhood that provided a sense of community. Pedestrian access to the shops and services in downtown Winslow was integral to the development's plan.

The Site and Its Surroundings

Winslow Mews is located on a 1.5-acre (0.6-hectare) site that previously housed two small, single-story duplex offices and a loop road around the buildings. The development is within walking distance of Winslow Way, the town's main street, with its professional offices, shops, and restaurants, and is a ten-minute walk to the ferry dock.

To the north of the site are low-rise office buildings; to the south, a single-family home on a tree-filled lot; to the east, small houses converted into offices; and to the west, an apartment complex. A trail that leads to the ferry dock runs parallel to the site, along the west side, and preserved cedar trees line the east and west sides of the site.

Planning and Design

Winslow Mews is the first development of its kind in the town of Winslow, and the developer worked closely with the town to ensure that the project fit into the municipal master plan. The 22 units are set in a circle around a central green and an interior road; four units also face Wyatt Avenue, a public street. The central green provides open space, which the homeowners' association uses for gatherings. The three-story residences are

a mix of single-family homes and duplexes. With a density of 14 dwelling units per acre (35 per hectare), Winslow Mews still maintains a sense of openness.

The neighborhood was designed to be pedestrian oriented. In keeping with the developer's desire to deemphasize the impact of the automobile on the residential environment, the garages for the homes that front Wyatt Avenue were moved to the rear of the houses, and pedestrian entranceways to the neighborhood's interior were provided. Garages that face the interior road are discreetly tucked under overhangs or second-story porches, to lessen their visual impact. A sidewalk lined with street trees offers a pleasant place to walk along Wyatt Avenue. The entrance to the community provides passersby with a view of the common green and cherry trees, while separating the street from the quiet inner courtyard. Community mailboxes are located along both sides of the entrance, under a pair of covered passageways.

Front porches and small front yards emphasize the connection between the homes and the street. In the common courtyard that serves as a gathering place for residents, newly planted trees will eventually provide shade. The Winslow Mews Homeowners'

The homes fronting Wyatt Avenue have garages located in the rear. Street trees enhance the pedestrian-oriented environment.

Architectural details and bold colors reign at Winslow Mews. The builder describes the homes as "San Francisco in style with Bainbridge charm and Scandinavian colors."

Association has built a cedar fence with a lattice top to encircle the electrical boxes on the green, and hopes to add a gazebo at a later date.

Interesting architectural details and bold colors reign in Winslow Mews. The gabled roofs, with their variety of dormers and ridge lines, are reminiscent of the local traditional architecture. Craftsman-style trim, trelliswork, and a mix of window types add to the neighborhood's lively appearance and help to set it apart from other developments. McKenzie describes the homes as "San Francisco in style with Bainbridge charm and Scandinavian colors." He is known around the island for his vividly colored homes and for his abhorrence of what he calls "builder beige." The blue, yellow, green, and brown fiber-cement siding is trimmed with wood, and the front doors are painted in strong, contrasting colors of teal, red, and blue.

The single-family homes and duplexes all have a one- or two-car garage and the option of a ground-floor bonus room that can be used as a home office—a design element that was encouraged in Winslow's master plan. Some residents who have opted for a home office include an artist, an architect, and a small-business owner. The main living space of the homes is on the second floor, and bedrooms are on the third floor. Homes feature second-level porches or decks, and some have an additional porch on the ground floor.

Affordable Housing

As part of Washington's Growth Management Act of 1998, towns can offer incentives to developers to include affordable-housing units in exchange for greater allowable density in a development. The act requires that in any residential development made up of more than eight units, 10 percent of the units must be set aside for affordable housing. McKenzie was the first developer in Winslow to include affordable housing in his development in accordance with the Growth Management Act.

Residents whose incomes are 80 percent of the median for Kitsap County (in which Bainbridge Island is located) qualified to buy the affordable units. However, because buyers who met this requirement could not afford the $160,000 price tags, the low-income units sat empty for nine months. In order to find qualified buyers, McKenzie worked with the town to change the income requirements to 80 percent of the median income for the city of Seattle. A special advertisement was created to sell the low-income units, and the developer worked with 65 individuals before finding qualified low-income buyers.

The two affordable-housing units—both halves of a three-story duplex on the east side of the development—blend seamlessly into the community. Deed restrictions on these duplexes require that the terms of their resale follow the affordability requirements outlined for initial buyers; they also state that, for 20 years from the initial sale, the appreciation on the value of each home cannot exceed the increase in the Consumer Price Index.

Financing and Marketing

The project was financed through a conventional construction loan with Continental Bank (now Homestreet Bank). Home prices averaged $200,000 to $225,000 without builder options. The 20 market-rate units were sold at full price within seven months of the start of construction, without buyer incentives or points paid.

Marketing for Winslow Mews began while homes were being framed, and the effort was very successful. Home were sold so quickly that the developer decided not to build a model. All but two units sold within seven months of the start of construction.

Signage was the key ingredient of the project's marketing success: more than 80 percent of buyers learned of Winslow Mews through on-site signage. The sales center was open every weekend—and, although the project is not located on a heavily traveled street, the signage led buyers to the project.

Word of mouth and newspaper publicity drew many customers, so minimal advertising was required. Print advertisements in *Coldwell Banker* magazine (which is available free on the ferry) attracted the interest of Seattle residents and of visitors to the island. When the community was nearly completed, a broker's open house was held to acquaint the close-knit real estate community with the project. An article on density and design in the *Seattle Post-Intelligencer* brought added attention. Although the article made no direct mention of the project, it sparked interest in Winslow Mews because it featured a rendering of the development. Most of the buyers were young professionals or empty nesters from Bainbridge Island; one was from Seattle; and a few were from out of state.

In the interior of the project, where garages face the courtyard, they have been visually minimized, tucked under second-story porches.

Experience Gained

Winslow Mews was a small site, which necessitated tight lots, so the developer had to be attentive to privacy issues. Also, in such a close environment, architectural details gain importance.

Curb appeal is important; the project will not succeed if it does not look good from the street. For the four houses facing Wyatt Avenue, the architecture of the porches sets the tone and provides separation from the street.

Location, knowing the market, and fine-tuning the product type are vital to a project's success. Winslow Mews was the right product at the right location, price, and time.

The developer provided a basic product at a price that allowed for upgrades. More than 60 percent of buyers took advantage of builder options, adding $35,000 to $40,000 to their home's base price.

Developers in a small town have a responsibility to provide a high-quality product. To produce Winslow Mews, McKenzie listened to the city's needs and combined them with his sense of good development.

At the entrance to the project, covered pedestrian passages shelter community mailboxes. The entrance shown here provides a view of the common green to passersby while separating the street from the inner courtyard.

Winslow Mews

Project Data

Land Use Information

Site area (acres/hectares)	1.5/0.6
Total number of dwelling units	22
Gross density (units per acre/per hectare)	14/35

Land Use Plan

Use	Area (Square Feet/ Square Meters)	Percentage of Site
Residential	16,932/1,570	26
Roads	16,500/1,530	26
Common open space	20,000/1,860	31
Other	11,000/1,020	17
Total land area	64,432/5,980	100

Residential Unit Information

Unit Type	Unit Size (Square Feet/ Square Meters)	Number of Units	Sales Prices
Three-story detached	1,336–1,505/ 120–140	12	$200,000– $225,000
Three-story duplex	1,590/150	8	$220,000
Three-story duplex (affordable)	1,090/100	2	$160,000

Development Cost Information

Site Acquisition and Improvement Costs

Site acquisition	$530,000
Site improvement	25,000
Excavation, grading	120,000
Sewer, water, drainage	22,000
Landscaping, irrigation	30,000
Subtotal, site acquisition and improvement costs	$727,000

Construction Costs

Superstructure	$1,035,000
HVAC	129,000
Electrical	126,000
Plumbing, sprinklers	129,000
Finishes	400,000
Fees, general conditions	115,000
Subtotal, construction costs	$1,934,000

Soft Costs

Architecture, engineering services	$95,000
Project management	70,000
Marketing	30,000
Commissions	420,000
Legal, accounting services	15,000
Taxes, insurance	16,000
Construction interest	132,000
Permits and fees	200,000
Subtotal, soft costs	$978,000
Total development costs	$3,639,000

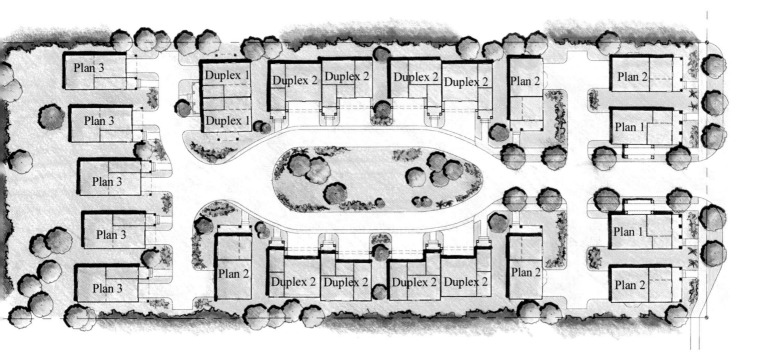

Development Schedule

Site purchased	April 1997
Planning started	June 1997
Construction started	April 1998
Sales started	June 1998
First closing	December 1998
Sales completed	January 1999
Construction completed	July 1999

Development Team

Developer

Rod McKenzie
McKenzie Holdings, LLC
427 Lovell Avenue, S.W.
Bainbridge Island, Washington 98110
206-842-9415

Architect and Site Planner

Hackworth Architecture
1927 Post Alley
Seattle, Washington 98101
206-443-1181

Landscape Architect

Verdigris Landscape Design
1402 Third Street, Suite 800
Seattle, Washington 98101
206-842-9217

General Contractor

Fairbank Construction
127 Parfitt Way, S.W.
Bainbridge Island, Washington 98110
206-842-9217

Real Estate Sales

Coldwell Banker/Marie Gallagher and Associates
337 High School Road
Bainbridge Island, Washington 98110
206-799-6851

The Fields of St. Croix

Lake Elmo, Minnesota

One of the most serious sprawl-related problems nationwide is the development of large residential lots on the urban fringe. In many metropolitan areas, where open land is scarce and property owners are seeking a slice of the countryside, farmland is being gobbled up by two- to ten-acre (one- to four-hectare) lots. Although the resulting leapfrog development is one of the major contributors to sprawl, many cities and townships on the urban fringe are unwilling to allow denser development, for fear of losing their rural character. The Fields of St. Croix, a 113-unit conservation community in Lake Elmo, Minnesota, an eastern suburb of the Twin Cities, offers a creative solution to this conundrum.

Developed by the Robert Engstrom Companies, the Fields of St. Croix—the first cluster

development of its kind in Minnesota—was designed to allow for growth while preserving a sense of the area's rural past. The development has achieved a number of groundbreaking objectives, including protecting the area's ecology and hydrology; preserving the farmland along an adjacent, heavily-traveled road (Highway 5); preserving a historic barn; using architectural standards to create a sense of place and community; and preserving common open space for the use and enjoyment of all residents.

Situated on lots that range from one-third of an acre to one acre (0.13 to 0.4 hectares), the homes at the Fields of St. Croix are located in two clusters. Most homes sell for between $350,000 and $550,000. Phase I has been entirely built out since its 1997 opening. Phase II, which opened in September 2000,

The Fields of St. Croix, a 241-acre (98-hectare) conservation community of 113 homes nestled in the prairies and marshes of Lake Elmo, Minnesota.

The development consists of two clusters, the second of which is along the south side of Goetschel Pond. The pond's shoreline has been left in its natural state.

sold at an even faster pace, with most of the lots sold by March 2001 for prices between $75,000 and $125,000. A third phase, adjacent to Phase II, will add 14 townhouse units. A proposed farmstead market and commercial area immediately adjacent to the townhouses was rejected by the city of Lake Elmo.

The Site

The gently rolling, 241-acre (98-hectare) site is located along Highway 5, between the Twin Cities's contiguous metro area and the distinctly rural development near the St. Croix River. Until ground was broken on the current development, the site was mostly farmland and a lake. Today, a large amount of the farmland remains, and the lake's shoreline is still relatively untouched. Also remaining is a Civil War–era barn, which has been restored for use as a community center.

Phase I consists of 45 homes and is nestled into the hillside overlooking Lake Goetschel. This cluster is incorporated into the Natural Harvest Community Supported Agriculture (CSA) farming operation. Phase II, on the south side of the lake, contains 68 housing units. The cluster concept enables residents to live near each other in small, villagelike communities, while leaving more rural space

open and accessible to all. The Fields of St. Croix offers open-space amenities such as walking and recreation paths around Lake Goetschel, a soccer and ballfield, and preserved views. The open space enables residents to enjoy a piece of the countryside without owning and maintaining individual large lots.

Planning and Approval Process

The city of Lake Elmo had historically resisted suburban-style development, limiting residential development to a sparse one unit per ten acres (four hectares), with some allowance for 2.5-acre (one-hectare) lots. Robert Engstrom, whose company has been developing residential property in the Twin Cities for nearly 30 years, wanted to offer an alternative to the large-lot development that is consuming the countryside, and to pursue his vision of what an urban fringe development could be. Engstrom and other residential developers requested a zoning change; and, in 1996, with the support of a city council that was open to new ideas, the city of Lake Elmo granted a zoning variance for clustered development: the variance increased allowable density to nine homes per 20 acres (eight hectares), and provided for over half of the land to be

The landscaping takes advantage of native prairie grasses and wildflowers.

preserved for open space. Engstrom placed a conservation easement on the open space and assigned it to the Minnesota Land Trust, an organization that oversees conservation easements across the state.

Architecture and Engineering

An interesting aspect of the Fields of St. Croix is the integrity and cohesiveness of its architecture. The developer deliberately avoided the common practice in today's new subdivisions, in which the combination of different architectural styles creates a dissonant and somewhat artificial look. He chose instead to create a sense of community and place through architectural practices: in other words, to recreate some of the qualities that made rural America look so friendly.

For Phase I, the developer and Jack Buxell, of J. Buxell Architecture, Ltd., oversaw the creation of the master plan, the development of an architectural control process, and the determination of architectural standards. Although all the homes were custom designed for their owners, they were built (by some 15 different builders, working with a variety of architects) in accordance with the defined guidelines. Because of their historic promi-

nence in the region, Prairie style, Craftsman style, and bungalows predominate. Garages are usually recessed to the rear, or side-loaded, increasing the homes' curb appeal. Thanks to the guidelines, the homes at the Fields of St. Croix seem friendlier, more genuine, and more inviting than those in typical subdivisions. Because of the success of this approach, a similar method is being used in Phase II.

Although the architectural integrity of the Fields of St. Croix goes a long way toward establishing the character of the development, the restored barn, located in Phase I, makes at least as significant a contribution. Located on a hill overlooking Lake Goetschel, the Civil War–era structure enjoys serene views to the south and west. After witnessing many generations of farming, and even surviving a tornado, the barn now serves as a community center, playing host to a variety of functions and events. It was restored by the developer just as the first lots began to sell, and its popularity as a community gathering space has made it a major selling point for the lots and homes in the development.

Perhaps the most interesting aspect of the Fields of St. Croix is the stormwater and wastewater treatment system. First, narrow streets—and paved areas that are generally smaller than those in conventional subdivisions—help to reduce stormwater runoff. Then, a series of bogs, ponds, swales, and other detention devices treat the runoff that is collected. Many of these devices are planted with native vegetation, and are attractively incorporated into the open-space plan.

Wastewater is handled in a more thorough—and more innovative—way than in most suburban developments. To filter wastewater, the developer constructed an engineered wetland that consists of a series of four cells. The first element, a standard sealed septic tank, removes solids. In the first cells, lined wetland cells, bacteria consume waste materials. A variety of native wetland vegetation allows the system to better blend into the landscape. The third and fourth cells are unlined, allowing water to percolate into the ground.

Wastewater is drawn to the constructed wetland treatment area by gravity flow, much the same way that sewage is collected in most urbanized areas. But because the system has sufficient capacity to treat all waste-

water on site, one less Twin Cities community sends its wastewater though the metropolitan council's treatment plant and down the Mississippi River. Moreover, the passive treatment method used at the Fields of St. Croix is more environmentally friendly than traditional mechanized methods.

This wastewater treatment system was the first of its kind approved by the Minnesota Pollution Control Agency, and it has served as a model for dozens more like it around the state. Such systems are becoming increasingly common nationwide, especially in resort communities and other somewhat clustered developments that are not near a large city.

Other conservation efforts at the Fields of St. Croix include the planting of native grasses as a means of restoring the native prairie. To maintain the prairie, a "prairie burn" is conducted every two years, which clears out old, nonnative grasses and weeds and allows the native bluestone prairie grass to reseed itself.

The conservation easement, part of the 144 acres (58 hectares) of open space on

Some homes face a common green, where the homeowners' association maintains a cutting garden. The architecture reflects traditional local styles: Prairie, Craftsman, and bungalow.

the site, protects a sizable piece of open space from the threat of development. Often, developers set aside open space as an amenity, only to develop it or sell it off at a later date to maximize profits. Turning the conservation easement over to the Minnesota Land Trust eliminated this possibility.

The preservation of the farmland is also a major selling point for the Fields of St. Croix. Approximately 12 acres (five hectares) are planted and maintained by Natural Harvest CSA, a co-op farming operation. Members of the public can purchase a share for $330 annually, which allows a weekly pickup of food. Shareholders are also encouraged to help with planting and harvesting. Available products include fresh fruits and vegetables, fresh eggs, and special canned products such as jams and honey. The chickens, which are used for egg production, are a big hit with area children. The co-op is a practical way for community residents to maintain a connection to their land.

Marketing and Financing

The Fields of St. Croix was marketed as the first conservation community of its kind in

Minnesota, and as a viable alternative to land-consuming and unattractive large-lot development. Robert Engstrom Companies marketed the property, and because of the combination of a strong economy, the attractiveness of the project, and the developer's good reputation, very little promotion was required. Robert Engstrom Companies paid all development costs, including $250,000 for the restoration of the barn.

Experience Gained

Perhaps the greatest significance of this project is that it has become a model for several

similar cluster developments in the state of Minnesota. The Fields of St. Croix offers a unique combination of preserved farmland, permanently protected open space, high-quality architecture, and on-site wastewater management as a healthy alternative to the large lots and land-consuming practices that typify many developments on today's suburban and rural fringe.

The city of Lake Elmo is committed to retaining its rural character. The real, long-term benefit of cluster developments, such as the Fields of St. Croix, is that they require fewer lineal feet of paved streets and sewer lines, which represents a massive savings to the city over time. Lake Elmo now encourages this type of development, and has approved approximately ten more projects since the Fields's inception.

The Fields of St. Croix has received several awards for its commitment to conservation and its enhancement of the suburban and rural fringe. In 1998, the National Associa-

tion of Home Builders awarded the Fields of St. Croix its Best in American Living Award for the development's numerous conservation features and for the architectural design of its energy-efficient homes. The development also received the Minnesota Environmental Initiative's Fifth Annual Environmental Initiative Award—Land Use and Community Development, which rewards innovation, collaboration, leadership, and environmental excellence. Finally, the restored barn received the 1998 Adaptive Reuse Award of the Rivertown Restoration Society.

At first glance, nine housing units per 20 acres (eight hectares) may not appear to be smart growth, but it is; one might think of it as "smart suburban-fringe growth," a greener alternative to standard sprawl. Considering how many townships and urban-fringe cities allow only large-lot development, a development of cluster homes that has its own wastewater treatment system, maintains existing farmland, and preserves open space seems very smart indeed.

The Fields of St. Croix

Project Data

Land Use Information

Site area (acres/hectares)	241/98
Open space (acres/hectares)	144/58 (60 percent of total site area)
Total number of dwelling units	99 single-family detached, 14 townhouses
Average net density (units per acre/ per hectare, not including open space)	1.14/2.8

Land Use Plan

Lot sizes (acres/hectares)	0.35–1.0/0.14–0.4
Percentage of site	40

Development Schedule

Site purchased, Phase I	1995
Site purchased, Phase II	1997
Planning started	1996
Lot sales and construction began	1997
Estimated completion	2003

Development Team

Developer

Robert Engstrom Companies
4801 West 81st Street
Bloomington, Minnesota 55437
952-893-1001
www.engstromco.com

Land Conservator

Minnesota Land Trust
2356 University Avenue West, Suite 400
St. Paul, Minnesota 55114
651-647-9590
www.mnland.org

Architects

J. Buxell Architecture, Ltd.
129 North Second Street, Suite 101
Minneapolis, Minnesota 55401
612-338-3773

Design Forum, Inc.
4801 West 81st Street
Bloomington, Minnesota 55398
952-831-5926

Primary Builders

Senn & Youngdahl, Inc.
4606 Stillwater Boulevard
Stillwater, Minnesota 55082
651-351-1450

Landmark Homes
4732 Larkspur Lane North
Lake Elmo, Minnesota 55042
651-439-4995

Huntington Homes, Ltd.
9805 Cimarron Trail
Minnetonka, Minnesota 55305
952-546-1102

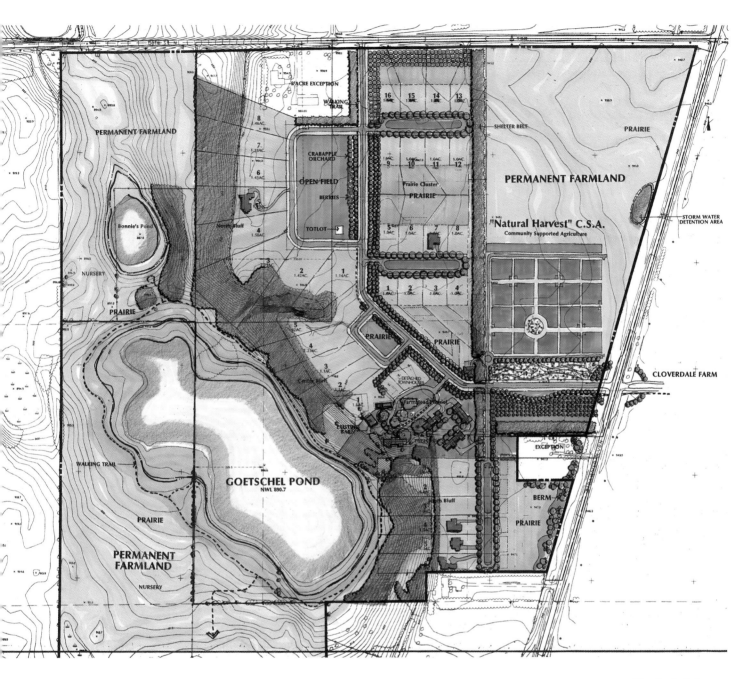

The plan includes preserved farmland, prairies, orchards, and ponds. Homesites are set back from the pond to preserve its natural shoreline.

Sonoma Villero

Bothell, Washington

Sonoma Villero is a 240-unit development of townhouses and flats in Bothell, Washington, a bedroom community located 12 miles (19 kilometers) north of Seattle, near the University of Washington's Bothell campus. The area is known for its mountain and lake views, outdoor recreation opportunities, and proximity to major employers, such as Microsoft, Eddie Bauer, and AT&T Wireless, as well as regional shopping and entertainment destinations. Designed as condominiums targeted to first-time homebuyers and active older adults, the Sonoma Villero units were rented at first, to avoid competition from a similar development nearby. Then, as the market became less saturated, the units were converted to condominium ownership.

Townhouses have front entries along a common walkway, facing green space and tree buffers.

The Site

Because of the difficulty of assembling parcels for development, the site had been

passed over by other large development companies. But the 160th Street Association, LLC, the developers of Sonoma Villero, recognized the opportunity and believed it was worth the effort. The principals assembled five properties to make up the 11-acre (4.5-hectare) site—a sloped, heavily treed parcel east of Interstate 405.

The land lies in an unincorporated part of King County, near the city of Kirkland, and borders the Bothell city limits to the north. To the east, the site borders a condominium community that is similar in density and size to Sonoma Villero. To the north are single-family homes, and to the south an interchange for I-405. Although the adjacent interstate might be considered a drawback, some residents of Sonoma Villero view its proximity as a benefit.

Development Process

A number of factors went into the decision to construct Sonoma Villero. First, the developer had noticed that real estate growth was headed up the I-405 corridor north of Seattle: a new University of Washington campus had just opened in Bothell, and Microsoft had recently opened its new headquarters in nearby Redmond. The area was quickly becoming part of Seattle's high-tech corridor, making it attractive to young adults.

Although the land was within the urban growth boundary and local planners favored the development of Sonoma Villero, the home-owners' association (HOA) of a bordering

community of single-family homes repeatedly opposed the project, claiming that new residents would overcrowd roads and burden services. The approval of a new, 209-unit condominium development across the street from the Sonoma Villero site strengthened the community's opposition. At the same time, the developer saw a potential market conflict—two similar communities across the street from one another, being built and marketed simultaneously—and searched for ways to differentiate the Sonoma Villero development. Although Sonoma Villero was originally planned for condominium ownership, the developer decided that a rental community of townhouses and flats would fill a distinct niche. The units would be rented at first, then offered for sale at a later date, once the market opened up.

When the neighboring HOA was unable to prevent Sonoma Villero from going forward, it began petitioning for lower unit counts, increased buffers between Sonoma Villero and the neighboring single-family homes, and for the protection of what the HOA regarded as "significant trees." The developer was able to address the needs of the single-family community without decreasing the number of Sonoma Villero units by increasing setbacks slightly, repositioning some buildings, and adding more trees between the developments—changes that not only appeased neighbors but enhanced the appearance and value of the community. The developer was aware of the HOA's opposition from the beginning, and attributed its success in assuaging the concerns of the neighboring community to careful planning and design during the early stages of the development.

Design and Construction

The sloped site offered the opportunity to regrade, creating the ambience of a European village. Buildings are stepped down from street level and follow the slopes. To break up the density of the project, the townhouses and flats are grouped into individual neighborhoods, each with 20 units per acre (49 per hectare). Within these neighborhoods, groupings of two to seven units reduce bulk. Thirteen different floor plans allow for individuality in each home. One-bedroom flats are located on the backs of two-bedroom townhouses. A greenbelt of trees surrounds Sonoma Villero, and specimen trees accent the landscaping.

Although units in the development were initially for rent, additional money was spent

during construction to prepare for the transfer to condominium ownership. For example, because of the project's proximity to the interstate, sound control was a major concern, and a sound engineer was added to the development team to address this issue. As a result of his recommendations, the builder used cast-iron sewer lines instead of PVC pipes, and layered extra subflooring between floors. All buildings that back up to the interstate have insulated, double-density sliding glass doors; laminate windows; and two-by-six-inch framed walls, which allow for more insulation than traditional two-by-four framing. In addition, all skylights, vents, and other areas where noise could penetrate the units were turned away from the freeway.

The units offer carefully chosen interior finishes and details—such as premium kitchen cabinets, high ceilings, and recessed lighting in the living rooms—and include many extra

The clubhouse at Sonoma Villero was a necessity for the rental community but has also been used as a sales office for the condominiums. The clubhouse features a pool, a heated spa, a gym, and a fully equipped business and conference center.

features, such as powder rooms, dens, walk-in closets, breakfast areas, kitchens with islands, and skylights in upper-level baths. Additional unit amenities include gas fireplaces and high-speed Internet access. Building exteriors are sheathed in vinyl siding in a variety of pastel earth tones, and the white trim on all exteriors unifies the design. In accord with the developer's specifications, architectural detailing is extended to all four sides of the buildings so that all residents would have an attractive 360-degree view.

To enhance the village ambience, plantings and rough-hewn rock walls were used instead of concrete walls to outline the slopes of the site. Playgrounds are tucked between buildings and are shaded by large trees. The clubhouse at Sonoma Villero, which was a necessity for the rental community but has supported condominium sales as well, features a pool, a heated spa, a gym, a fully equipped business and conference center, and community sales offices. Stone and cherry-stained millwork are the unifying materials throughout the development.

Approvals

The approvals process for Sonoma Villero posed many challenges for the developer. Besides the difficulties with the HOA of the neighboring single-family community, opposition also came from political leaders in surrounding jurisdictions, who were concerned that local roads lacked the capacity to handle the additional traffic the project would bring.

The site is located in an unincorporated portion of King County and borders the city of Bothell. In an attempt to thwart the development, both the city of Bothell and the King County council resisted extending public services, such as sewer, water, and roads, to the project. To complicate matters further, the interstate intersection at N.E. 160th Street is state owned, but all other local roads are owned by King County. It was difficult to bring together state and local officials to discuss these issues, but the developer's team worked with those involved to add extra turn lanes to the local road that fronts Sonoma Villero and to change the development's entrance to

The community offers 109 three-level townhouses. The two-car garage included with each unit comes in one of two designs: in one, cars can be parked side by side; the other allows them to be parked in tandem. A greenbelt of trees surrounds Sonoma Villero, and mature trees accent the landscaping.

better fit the county's sight-distance criteria. In addition, a transportation management plan was developed to encourage Sonoma Villero residents to park and ride to employment centers in Bellevue, Redmond, and Seattle.

Because the site is located in a watershed that drains into an environmentally sensitive area, extra land was needed for biofiltration. A small strip of land located on the west side of the project, between the project site and the interstate, was identified as a potential drainage area. This little piece of land is owned by a church, but was separated from it by the interstate. The developer worked out an easement with the church to use the land for biofiltration.

Financing, Marketing, and Management

Marc, Harry, and Curt Pryde, who have developed and managed residential and commercial properties in the Seattle area for almost 50 years, formed the 160th Street Association,

LLC, for the development of Sonoma Villero. Pryde Corporation, a closely held private company that was founded in 1957, was involved in every aspect of the project, including development, building management, and sales of the properties. The development was financed using short-term construction loans and conventional loans from Bank of America.

During the spring of 2000, when market conditions indicated a demand for low-priced, for-sale housing in the Seattle market, the developer began to select unit types to be sold as condominiums when residents did not renew their leases. The process was gradual, to ensure a balance between supply and demand for the condominium units. Transforming the rental units into condominiums was not difficult, as units generally required only fresh paint and new carpeting before being put up for sale.

The majority of units are priced under $200,000 and are affordable to first-time buyers. One-bedroom units start at $120,000, two-bedroom units at $180,000, and three-bedroom units at $200,000. Homes that back up to the community's greenbelt command a $15,000 to $20,000 price premium for their views of the thick tree buffer. All townhouses have garages, a desirable convenience that also reduces the number of cars parked on the community's streets.

The marketing strategy for Sonoma Villero includes brochures, newspaper advertisements, and a Web site. Marketing materials focus on the value of the units, the amenities, and the reasonable prices. Condominium sales targeted first-time homebuyers and others interested in value. Single professionals, newlyweds, and young families generally preferred the townhouses, while empty nesters usually preferred the flats.

Initially, the developers expected current renters to be the primary source of buyers at Sonoma Villero, particularly since rents were approximately equal to the principal and interest on most mortgage payments for each unit. However, most renters did not buy at Sonoma Villero, citing credit issues, an inability to come up with a down payment, and lifestyle concerns about renting versus owning.

Experience Gained

If the developers had known beforehand about the challenges and opposition they would face during the approval process, they might have given more consideration to the time frame needed to complete the project, and to the market projections for that time frame.

The developers carefully considered design and floor plans, creating a "for-sale experience" in a rental community so that the project would ultimately enjoy buyer acceptance. However, knowing that the development would be transformed from a rental community into a condominium community made it difficult to determine the right mix of project amenities. Although items such as noise mitigation would not have changed, some interior features and finishes—such as plumbing in the garages for washers and dryers—were not included during construction, but would have been desirable later, with the for-sale market. In addition, if Sonoma Villero had been a strictly for-sale product, the developer would have designed for a lower density. (Nevertheless, greater density has improved affordability.)

Teamwork was essential in overcoming many obstacles. By working closely together, team members can better anticipate and solve problems early in the process. At every point during the evolution of this project, consultants were brought in to address specific challenges.

Sonoma Villero

Project Data

Land Use Information

Site area (acres/hectares)	11/4.5
Total number of dwelling units	240
Gross density (units per acre/per hectare)	21.8/53.8
Parking ratio (per unit)	2.6

Land Use Plan

Use	Acres/ Hectares	Percentage of Site
Attached multifamily residential	3.7/1.5	33.5
Roads and parking areas	2.9/1.2	26.5
Common open space	4.2/1.7	38.0
Community building	0.1/0.04	1.0
Pool and pool deck	0.1/0.04	1.0

Residential Unit Information

Unit Type	Unit Size (Square Feet/ Square Meters)	Number of Units Built	Current Sales Prices
Flats	700–1,050/70–100	60	$120,000–$170,000
Townhouses	1,150–1,550/110–140	180	$180,000–$220,000

Development Cost Information

Site Acquisition and Improvement Costs

Site acquisition	$3,500,000
Excavation, grading	2,000,000
Sewer, water, drainage	600,000
Paving, curbs, sidewalks	300,000
Landscaping, irrigation	500,000
Easements	200,000
Fees, general conditions	2,000,000
Subtotal, site acquisition and improvement costs	$9,100,000

Construction Costs

Superstructure (including HVAC)	$20,000,000
Electrical	600,000
Plumbing, sprinklers	600,000
Graphics, other	600,000
Subtotal, construction costs	$21,800,000

Soft Costs

Architecture, engineering services	$350,000
Project management	250,000
Marketing	500,000
Taxes, insurance	200,000
Permits, impact fees	700,000
Subtotal, soft costs	$2,000,000
Total development costs	$32,900,000

Development Schedule

Planning started	January 1995
Site purchased	January 1996
Construction started	April 1997
First rental occupancy	September 1998
Project completed	April 1999
Sales started	July 2000
First closing	August 2000

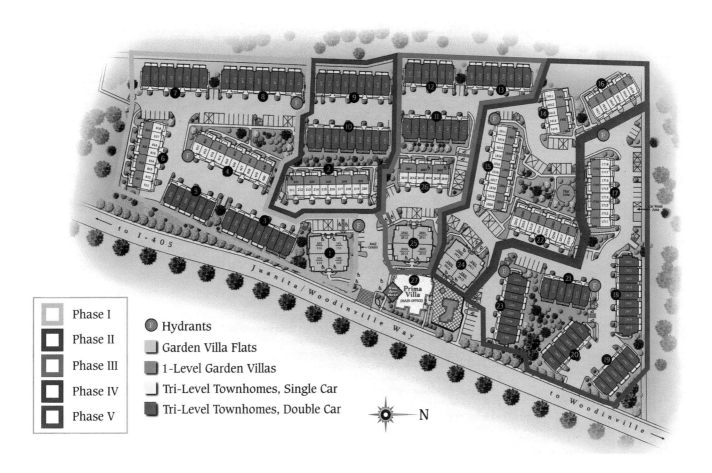

Phase I
Phase II
Phase III
Phase IV
Phase V

Ⓕ Hydrants
☐ Garden Villa Flats
☐ 1-Level Garden Villas
☐ Tri-Level Townhomes, Single Car
☐ Tri-Level Townhomes, Double Car

N

Site plan.

Development Team

Developer
160th Street Association, LLC
50 116th Avenue S.E., Suite 200
Bellevue, Washington 98004
425-451-4700
www.sonomavillero.com

Architect and Site Planner
Kohler Associates, Architects and Planners, PS
200 N.E. Pacific Street, Suite 103
Seattle, Washington 98105
206-675-9100
www.kohlerassociates.com

Landscape Architect
Thomas Rengstorf Associates
911 Western Avenue, Suite 444
Seattle, Washington 98104
206-682-7562

Civil Engineer
Group Four, Inc.
16030 Juanita Woodinville Way
Bothell, Washington 98011
206-362-4244

Structural Engineer
Anderson-Peyton
31620 23rd Avenue South, Suite 321
Federal Way, Washington 98003
206-941-9929
www.anderson-peyton.com

Farrcroft

Fairfax, Virginia

LESSARD ARCHITECTURAL GROUP

Farrcroft, a 70-acre (28-hectare) infill development, is strongly linked to the surrounding town and offers a lifestyle based on walkability and social connections.

Farrcroft is a 70-acre (28-hectare) residential community located on an infill site in the city of Fairfax, Virginia, 18 miles (29 kilometers) from Washington, D.C. It was among the first developments in the northern Virginia market area to use modified new urbanist planning concepts, including side and rear alleyways, and homes that directly engage the street. Farrcroft is located within walking distance of the shops, restaurants, and services of Old Town Fairfax, a historic town dating from the 1790s. The community of single-family and attached homes features a pool, pocket parks, trails, and a community building.

The firm of Basheer & Edgemoore Communities, which developed Farrcroft, was founded through an alliance between Diane Cox Basheer Communities, a developer, and Edgemoore Homes, a local homebuilder. The firm acquires, develops, builds, and markets residential communities in the northern Virginia suburbs.

Site and History

Farrcroft is built on the historic estate of the Farr-Ratcliffe families, on land that the Queen of England granted to Samuel Farr in 1797 and that was used as a campground for soldiers during the Civil War. Ballynahown, the Georgian manor house built by Wilson Farr, was surrounded by woods and cow pastures when Basheer & Edgemoore acquired the site in 1995. Restored by the developer, Ballynahown has become a community focal point that is used for public and private events.

To the east of Farrcroft is Old Lee Highway, which leads to Old Town Fairfax and the Fairfax/Vienna Metro Station. To the west are conventional, 1950s-era subdivisions. An elementary school and soccer fields are to the north, and Main Street—the commercial hub of the city of Fairfax—borders the development to the south. George Mason University, less than one mile (1.6 kilometers) away, offers educational, cultural, and other facilities.

Development Process and Planning

The city of Fairfax's 20/20 Vision Plan designated the Farr tract, the last large undevel-

oped parcel remaining in the town, as a potential traditional neighborhood development (TND). This designation offered the opportunity for a creative concept that would enhance the center of town and attract significant new—and more upscale—residential construction within the city's limits. Until Farrcroft was developed, most of the city's housing stock consisted of small, moderately priced, post–World War II homes, and the city wanted to broaden its appeal to potential residents by adding homes that were targeted to a more affluent market.

Basheer & Edgemoore used the 20/20 Vision Plan as a guide for creating a modified new urbanist neighborhood, borrowing the particular elements of new urbanism that would work for this project—such as rear alleyways and garages, and the mixing of housing types. One goal was to attract residents who were at various stages of life. Homes are set on narrow, deep lots, with the narrow dimension facing the street (in contrast to conventional suburban lots, where the wide dimension faces the street). The modified new urbanist elements fit the site's infill location and enabled the developer to complement the city's early-American character and continue the existing street grid. Farrcroft was designed to be a sought-after community offering a lifestyle based on walkability.

ParkerRodriguez, Inc., the land planning firm, was familiar with the concepts of new urbanism, having worked on two very well known new urbanist communities: Kentlands, Maryland, and Celebration, Florida. ParkerRodriguez

used Farrcroft's history and surroundings as the basis for design themes and early conceptual drawings. The drawings were made into a slide presentation that was shown to community groups, and were also used in a brochure detailing the history of the site and the developer's vision for the project.

Although the city endorsed the project, surrounding residents had hoped to retain the open space in the middle of the city and felt that if the property were to be developed at all, the homes should be of the conventional suburban style that was originally master planned for the site. The planned density of seven units per acre (17 per hectare)—versus the original zoning of two units per acre (five per hectare)—also drew complaints. Basheer & Edgemoore's principal partner held meetings with 5,000 citizens, from 50 civic groups, to discuss the concept for Farrcroft, to educate community members about traditional neighborhood design, and to listen to neighbors' views. In response to the concerns voiced at these meetings, the developer created 15 different versions of the land plan during the two and one-half years that preceded the final zoning decision, which was made in the summer of 1997.

The richly detailed bridge that leads to one of the two entrances to the community creates a sense of arrival and sets the tone for the development. The sidewalks outside the development are paved with brick, continuing Farrcroft's design theme.

George Mason University, also use Old Lee Highway. To mitigate potential traffic problems, the developer made some road improvements and installed new traffic lights at both Farrcroft entrances.

Because of the project's grid street pattern, city officials were concerned that students from George Mason University would use the neighborhood as a shortcut to campus. To prevent this, the land planners created a maze of streets that would make a direct drive through the neighborhood very difficult. In addition, the developer installed traffic arms on the neighborhood's main interior road, hidden inside brick columns. These arms, which Farrcroft residents can operate electronically (by using a remote-control device similar to a garage door opener), remain closed during peak morning and evening commuting times.

Design

Farrcroft's courtyard, village, and manor homes are clustered into neighborhoods of similar product types. Natural land features and pocket parks provide transitions between clusters.

The developer offers five different floor plans for each product type. Attached courtyard homes are configured in a "manor" style, with a center home and one home on each "wing." Each home is approximately 2,700 square feet (250 square meters). The courtyard homes were the most popular product type and sold out quickly. Village homes, single-family homes of approximately 3,200 square feet (300 square meters), are set on narrow, deep lots. Both the courtyard and village homes offer rear garages accessed by alleyways and feature private, fenced backyards with trellised gates. Manor homes, the largest product type, are traditional detached homes that range from 3,200 to 4,000 square feet (300 to 370 square meters) and are set on quarter-acre (0.10-hectare) lots.

The attached courtyard houses are configured in a "manor" style, with a center home and one home on each "wing."

Over time, local residents grew more comfortable with the new land plans and even expressed interest in some of the proposed product types. For example, the plans for Farrcroft appealed to empty nesters who wanted to remain in Fairfax but wanted smaller lots to maintain. The developer offered attached and village-style homes that provided owners with the square footage they wanted but with less yard space. After discussions with city officials and local citizens, the developer made several concessions to facilitate acceptance of the project, including honoring adjacent setbacks and creating conservation buffers.

Traffic was a major concern for both local residents and city officials. The entrances to Farrcroft are located on Main Street and Old Lee Highway—both extremely busy roads—and nearby residents were afraid that the additional traffic generated by the development would aggravate the already serious traffic problems in the area. Main Street, which borders the community on the south, serves as a primary east-west commuting road between the Washington Capital Beltway and surrounding suburban communities. Commuters, particularly those traveling to

LESSARD ARCHITECTURAL GROUP

All homes have four bedrooms and three and one-half baths. They feature nine-foot (2.7-meter) ceilings on the first and second floors, two-story foyers, covered entranceways, and exterior facades in Federal, Georgian, English, or Southern styles. Residents can choose from a list of optional features and upgrades, including sunrooms, bay windows, upgraded kitchens and baths, and a finished "club room" in the basement, with optional wet bar, bath, and home office or craft room.

The developer was careful to preserve the mature trees and historic features of the site and used them to define clusters of homes. Village homes line the oval drive surrounding Oak Hill Park, where a great white oak that is over 200 years old has been carefully preserved. The courtyard homes, which reflect the architecture of Ballynahown, encircle the former Farr family residence, now painstakingly restored to its former glory. Daniel's Run Stream meanders through the site and is

HUGH BROADUS

LESSARD ARCHITECTURAL GROUP

bordered by a stream-valley park, with walking trails. The Farrcroft pond, a stormwater management pond that doubles as a water amenity for the community, is spanned by a new entry bridge that links the neighborhood to Old Lee Highway. The bridge, with its arch and balustrade leading to a circular drive at the entrance to the community, brings a new architectural feature to the city.

Financing, Marketing, and Operations

Traditional bank financing was used for the construction loans, with a four-stage takedown of the land as each cluster of homes was built. Lots in each phase were sold out one year before construction began.

Developing Farrcroft as a modified new urbanist project was a marketing decision based on demographics. Basheer & Edgemoore believed that there was pent-up demand for this type of community in an advantageous location near commuting routes and the Metro system, and within walking distance of schools, shopping, and government services. Although the developer considered basing Farrcroft on a more strict interpretation of new urbanism, in which lot sizes and house

Pocket parks are spread throughout the community, providing transitions among housing types.

The homes feature Georgian, Federal, Southern, and English facades. Brick-paved sidewalks link the houses with community amenities and the city of Fairfax.

HUGH BROADUS

types would have varied on the same block, Basheer felt that the pace of sales would have been too slow to make financial sense for this particular project.

Word of mouth and drive-by visits were important for selling the community. Most buyers moved from within a five- to ten-mile (eight- to 16-kilometer) radius of the site, and many Farrcroft residents helped to sell the neighborhood to friends and relatives. Before ground was broken, a triple-wide sales trailer and visitors' center was set up on the property to provide marketing materials and information. Joann MacHamer, vice president of Basheer & Edgemoore, attributes the community's sales success to the time and effort put into the design of the homes.

The homeowners' association (HOA) was turned over to the residents in 2002. A Farrcroft resident hired by the HOA serves as an on-site property manager and works out of an office in Ballynahown. The property manager responds to residents' questions, passes along community information, and acts as a "point person" for the community.

The neighborhood has a very strict set of covenants, conditions, and restrictions, including architectural covenants that regulate the use of the property and any improvements. To ensure that landscaping would be consistent, and that the community would have the appearance that the developer desired once the plants and trees had achieved full growth, predetermined plantings were installed before residents moved in.

Basheer believes that "the developer should take on a social role as part of developing a community." To help neighborhood residents get to know each other and to integrate Farrcroft into the surrounding area, the developer allowed the city to use Ballynahown and Farrcroft model homes to host public events, such as the annual Chocolate Lovers' Festival. The developer has also sponsored the city's Fourth of July celebration and fireworks. Before the community pool was completed, arrangements were made for homeowners to have memberships at another community's pool so that neighborhood children could meet each other before the school year began. In Basheer's words, "The neighborhood is now an extremely social animal." Its connections to the surrounding environment strengthen the neighborhood, and the social life of the development is real—not fabricated.

In the summer, the pool complex is the focus of the community's social life.

Experience Gained

Because most developers want to begin a project as quickly as possible, they are sometimes reluctant to take extra time to fine-tune plans. But according to Basheer, it is important to take the extra time, listen to the community's needs, and design accordingly, when possible and financially feasible.

Developers should work with the best professional consultants, who will help sort through citizens' comments, determine what design changes are reasonable, and identify those that will benefit the proposed community.

Basheer notes that a developer cannot take a product that has already been built elsewhere and "just plop it down in an infill community." Although designing homes specifically for a particular infill site is more expensive and requires extra time in the planning stages, the effort will reap returns at the end of the project, in the form of higher home prices.

Farrcroft
Project Data

Land Use Information

Site area (acres/hectares)	70/28
Total number of dwelling units planned/completed	270/188
Gross density (units per acre/per hectare)	4/10
Average net density (units per acre/per hectare)	7/17

Land Use Plan

Section 1

Detached homes	42
Attached units	37
Roads (linear feet/meters)	2,040/620
Open space (acres/hectares)	9.9/4

Section 2

Detached homes	45
Attached units	37
Roads (linear feet/meters)	1,980/600
Open space (acres/hectares)	4.38/1.8

Section 3

Detached homes	54
Attached units	22
Roads (linear feet/meters)	1,040/320
Open space (acres/hectares)	9.6/3.8

Section 4

Detached homes	37
Attached units	12
Roads (linear feet/meters)	1,723/525
Open space (acres/hectares)	1.31/0.53

Residential Unit Information

Unit Type	Lot Size (Square Feet/ Square Meters)	Unit Size (Square Feet/ Square Meters)	Number of Units	Final Base Prices
Courtyard	3,200–3,500/ 300–325	2,642–2,790/ 250–260	92	$401,900– $426,900
Village	5,000–7,000/ 470–650	3,145–3,300/ 290–310	111	$549,000– $565,000
Manor	10,000/930	3,183–3,943/ 300–370	67	$584,000– $627,500

Development Cost Information

Site Improvement Costs

Offsite improvements, utilities	$1,750,000
Surveying, engineering	480,000
Earthwork	2,150,000
Sewer, water	1,435,000
Storm drainage	1,550,000
Paving, curbs, sidewalks	1,910,000
Landscaping	875,000
Amenities, proffers	3,400,000
Miscellaneous	500,000
Total	$14,050,000

Engineering and Design Costs

Preliminary studies, zoning	$670,000
Wetlands	185,000
Off-site design	180,000
On-site design	575,000
Architecture fees	300,000
Miscellaneous fees, permits	560,000
Total	$2,470,000

Home Construction Costs

Indirect housing construction cost	3.7 percent

	Per Square Foot/ Square Meter
Courtyard Homes	
Interior units	$62/$667
End units	$66/$710
Village Single-Family Homes	
Front garage	$61/$656
Rear garage	$60/$645
Manor Single-Family Homes	
All types	$61/$656

Development Schedule

Site purchased	October 1997
Construction started	April 1998
Sales started	March 1998
First closing	January 1999
Phase I completed	January 2000
Project completed	December 2002

Development Team

Developer

Basheer & Edgemoore Communities
2071 Chain Bridge Road, Fifth Floor
Vienna, Virginia 22182
703-749-0140
www.basheerandedgemoore.com

Site Planner

ParkerRodriguez, Inc.
101 North Union Street, Suite 320
Alexandria, Virginia 22314
703-548-5010

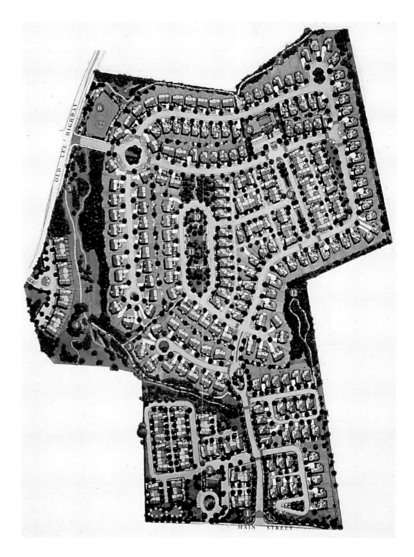

Architects

Lessard Architectural Group
8603 Westwood Center Drive, Suite 400
Vienna, Virginia 22182
703-760-9334

Burke Smith Architects
3609 Chain Bridge Road, Suite D
Fairfax, Virginia 22030
703-352-0116

Engineering and Site Planning

Dewberry and Davis
8401 Arlington Boulevard
Fairfax, Virginia 22031
703-849-0100
www.dewberry.com

Vehicular and pedestrian connections—both within the development and to the surrounding community—are an important feature of the site plan. To keep outsiders from using the community as a cut-through, the streets were designed to meander, and can be closed off during rush hour. Natural features were preserved where possible.

Orange Shoals

Cherokee County, Georgia

One morning, Chaunkee Venable—farmer, musician, Atlanta native, and developer —awoke from a dream. In that dream he saw a community within a forest. More precisely, a community within a forested preserve—a community whose roads and other developed areas did not interrupt or cordon off one part of the preserve from another.

This preserve, or "integrated greenbelt," was a place where people could walk freely without crossing streets, and where wildlife could exist near a human settlement while still roaming freely in an uninterrupted forest. In Venable's dream, all the residents of the community could walk out of their homes directly into what would become this "100-

acre [40-hectare] shared backyard." Venable the farmer got on his tractor and spent five years surveying the property and hand stenciling lots carefully around streams and woods—exercising great care for the land, and for the delicate watershed areas on the property.

The result, ten years later, is Orange Shoals, the best-selling community in Cherokee County, Georgia, and one of the top-five–selling communities in the Atlanta metropolitan area: a model of ecological stewardship that has met success in the marketplace. In a gesture that is rare—and rarely possible—in conventional subdivision development, the project is named after a natural feature that still exists on the property, and that continues to be a source of value to residents, homebuilders, and the developer.

Background

Located about 25 miles (40 kilometers) from downtown Atlanta, Orange Shoals lies directly in the path of regional growth in the favored quarter. Gwinnett County, to the south, is approaching buildout, and Cherokee County is on the northern fringe of new development that is beginning to flood over from Gwinnett. Orange Shoals, in the southern part of Cherokee, is at the very frontier of Atlanta's growth.

An environmentally sensitive community, Orange Shoals holds a unique position in the exurbs as a sustainable, value-added community in the midst of low-cost development that is driven primarily by land economics.

Value is far from absent on the fringe, but whereas conventional amenity packages may include a golf course and a clubhouse or country club facilities, Orange Shoals offers a different kind of added value: one that is sustainable, environmentally friendly, and low cost. Because Orange Shoals is oriented to existing resources, it was possible to avoid the high cost of adding manufactured value. Instead of creating a location, the community improves and capitalizes on the "location" that is already there.

As traffic and air quality worsen in the Atlanta region, quality of life is becoming more important to consumers, and is exerting an increasing pull on real estate markets: locations that offer an escape to nature can command high premiums and garner high absorption rates. Surveys commissioned by builders and developers are finding that, both for recreation and for aesthetic reasons, more and more

A stone feature marks the entrance to a neighborhood in Orange Shoals.

Facing page: Orange Shoals capitalizes on its natural features. This aerial view shows how the development meanders through wooded habitat without disturbing it more than necessary. A large contiguous natural area is important for wildlife preservation.

consumers want green space in their communities. When green space takes the form of a preserve, it has added benefits: the protection of wildlife and of natural resources like clean air and water. At Orange Shoals, open space is taken to the next level: instead of creating a centralized amenity and distributing its value to a limited number of homes (in return for a premium), the developer devised a plan in which the amenity—open space—is shared by every lot.

At the core of Orange Shoals is the integrated greenbelt. Venable says that his first concern was to preserve the land, and the design of the community was based on that goal. His second concern was to build a community that residents would like to live in (Venable himself lives in Orange Shoals).

While many communities are designed either to maximize profits (the most lots possible), or to maximize absorption (design as a sales tool), Orange Shoals is designed to preserve a wildlife habitat, specific topographical features, and delicate watersheds. It is also designed to minimize the impact of grading and the built environment. Because the greenbelt is all one piece, an animal can travel to any part of the habitat without having to cross a road. The land plan, the integrated greenbelt, and the streets are designed around 11 natural springs that Venable refused to sacrifice. Venable, who refers to these springs as the "lifeblood of the ecology," believes that if he had sold the property to a conventional developer, the springs would have been paved over. Paramount at Orange Shoals is a concern for the diversity of the natural habitat, and for the integration of human habitats with those of native plant and animal species. Although Venable's concept and design certainly succeeded in attracting residents, marketing

Several miles of trails turn the greenbelt into an amenity for residents.

had very little influence on the design of Orange Shoals.

To permanently protect Orange Shoals as a preserve and habitat, Venable enlisted the help of the Georgia Wildlife Federation and the Audubon Society to make Orange Shoals the first community in Georgia to become a certified wildlife habitat. The development also has earned certification from the National Wildlife Federation as a wildlife habitat.

The Project

The 400-acre (160-hectare) property is planned for 317 single-family detached homes at build-out, a gross density of 0.8 homes per acre (two per hectare). Approximately 25 percent, or 100 acres (40 hectares) of the site is designated as preserved forests, and includes trails, springs, creeks, bird feeders, bat houses, a butterfly garden (with over 40 varieties of plants that attract butterflies), and the shoals themselves. Amenities include a swimming pool with a 50-foot (15-meter) water slide; a playground; and lighted tennis courts. Every home in the project backs up to the nature preserve, so that all residents have immediate access to a 100-acre (40-hectare) common backyard. Because the preserve acts as a buffer between homes that might otherwise back up to one another, this design also affords a good deal of privacy. The result is a rural, low-density feel in an area that is rapidly becoming a suburban location.

Homes at Orange Shoals began selling at $150,000 in 1996, but since the first phase was completed, prices have increased to $250,000 and go as high as $450,000. Minimum lot size is about 0.6 acres (0.2 hectares), and ranges to about 1.5 acres (0.6 hectares). Density in the developable area of the property is about 1.2 units per acre (three per hectare).

Homes range in size from 2,500 to 4,000 square feet (230 to 370 square meters). At this writing, nearly all the lots had been sold,

at an average of about 45 sales per year. The developer and homebuilder have reduced inventory somewhat to slow sales down while the lots continue to appreciate.

At the beginning of the project, homebuyers could select from a number of small builders. In 2001, Haven Properties, a custom home-builder, purchased all the remaining lots. The firm is building Colonial and Craftsman-style homes with large front and back porches that take advantage of the natural beauty of the lots.

The site itself is situated in the foothills of the Appalachian Mountains, on land that Venable acquired in 1989. For many years, Venable acquired land for other developers, but he had a change of heart after seeing one farm after another transformed into homogenous, maximum-density, built-to-sell communities planted on flattened earth and marketed as

A rustic playground is nestled in the woods, providing a setting for both play and social activity.

The land plan and integrated greenbelt are designed to protect the 11 springs that run through the property.

within development, the integrated greenbelt in Orange Shoals is one uninterrupted space with small islands of development in its midst. In addition to the potential price premium associated with direct frontage on a large nature preserve, the preserve serves as a buffer, bringing privacy—a particularly valuable amenity—to the community. The atmosphere engendered by the forest is part of a larger rural aesthetic at Orange Shoals that differentiates the community from others in Cherokee County, which is quickly losing its rural character as development takes on a decidedly suburban quality.

The unique design features at Orange Shoals have translated into a similarly unique—and successful—market position, attracting buyers from a wide range of ages, family types, life stages, and backgrounds. The majority of buyers are families, many of whom are drawn by the promise of safety that the wooded greenbelt offers for children, by providing play areas that are cordoned off from the outside world. But many retirees are buying in the community as well, because of the uniqueness of the lifestyle that Orange Shoals offers.

Amenities

Orange Shoals has miles of trails and a swimming pool with a fifty-foot (15-meter) water slide. Venable says that he put the pool next to the entrance and at the top of a hill so that residents would have some privacy from potential homebuyers who drive into the community—adding that if he had designed the community to be marketed rather than lived in, he would have put the pool at the bottom of a hill, visible from the point of entry. The landscaping around the pool area is in keeping with the rural aesthetic: the forest is allowed to encroach into the fenced area, so that the concrete surrounding the pool does not extend all the way to the fence. According to Venable, this approach adds privacy and makes use of an attractive natural

upscale, country club locations. According to Venable, many farmers in Cherokee County who had sold their land felt so humiliated by what was done with it that they moved away from the county.

The Integrated Greenbelt

A green space is an open space, often a park or a wildlife refuge. A greenbelt is a network of these spaces, often linear, that is generally designed along stream corridors or ridges, rights-of-way for gas pipelines, or power-line easements, and that offers a number of benefits—including animal habitats and stormwater filtration—as well as opportunities for exercise, social interaction, and the peaceful contemplation of nature and the cycle of the changing seasons.

Unlike the green spaces in conventional communities, which are scattered islands

buffer. The paved pool deck is straight on only one side—and, like the pool, is rounded in parts, creating the sense of an old-fashioned swimming hole rather than a modern, junior Olympic pool. With the exception of those in the houses, the community is free of stairs and is entirely wheelchair accessible—including the sales office, pool, water slide, and gazebo.

In addition to the 100-acre (40-hectare) preserve, 150 acres (60 hectares) of forest have been "added" to the greenbelt, as buyers have chosen not to grade and plant grass on the entirety of their backyards. Including this privately owned preserve, total greenbelt acreage has increased to 300 acres (120 hectares), or about 75 percent of the community. The trails throughout the greenbelt, which are unpaved, are kept up on a voluntary basis by residents, and maintained naturally by foot traffic. Among the plants along the trails are species that were rescued from homesites. In addition to cutting down on landscaping costs, this "native plant rescue program" exemplifies the conservation ethic at Orange Shoals: though neither is at the mercy of the other, the community was not developed at the cost of native plant life. Some nonnative plants were brought in and placed at entrances to different development pods (neighborhoods) to enhance the community's appearance.

Conclusion

Orange Shoals's creative, integrated greenbelt design—with its attention to animal habitats, ecological processes, and the unique attributes of the land—has made it successful in the marketplace. The community's approach to development is a radical one—both in the conventional sense and in the deeper sense of the word: "from the root."

Design with nature, and from nature, is radical at its core, in its concern for the land as the root of the built environment. The success of Orange Shoals suggests the possibility of developing communities that do well while doing good.

Many of the homes at Orange Shoals are situated on wooded, gentle slopes along the shoals.

Orange Shoals

Project Data

Land Use Information

Site area (acres/hectares)	400/160
Gross density (units per acre/per hectare)	0.8/2
Average net density (units per acre/per hectare)	1.1/2.7

Land Use Plan

Detached residential (acres/hectares)	200/80
Common open space (acres/hectares)	100/40

Residential Unit Information

Lot sizes (acres/hectares)	0.6–1.5/0.2–0.6
Unit sizes (square feet/ square meters)	2,500–4,000/230–370
Total number of dwelling units planned/sold	317/306
Final price range	$240,000–$450,000

Development Cost Information
(In Millions)

Site acquisition	$3.8
Site improvement	2.4
Soft costs	1.3
Total development costs to date	$7.5

Development Schedule

Site purchased	1989
Planning started	1994
Construction started	1995
Sales started	1996
First closing	1996
Phase I completed	1997
Project completion	2003

Development Team

Initial Developer

Global Development
Canton, Georgia 30115

Land Planner

Bilson & Associates
40 Powder Springs Street
Marietta, Georgia 30060
770-419-0006
www.bilsonassociates.com

Builder and Developer

Haven Properties, Inc.
11660 Alpharetta Highway, Suite 265
Roswell, Georgia 30076
770-752-0920
www.havenproperties.com

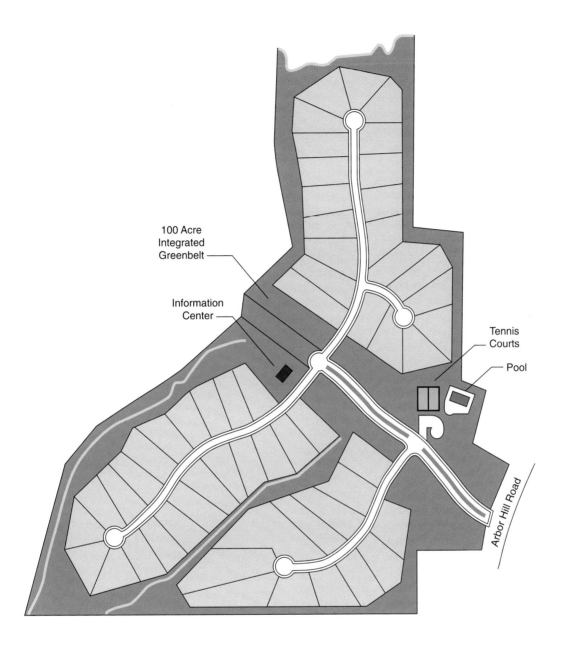

100 Acre
Integrated
Greenbelt

Information
Center

Tennis
Courts

Pool

Arbor Hill Road

The Parks of Austin Ranch

The Colony, Texas

The Parks of Austin Ranch ("the Parks") is the first of its kind—an entirely rental, multifamily, master-planned community. It is the residential component of the expansive Austin Ranch development site, 20 miles (32 kilometers) north of downtown Dallas. Austin Ranch, master planned by RTKL Associates, consists of 1,900 acres (770 hectares) of rolling landscape and will host office, retail, and residential uses. The Parks, comprising 300 acres (120 hectares) in the eastern section of the site and now in its second phase of construction, offers thoughtfully designed market-rate lofts, townhouses, and garden apartments, as well as convenience retail. All the units are for rent and were built to meet the growing market of young professionals who prefer to postpone homeownership.

Developer Lucy Billingsley wanted to create a singular community based on new urbanist principles, and she imbued the project with one-of-a-kind amenities and personal touches. Working with a dedicated team of designers, Billingsley created a community that is not only contemporary and pedestrian-friendly, but also embraces the natural environment. When completed, the Parks will consist of 5,000 units and make use of dozens of different one-, two-, and three-bedroom floor plans that can be viewed (and sometimes altered) online by prospective tenants. Phase I of the project has just been completed and offers 548 units, with rents ranging from $735 to $1,435. Amenities include a swimming pool, a fitness center, a communal lodge, high-speed communication access, and hike-and-bike trails. The Parks is conveniently

located near several national corporate head-quarters and highways, yet is buffered by old-growth trees, natural lakes, and pristine views. The Parks has won several awards, including the National Association of Home Builders's "Pillars of the Industry" award for Phase I.

The Site

Austin Ranch stands on atypical terrain for North Dallas. In place of a flat brown land-scape is one in which 100-year-old oaks dot green hillsides and cows graze near split-rail fences. Los Robles Nature Preserve and the Arbor Hills Nature Preserve neighbor the site to the south, and Lake Lewisville lies to the northwest. In contrast to these natural assets, typical low-density suburban office parks and upscale gated communities frame the nearby Dallas North Tollway and State Highway 121. The affluent city of Plano forms the northern and eastern borders. Although the site touches

four different municipalities, Austin Ranch was eventually annexed by the city of the Colony.

Many of the nearby corporate headquarters and office parks employ the Parks's tenants, but Austin Ranch will eventually include ap-proximately 39 million square feet (3,623,220 square meters) of office space, which will provide on-site employment for some resi-dents. Freddie Mac's HomeSteps Asset Services is the development's first business tenant. Industrial and residential space at buildout will be about 7 million and 23 mil-lion square feet (650,320 square meters and 2,136,770 square meters), respectively.

Development

Founded in 1978 by Henry and Lucy Billingsley, the Billingsley Company is involved in a broad range of real estate activities, including project development, property management, and the acquisition of raw land. Until the Billingsley Company began developing the Parks of Austin Ranch, industrial and office development had been the company's primary focus. The Bill-ingsley Company assembled the Austin Ranch land piecemeal, over a 15-year period; the com-pany knew that because of the site's natural beauty, a special project would have to be designed for it. Lucy Billingsley envisioned a forward-thinking, multiuse community that offered the latest technologies, yet respected the natural setting and the pedestrian.

The 1,900 acres (770 hectares) of former farmland consist of rolling hills and numerous old-growth trees. The landscape reminded

The interior of the leasing center is filled with light. Rich wood floors and fine furnish-ings set the tone.

Facing page: The leasing center.

Billingsley of areas surrounding Austin, Texas —thus the name Austin Ranch. Billingsley also believes that Austin is the "heart" of Texas, and wanted the community to reflect Texans' fondness for the spirit of their state capital. Austin Ranch represents, according to Billingsley, "the Texas you wish you were from."

Because of the numerous nearby corporations employing young professionals, there was a pent-up demand for rental units. Most of the existing garden apartments were older and offered few amenities. The Addison Circle project (a potential competitor located ten minutes south of Austin Ranch) is made up of high-density rentals, but Billingsley wondered if a garden apartment product (at a slightly lower density) could be reconfigured and still perform financially. Billingsley had never developed a multifamily project but believed that a different kind of apartment community, based on new urbanist principles, could be successfully developed on the site.

Billingsley assembled a team of experienced professionals and created a plan for the Parks that included rental residential units, convenience retail facilities, and a host of amenities and design styles rarely seen in rental properties. She made sure that basic new urbanist principles were incorporated into the project: the community would be pedestrian-friendly, respect the undeveloped land, not be fenced off from surrounding communities, contain a town center, and attract a varied population. The development team aimed for moderate density (about 30 dwelling units per acre—74 per hectare), which would allow for less costly construction and, in turn, reasonable rents.

The Parks is the first significant development within the Austin Ranch site, and its success will enhance the rest of Austin Ranch's future. The Parks will consist of eight phases, the first of which has been completed. Two-story and three-story townhouses and lofts, as

Unlike most garden apartments, which are surrounded by parking lots, the buildings at the Parks line the sidewalks, and most parking is in garages with direct access to units. The plan is truly urban in form.

well as retail, are now being constructed in Phase II. Phase III will consist of 457 units—including villas, townhouses, granny flats, and lofts—that will feature urban residential modules designed by Peter Calthorpe. A town center is planned for Phase IV, when the population has reached a serviceable level. Additional retail and residential uses will follow in subsequent phases.

Planning and Design

To help implement her vision for the Parks, Billingsley collaborated with Peter Calthorpe, a leading figure in new urbanism. Billingsley and Calthorpe agreed that they wanted the Parks to defy the conventional model of a suburban, master-planned community that is proliferating not only in North Dallas but throughout the entire country. Calthorpe created the master plan for the 300-acre (120-hectare) site and produced a pedestrian-

scale community where residents can meet their basic consumer and social needs without getting into a car.

Billingsley, Calthorpe, and Lucilo Peña, Billingsley's president of development, went one step further and decided to save as many of the old-growth trees and as much of the natural landscape as possible—a decision that created challenges but that added immeasurable visual appeal. Scholar's Park, for example, is a green space in which the designers retained the naturally occurring berms. Flowing water lit by fiber-optic cable mimetically frames the undulating grassy "bumps" and empties into a small koi pond. Benches, streetlights, and a sidewalk inlaid with granite slabs engraved with humorous and inspiring quotes form the exterior border of the park and provide an eye-pleasing view from the balconies of nearby units. Nearly all the units in the development have views of green space or water features.

The Parks's numerous vistas and paseos are enhanced by a purposeful lack of fencing. Billingsley and her team wanted to encourage visual connections as well as community connections—or, in Billingsley's words, to "build an apartment complex without the 'complex'." The Parks's entrance portals are subdued and welcoming; and, unlike many of the surrounding residential developments, the site is not surrounded by high masonry walls or wrought-iron fencing. Instead, woods, outcroppings, and fields provide natural boundaries and help distinguish the Parks from its competition.

Public art is also an important feature. Billingsley chose works by a variety of artists and installed them throughout the grounds. A freestanding street clock from Amsterdam stands in a square in Phase I; a life-size chess set will be built in Phase II; and, at the center of the Parks, three large, steel-mesh horses, by Connecticut artist Peter Busby, appear to gaze perpetually at passersby.

The project's common interior spaces and model units are decorated with Billingsley's personal touches. Instead of stocking reception areas with mass-produced, everyday furnishings, Billingsley and Peña chose warm, earth-colored materials that reflect Texan culture and mixed them with one-of-a-kind objects Billingsley had bought on trips to Europe and the Near East. Billingsley's attention to detail immediately draws the visitor in, and the unique furnishings add an extra dimension to the spacious and light-filled interiors.

The building exteriors make use of traditional southwestern colors and materials, such as stone and brick. To avoid strict homogeneity, a different team of architects will design each phase. Calthorpe designed a template, consisting of six modules, that will be executed in various ways during the development of Phase II and will accommodate 25 to 30 different floor plans for the rental units. Using this "kit of parts," Billingsley and her team have set out to create a functional garden apartment product in a unique context.

The Parks's wide sidewalks and narrow streets successfully accommodate the pedestrian,

Architectural styles vary at the Parks. One section, called the Mews, is modeled after London's 19th-century mews. Each townhouse has a private first-floor entry. A freestanding street clock from Amsterdam stands in the square.

The swimming pool appears to empty into a waterfall.

picion by residents of surrounding communities, who feared that such a large rental project would lower property values. Similar problems are encountered by many developers throughout the country as zoning and building codes lag behind newer design trends and neighbors fear the changes brought by new developments. After being annexed by the Colony, the Parks received all approvals —and even some of the once-dubious jurisdictions have asked Billingsley to consider developing projects in their communities.

As a contribution to the Colony's public infrastructure, Billingsley constructed a four-lane divided road and underpass; the company also contributed a significant amount of parkland to the city and created a private nature reserve adjacent to the Parks.

Financing, Marketing, and Management

Lenders were initially wary of the innovative aspects of the development, but Billingsley

although this was a difficult goal to accomplish. The development team had to work diligently with city engineers to modify many of the existing development codes and standards. Because of the site's suburban location, regulations called for street widths, setbacks, and curb cuts that were much larger than what the developer and designers envisioned. Adding to this struggle was the fact that the entire plan for the project was met with sus-

was able to persuade them of the validity of her vision. The development team believed that if the project could not only fill a need in the market but exceed expectations, it would be a success. The project is divided into large phases. Phase I has proved to be a resounding success: within two months of completion, 99 percent of the units had been leased, and Phase I now maintains a 96 percent occupancy rate.

The Billingsley Company has had to do relatively little marketing for the Parks and finds that most tenants hear of the project through word of mouth or newspaper articles. The application process and one-year lease are standard, and pets are allowed for a fee. The Billingsley Company manages the property—and, although overseeing an amenity-rich multifamily complex is a challenge, the company is learning as it goes. Since each unit is equipped with high-speed Internet access, residents can interact with the management office and concierge services through the Austin Ranch Web site.

Experience Gained

The entire process was a learning experience for Billingsley, as she had never before developed a multifamily residential project. Because she was new to the experience, she sought advice from industry leaders and assembled a seasoned development team. Billingsley and her team saw a need in the rental market and sought to fill it—but, because they believed that market studies merely reflect what is available, rather than what consumer needs *could* be satisfied, they chose to go beyond what could most easily have been accomplished. Instead of plowing down and paving over natural features, and maintaining the status quo, they worked to create a place that would appreciate with age and stand far above the competition.

Most of the newer rental projects in the area were built at much higher densities and

therefore commanded higher returns per acre. The Parks at Austin Ranch was an experiment to determine if medium-density garden apartment product types could be built within a different context and still perform financially.

Billingsley stood firm in what she wanted to accomplish. Gaining changes in the development codes was a challenge, as was meeting the resistance from some of the surrounding communities. In the end, the project received its approvals and has gained numerous accolades and positive recognition from once-dubious parties.

It is important, when designing a multifamily project, to respect the residents and anticipate their needs. The designers were careful, for example, not to put the pool near the leasing office, so that residents could relax without interruptions from prospects coming and going. Additionally, each apartment has an attractive view: no one has to look at a brick wall or trash bins. Although it is difficult and costly, Billingsley recommends saving as much of the natural tree cover as possible. The visual and environmental benefits are immeasurable.

Original works of art enhance the public space at the Parks.

The Parks of Austin Ranch: Phase I

Project Data

Land Use Information

Site area (acres/hectares)	24.4/9.9
Percentage completed	100
Total number of dwelling units	548
Floor/area ratio	0.68
Parking spaces	980
Parking ratio (per unit)	1.8

Land Use Plan

Use	Acres/ Hectares	Percentage of Site
Buildings	2.1/0.85	8.6
Streets and surface parking	7.7/3.2	31.5
Landscaping and open space	14.6/5.9	59.8
Total	24.4/9.9	100.0

Gross Building Area

Use	Square Feet/ Square Meters
Residential	714,630/66,390
Other	8,710/810
Total	723,340/67,200

Residential Unit Information

Unit Type	Unit Size (Square Feet/ Square Meters)	Number of Units Built/ Leased	Monthly Rent
1 bedroom/ 1 bath	607–1,045/ 60–100	333/319	$735– $1,040
2 bedroom/ 2 bath	1,082–1,177/ 100–110	191/178	$1,345
3 bedroom/ 2 bath	1,348/130	24/21	$1,305– $1,435
Total		548/518	

Development Cost Information

Site Acquitision and Improvement Costs

Site acquisition	$5,206,000
Excavation, grading	519,998
Sewer, water, drainage	591,983
Paving, curbs, sidewalks	1,080,425
Landscaping, irrigation	923,040
Street landscaping	54,400
Subtotal, site acquisition and improvement costs	$8,375,846

Construction Costs	**$28,297,303**

Soft Costs

Architecture, engineering	$575,992
Marketing	51,000
Legal, accounting services	65,000
Taxes, insurance	18,166
Title fees	114,524
Construction interest, fees	2,672,700
Subtotal, soft costs	$3,497,382

Total development costs	$40,170,531

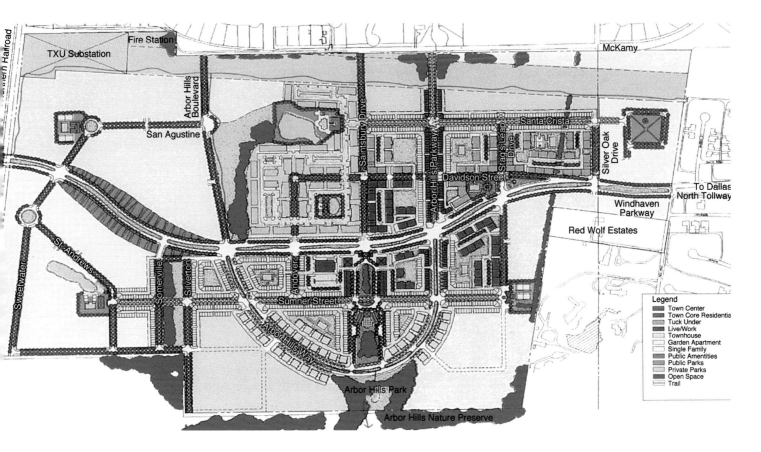

Development Schedule

Site purchased	October 1984
Construction started	May 1999
Sales/leasing started	January 2000
Phase I completed	June 2001
Project completed	Phase II partially complete

Development Team

Developer

Billingsley Company
4100 International Parkway, Suite 1100
Carrollton, Texas 75007
972-820-2244
www.billingsleyco.com

Architect

BGO Architects
4245 North Central Expressway, Suite 300
Dallas, Texas 75205
214-520-8878
www.BGOarchitects.com

Planner

Calthorpe Associates
739 Allston Way
Berkeley, California 94710
510-548-6800
www.calthorpe.com

Landscape Architect

Mesa Design Group
3100 McKinnon Avenue, Suite 905
Dallas, Texas 75202
214-871-0568
www.mesadesigngroup.com

Site plan.

Belle Creek

Commerce City, Colorado

The developers of Belle Creek are building a traditional town by creating a mix of housing types on a connected grid of pedestrian-oriented streets. Affordable housing is part of the mix and is scattered throughout the community.

Belle Creek is a 171-acre (69-hectare) development of over 900 dwelling units located in Commerce City, Colorado—a suburban area about eight miles (13 kilometers) northeast of downtown Denver and west of Denver International Airport (DIA). The site is largely surrounded by farms and industrial sites. It was once part of the industrial corridor that supported Stapleton Airport and was originally planned for industrial uses. But when Denver's principal airport was moved

from Stapleton to the new site, the jurisdictions in this northeast corridor rapidly revised their master plans to include new residential, office, and retail areas.

Commerce City, which has been a leader in such efforts, has taken a number of steps to add new dimensions to the city's historically industrial character. For example, the city has aggressively developed a "new lands" program to improve the quality of new devel-

MICHAEL PECK

Elevations

Main street level

Lower street level

Upper level

opment, and has constructed new water and sewer infrastructure between the city and the new airport. City leaders have encouraged the construction of a "beltway" connection to the highway system that is already linked to the employment centers of downtown Denver, DIA, and the Boulder Corridor, along U.S. 36. City leaders have embraced a well-coordinated planning and design program that is based on the new urbanism, and that was written with the help of Belle Creek's developers. Belle Creek was the first development to be approved under the new standards.

Homes at Belle Creek are a mix of single-family homes, townhouses, and multilevel rental apartments. Many of the single-family homes have optional carriage units above garages, and the town center, which is not yet complete, will include market-rate live/work units above retail space. The project's focal point is a "family center," fronting the town green, that includes an early-child-hood learning center, a school, and other community amenities. Convenience retail, office space, and pocket parks complete the community.

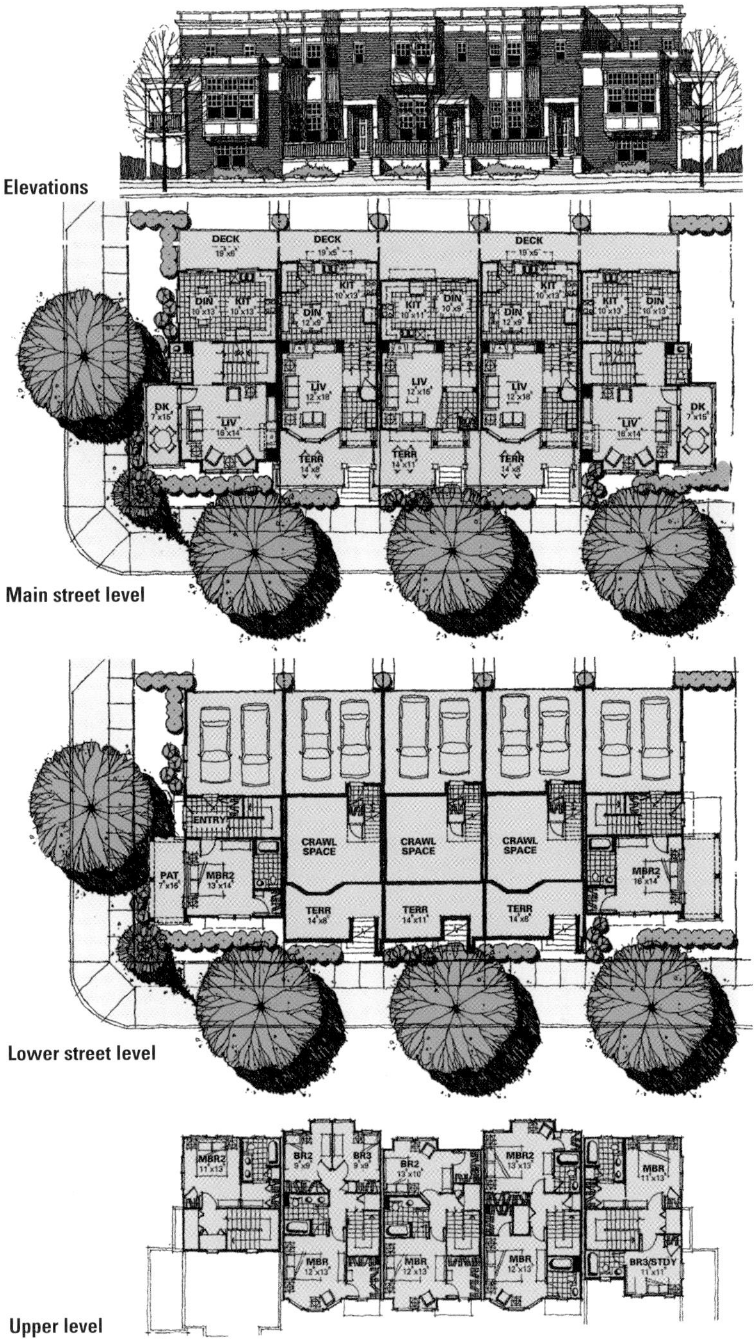

Goals and Objectives

The goal of the developers of Belle Creek was to create a mixed-income community with a walkable lifestyle. Fifty-one percent of the units were designed to be affordable to households earning 80 percent of the local median income, and the range of housing types and price points was made wide enough to allow residents to move up or down with-

out leaving the community and their social connections.

The vision for the community is based on giving residents the setting, the tools, and the added capacity to better manage the homes and neighborhoods in which they live. Central to this vision are the relationships formed between and within families through the

The townhouses, which are built in small clusters throughout the development, include integral two-car garages that are accessed from rear alleys.

MICHAEL PECK

Each house type is available in several styles inspired by traditional local architecture: Craftsman, four-square, cottage, and Victorian. Most homes feature front porches.

activities of raising and nurturing children—hence the focus on the family center.

In addition to paying a fair-market price for the land, the master developer agreed to the following covenants as a part of the land purchase agreement:

- The plan would disperse buyers and renters of various income levels throughout the community;
- A family center, featuring a high-quality child care facility, would be included;
- The developer would provide incentives to attract a neighborhood elementary school;
- The site plan would include pocket parks and pedestrian circulation;
- The developer would establish a down-payment assistance program for 10 percent of the for-sale residential units and a homebuyer education and counseling program;
- Public transit would be integrated into the community.

A focal point of the community is the 22,817-square-foot (2,120-square-meter) family center. The facility is shared by the residents of Belle

Creek and Commerce City at large. It houses an extensive early-childhood learning facility, a computer center, a gymnasium, an exercise room, and meeting and multipurpose areas. A charter school for kindergarten through eighth grade—which will open in September 2003—will also use the facility as an extension of its campus. The amenities were put in place as early as possible so that they would be available to the first residents.

Background

Belle Creek was conceived by a partnership consisting of Sam Gary, Gene Myers, and Rocky Mountain Mutual Housing. Sam Gary, of Gary-Williams Energy and the Piton Foundation, is a pioneer and longtime advocate of communities that enable families to move from poverty and dependence to self-reliance. The goals and objectives for Belle Creek were based largely on Gary's direct experiences with community services and affordable housing; they also drew on his experience as a member of the boards of the Enterprise Foundation, the Stapleton Redevelopment Foundation, and the Warren Village Foundation.

Gene Myers, of Greentree Homes and New Town Builders—a production, custom, and niche-market home developer—is well versed in the homebuilding and land development process and shares Gary's community vision; Myers also has a particular interest in the aesthetics of community planning.

Rocky Mountain Mutual Housing—a nonprofit with a solid track record in low- and moderate-income housing—joined the team to manage the rental apartments and the family center. In addition to providing affordable housing, Mutual offers residents the tools they need to reach self-sufficiency, including job training, daycare, assistance in equity-building to facilitate homeownership, and education in financial management. Residents make up over half of the board of directors and are involved in management decisions.

Planning and Design: Not Another 1,000 Beige Boxes

The developers began with a conventional suburban land plan but quickly realized that to make the development financially feasible, they would need higher densities than such a plan would yield. A new urbanist approach added 140 units to the original plan, enabling the developers not only to achieve higher density but to create a design that emphasizes a sense of community and place. The higher density was also needed to support the family center, which was crucial to the community vision.

In the fine-grained, mixed-use land plan, each home, lot, and block is seamlessly integrated with the town center and square, the family center and surrounding park, and the 12 neighborhood pocket parks. Rental apartments are in small buildings dispersed throughout community. The majority of homes are within one-quarter mile (0.4 kilometers) of the family center by way of a walkable grid pattern of streets and sidewalks. Vistas are carefully planned so that the turn of every corner holds an interesting view. Because landscaping is so vital to attractive streetscapes, the plan includes meticulously placed street trees and landscaping; this approach enabled the builders to use less expensive exterior materials on the more affordable product types without sacrificing the high overall design standards. Curbside planting strips are a generous ten feet (3 meters) in width on

Comparing the Costs of New Urbanist and Conventional Development

Belle Creek's developers created a cost simulation to compare a new urbanist development plan with a conventional suburban plan. Although the total costs are higher for the new urbanist plan, the plan yields more lots, which brings down the cost per lot and makes the overall plan more cost-effective. ▲

Cost Item	New Urbanist Development[a]		Conventional Suburban Development[b]	
	Total Cost	Cost per Lot	Total Cost	Cost per Lot
Fees	$16,606	$78	$16,606	$95
Professional fees	629,793	2,971	556,015	3,177
Earthwork	466,826	2,202	460,802	2,633
Sanitary	472,971	2,231	393,516	2,249
Drainage	398,338	1,879	398,338	2,276
Water, irrigation	1,028,930	4,853	1,003,430	5,734
Streets, alleys	1,302,365	6,143	1,139,240	6,510
Private utilities	1,033,980	4,877	1,021,030	5,834
Landscape	598,103	2,821	598,103	3,418
Contingency	171,203	808	141,400	808
Taxes, insurance	54,003	255	54,003	309
Overhead	300,000	1,415	300,000	1,714
Interest, loan fees	431,020	2,033	418,089	2,389
Total	$6,904,138	$32,567	$6,500,572	$37,146

a. Yield of 212 units: 183 single-family units and 29 townhouses.
b. Yield of 175 units: 146 single-family units and 29 townhouses.

MICHAEL PECK

main streets, and five feet (1.5 meters) on secondary streets.

Just as the developers came to the new urbanist plan for practical reasons, the traditional architectural styling was a cost-based decision: traditional homes are very efficient to build. The original architectural designs, which were based on the popular early-20th-century motifs found in and around Denver's acclaimed Washington Park area—include cottage, Victorian, Craftsman, and four-square styles. The product mix includes

- 304 rental apartments;
- 108 townhouses;
- 515 single-family homes;
- Approximately 50 carriage houses above garages accessed via alleys;
- 5,000 square feet (460 square meters) of town center retail and office space;
- The 22,817-square-foot (2,120-square-meter) family center;
- Six development pads for a church and for over 300,000 square feet (27,870 square meters) of convenience retail uses.

Although 5,000 square feet (460 square meters) of the community's commercial development will be located in the town center, most will be at the edge of Belle Creek (the intersection of 104th Avenue and Highway 85), where it is more supportable. The main retail site—approximately 9.5 acres (3.8 hectares) of developable land—will include pad sites for a gas station, a drugstore,

and various services. All parcels, which range in size from just under one acre (0.4 hectares) to just over three acres (1.2 hectares), are being marketed for sale. At this writing, two parcels are under contract—one to a church and one to a gas station. Ultimately, the developers envision a combination of freestanding convenience retail and service uses, and a 12,000-square-foot (1,120-square-meter) retail center.

The town center retail component is the street level of the three-story buildings at the center of the development, adjacent to the town square. The retail spaces have been designed to be convertible to residential uses should retail not be successful at this location.

Different housing types come together at the parks. The town square, for example, is faced by three different product types: rental apartments, townhouses, and single-family homes are on each of three sides (the family center is on the fourth). Housing prices span a wide range, from apartment rents that begin at $346 per month to single-family homes that sell for more than $300,000. Single-family homes range in size from 1,200 to 2,600 square feet (111 to 242 square meters), and all include full basements. The marketing effort, which emphasizes the fact that "real" towns have a mix of income and housing types, has focused on selling community over selling houses, and the owners of higher-priced homes have shown little resistance to being in close proximity to lower-priced housing.

MICHAEL PECK

Belle Creek was developed with sustainability in mind. Dual water systems provide nonpotable water for irrigation. Open space accounts for 30 percent of the community's land area. Homes are built to "Built Green" energy efficiency standards. Built Green Colorado, the largest green building program in the nation, is a voluntary program that encourages homebuilders to use technologies that improve energy efficiency, preserve natural resources, and reduce pollution. Built Green conducts random testing of homes for quality control. Fannie Mae and other lenders accept the Built Green standards for their Homestyle (energy-efficient mortgage) program, which recognizes the lower operating costs of such homes when qualifying buyers for loans.

Development and Marketing

Zoning approvals took seven months to obtain, and final plat approval required another four months. Entitlements were relatively easy to secure, in part because the municipality liked the housing mix and the family center, and welcomed the opportunity to get a project built with the city's new design standards. Also, because the development is so well designed, it did not draw neighborhood opposition. Local groups met with the developers and were satisfied with the product being presented. The major question was whether the project would lower nearby property values, but since much of the Belle

Creek housing was higher priced than existing homes in the area, this did not become an issue. Following more than two years of research and planning, Belle Creek officially broke ground in the summer of 2000. At present the project is in the second of four phases, with several sections of single-family homes and townhouses complete. The family center is open to the public, and the first 150 units of multifamily housing became available for occupancy at the end of 2002.

A homeowners' association has been established, mainly to administer architectural controls. Common areas are public, and are maintained by the Belle Creek Metropolitan District, a governmental entity. The metropolitan district funded the capital costs for the family center, and the center's operating costs will be shared by the metropolitan district, the city, and the charter school. Under a contract with the metropolitan district, Rocky Mountain Mutual Housing will manage the family center.

Homes began selling in 2000, with no more than a sign at the entrance. Press coverage and word of mouth have made advertising virtually unnecessary. The charter school is expected to become a major selling point once it opens. Consumer demand at Belle Creek has outpaced production: during the first year of sales, there was a waiting list of more than 300 prequalified buyers. This success contrasted dramatically with conventional communities in the trade area, which had experienced slow sales during the same period. During 2002, however, in a very weak overall market, sales diminished, especially for the townhouses, and the developers initiated an advertising campaign.

Financing

Because the developers wanted Belle Creek to serve as a model for other developers, it was critical that all those involved pay market prices and earn market returns. Thus far, Belle Creek is meeting community goals and staying on budget.

Belle Creek is a model of public/private partnerships. A city-approved metropolitan improvement district financed a portion of the public infrastructure and facilities, and, for the first five years of operation, will provide $150,000 per year in operating support for the family center. The developers would not have been able to obtain bond issues without city funds.

The facility for the early-childhood learning center is provided free to the operator. Belle Creek residents get first priority and a discount on child care. The developers voluntarily provided the charter school with land and school-impact fees, and contributed to the cost of "oversizing" the shared gymnasium in the

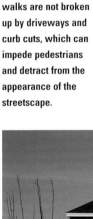

Rear alleys service most of the development. Because parking is in the rear, sidewalks are not broken up by driveways and curb cuts, which can impede pedestrians and detract from the appearance of the streetscape.

family center. In addition, the developers have voluntarily contributed funds to the school that are equal to the value of the school site (as if a school site had not been provided).

Key Bank provides debt financing on the home construction and shares in the land development equity with Bank One's Community Development Corporation through Key Community Development Corporation. Fifty-one percent of the rental housing will be occupied by households earning 80 percent or less of the area median income. In addition, 166 of the for-sale units are priced for households with incomes at or below 80 percent of the area median income. The developers will assist homebuyers with downpayments if needed.

Experience Gained

To ensure cooperation, developers must work with utility companies upfront on drainage issues and utility placement. In the case of Belle Creek, the developers did not foresee that it would be difficult to get utilities installed in alleys.

The developers were worried that detached garages—a common feature of new urbanist plans—would not sell. Buyers have a choice, and about 50 percent of buyers have chosen

MICHAEL PECK

A row of single-family homes faces one of several pocket parks.

detached garages. One reason is that optional accessory units ("granny flats") are available only above detached garages. Of the buyers who have chosen detached garages, about half have opted to purchase accessory units. Some buyers are using them as rental property, which helps them qualify for the mortgage.

Despite market research that showed low demand for the higher-priced homes, those homes sold out very quickly, and more could have been sold if they had been available. Increasing the proportion of the units at the higher end would also have been better for the bottom line and for the community's income mix.

Some of the lots are a little too shallow, and therefore place homes too close to the street. Lots are 65 feet (20 meters) deep for cottages and 85 feet (26 meters) deep for other single-family homes. Slightly narrower but deeper lots—about 95 feet (29 meters)—would probably have improved the streetscape.

Because they have fewer options, households at lower income ranges probably value community even more than those at the higher end. Therefore, it is even more important for projects targeted at low- and moderate-income households to provide the hard and soft infrastructure that fosters community relationships.

The developers are extremely pleased with Belle Creek but would like to raise the bar a little on their next project by placing a real focus on the town center. They would like to create a fully functional town center, with enough office space to provide an employment base for residents and to offer a complete "live, work, play, learn" community.

Any project has unique circumstances, but Belle Creek has many replicable elements. The success of such a project requires creativity, a cooperative municipality, and open-minded designers. The market for affordable housing is deep and currently not well served, and Belle Creek has proven that the market is ready for this kind of mixed-income community. Belle Creek shows that developers can provide affordable housing and still make a profit. Increasing density, carefully controlling costs, and partnering with local government and nonprofit agencies made for a bottom line that worked.

Those involved in Belle Creek have a strong sense of pride in it. During development of the town square, the owner of one of the construction firms was pleased to see the town square taking shape and wondered whether kids would eventually be playing in the proposed fountain. When he learned that they probably would, he agreed to contribute the full cost of the fountain.

Belle Creek

Project Data

Land Use Information

Site area (acres/hectares)	171/69
Percentage completed	61
Floor/area ratio	0.5

Land Use Plan

	Acres/ Hectares	Percentage of Site
Buildings	96.1/38.8	56
Streets and surface parking	35.9/14.5	21
Landscaping and open space	39.3/15.9	23
Total	171.3/69.2	100

Residential Unit Information

Single-Family Homes

Unit Type	Unit Size (Square Feet/ Square Meters)	Number of Units Planned/Sold	Initial Base Prices
Midtown Collection	1,222–1,525/114–142	255/76	$178,000–$201,000
Wellshire Collection	1,576–2,031/146–189	214/78	$219,900–$233,500
Platte Park Collection	1,833–2,600/170–242	46/14	$246,500–$265,900
Total		515/168	

Multifamily Units

Unit Type	Unit Size (Square Feet/ Square Meters)	Number of Units Planned/Leased	Monthly Rents
1 bedroom/1 bath	522/48	78/0	$346–$675
2 bedroom/1 bath	786/73	174/0	$409–$860
3 bedroom/2 bath	1,010/94	51/0	$473–$1,019
Total		303/0	

Townhouses

Unit Type	Unit Size (Square Feet/ Square Meters)	Number of Units Planned/Sold	Initial Base Prices
Hilltop Collection	1,215–1,747/113–162	108/27	$163,900–$188,500

Gross Building Area

Use	Existing (Square Feet/ Square Meters)	Planned (Square Feet/ Square Meters)
Retail and office	0	70,000/6,504
Family center	22,817/2,120	22,817/2,120
Total	22,817/2,120	92,817/8,624

Development Cost Information

Site Acquisition and Improvement Costs

Site acquisition	$3,209,046
Excavation, grading	1,136,697
Sewer, water, drainage	7,078,253
Paving, curbs, sidewalks	4,159,999
Landscaping, irrigation	2,077,443
Fees, general conditions	2,679,856
Other (private utilities)	2,907,680
Subtotal, site acquisition and improvement costs	$23,248,974

Construction Costs

Retail and office (estimated cost to complete pads and buildings)	$9,000,000
Residential	85,981,640
Family center	3,500,000
Subtotal, construction costs	$98,481,640

Projected Soft Costs

Architecture, engineering services	$1,363,503
Project management	1,522,849
Legal, accounting services	218,901
Taxes, insurance	308,618
Construction interest, fees	9,646,931
Other (land development loan fees)	1,033,166
Projected soft costs for New Town Builders	8,255,000
Subtotal, projected soft costs	$22,348,968
Total projected development costs	$144,079,582

Development Schedule

Planning started	June 1998
Site purchased	October 2000
Construction started	December 2000
Sales and leasing started	Fall 2000
Phase I completed	June 2002
Estimated completion	June 2003

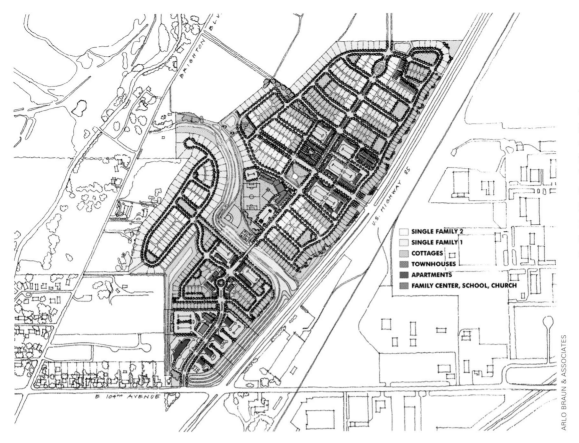

The developers needed an efficient plan that would yield enough density for financial feasibility. The final plan, created through an analytical process, did that and more: it yielded an attractive and livable community.

SINGLE FAMILY 2
SINGLE FAMILY 1
COTTAGES
TOWNHOUSES
APARTMENTS
FAMILY CENTER, SCHOOL, CHURCH

Development Team

Developer

Belle Creek, LLC
1805 Shea Center Drive, Suite 250
Highlands Ranch, Colorado 80129
303-707-4400
www.greentreehomes.com

Apartment Developer

Rocky Mountain Mutual Housing
1550 Park Avenue, Suite 200
Denver, Colorado 80218
303-863-8651
www.rmmha.org

Architect and Master Planner

Arlo Braun and Associates
1058 Delaware Street
Denver, Colorado 80204
303-623-0701
www.arlobraun.com

Architect (Apartments and Family Center)

Humphries-Poli Architects, PC
1215 Elati Street
Denver, Colorado 80204
303-607-0040
www.hparch.com

Landscape Architect

Nuszer Kopatz Urban Design Associates
1117 Cherokee Street
Denver, Colorado 80204
303-534-3881
www.nuszer-kopatz.com

Project Engineer and Land Surveyor

Carroll & Lange, Inc.
165 South Union Boulevard, Suite 156
Lakewood, Colorado 80228
303-980-0200
www.carroll-lange.com

Civil Engineer

ICON Engineering, Inc.
8100 South Akron Street
Englewood, Colorado 80112
303-221-0802
www.iconeng.com

Development Consultant

Inverness Properties, LLC
2 Inverness Drive East, Suite 200
Englewood, Colorado 80112
303-799-9500

Southern Village

Chapel Hill, North Carolina

Southern Village is located south of downtown Chapel Hill and the University of North Carolina. The project includes both rental and for-sale housing, as well as retail, office, and entertainment uses; a daycare center; an elementary school; and substantial open space.

Southern Village is a 312-acre (126-hectare) development located approximately two miles (three kilometers) south of downtown Chapel Hill and about a mile (1.6 kilometers) south of the University of North Carolina (UNC). The development is predominantly residential but includes a village center. Designed around a green—a formal open space for community residents—the village center offers a mix of commercial uses. Existing and planned components of Southern Village include 1,135 residential units (single-family homes, townhouses, condominiums, and rental apartments); 145,000 square feet (13,470 square meters) of office space; and 70,000 square feet (6,500 square meters) of retail, restaurant, and entertainment uses, including a four-screen movie theater. Noncommercial facilities complete the village center: Mary Scroggs Elementary School, a two-story brick structure designed in the tradition of an old schoolhouse; the Chapel Hill Day Care Center; and Christ United Methodist Church.

Approximately 30 percent of the project's acreage consists of open space, most of which is designated for recreation. An extensive trail system runs through Southern Village and is used by both pedestrians and bicyclists. A planned ten-foot- (three-meter-) wide greenway path will extend north and will connect with a sidewalk that leads to downtown Chapel Hill and UNC.

In an effort to preserve the site's trees, the developers established Arlen Park, a forested two acres (0.8 hectares) that offer trails, picnic tables, and a small historic cemetery surrounded by a stone wall. The trails that run through Arlen Park connect with the larger trail system of Southern Village. Open space is further organized into a series of smaller parks located throughout the development. Several of these parks include playground equipment, while others provide for passive recreation and relaxation.

A 400-space park-and-ride lot, operated by Chapel Hill Transit, is located at the southern portion of the community, adjacent to the village center. The lot is served by the north-south express-bus route during the workweek and by the Tarheel Express bus service for special events at UNC. The park-and-ride lot is adjacent to U.S. 15-501 and is well buffered from the rest of the community.

Southern Village also features a swim and racquet club that includes a swimming pool, a pool house, and six tennis courts. Membership in the club is voluntary for residents. The soccer field and basketball and volleyball courts adjacent to the club are open to all residents of Southern Village.

The Site and Its History

The Southern Village site, located west of U.S. 15-501 and south of Culbreth Road and Culbreth Middle School, in Orange County, consists of approximately 312 acres (126 hectares) of varying topography. The parcels that make up the site were first assembled in the 1970s, when Lake Tree, a mixed-use project, was proposed but rejected by the town of Chapel Hill. In the 1980s, the town approved a plan for a subdivision called Woodlake, but the developer's financial difficulties caused the approvals to lapse, and the project was never built.

No further plans were drawn for the site until the early 1990s, when the town of Chapel Hill amended its comprehensive plan to include small-area plans. Small-area plans were designed to provide more detailed land use plans for the undeveloped portions of the town's urban service areas and to ensure the coordination of public facilities. In June 1992, the town council adopted the plan for the Southern Area, which includes the Southern Village site. The planners considered three alternative development scenarios: the conventional

Homes in Southern Village are designed in an array of styles that take cues from the homes in the surrounding older neighborhoods.

pattern, the cluster pattern, and the village pattern. The town recognized that a one-unit-per-acre (three-units-per-hectare) conventional subdivision was not the appropriate development pattern for the site. Community leaders, town planning staff, and elected officials also agreed that it was critical to avoid haphazard development that would consume existing open space, and that—in order to preserve open space and minimize the impact of development—there should be a more distinct line between town and country. The village pattern, which is modeled on Chapel Hill's downtown area and other mixed-use traditional developments, was specified for the area that now encompasses Southern Village.

The town developed a conditional-use zoning process for the village area in order to coordinate the general design guidelines mandated by the village pattern. Soon after the revision of the town's comprehensive plan, D.R. Bryan, of Bryan Properties, Inc., purchased the unzoned Southern Village site and worked with the town to realize the urban village concept.

In accordance with the town's small-area plan, development of the site required a series of zoning approvals. The first set of approvals, consisting of the master plan, rezoning, and special-use permit for the eastern portion of the site, was granted in July 1993 and met with virtually no opposition. The second set of zoning approvals—for the western portion of the site—proved to be much more time-consuming and controversial because of ongoing construction on the eastern portion of the site, and the proximity of existing homes. The second set of zoning approvals was not obtained until 1996.

Development, Planning, and Design

The development of Southern Village was a collaborative effort between the town of

Chapel Hill and the developer. After he purchased the site, Bryan visited several new urbanist developments around the country, sometimes accompanied by the town's planning director. In the course of this research, the team gained insight into the design elements that make a new urbanist neighborhood function. The visits reinforced the value of the guidelines set forth in the Chapel Hill small-area plan for the Southern Area—including the development of a walkable, mixed-use community with an interconnected street system, access to public transit, neighborhood-oriented public spaces, and smaller residential lot sizes.

While some subdivisions construct their road network first and then encourage home-builders to spread out, in order to provide the appearance of a more built-out community, the Southern Village development plan focused on the development of homes and infrastructure on one street at a time. This approach emphasized the importance of the streetscape, and allowed a sense of place to develop in each phase of construction.

Single-family homes in Southern Village are designed in a diverse array of architectural styles that adhere to new urbanist design principles. Houses are close to the sidewalk and to each other, garages are accessed by rear alleys, and porches or verandas face the street, offering a transitional place between the public realm and private home. The apartments and condominiums have an urban form, with parking provided on the street and in lots behind the buildings. The community is well landscaped and contains a series of public parks and open spaces. The species of trees along the streets vary from one neighborhood to another, which gives the different parts of the community greater individuality.

Design elements integral to new urbanist developments can often conflict with a jurisdiction's long-established engineering regulations, and this was the case with Southern Village. The narrow streets, which slow traffic for the benefit of pedestrians and bicyclists while creating a more intimate space, presented challenges to regulations that dictated turning radii and the curvature of roadways. The alleys that provide access to approximately 90 percent of the homes also conflicted with the town's engineering and public works standards. Negotiation on these matters resulted in compromises— one of which was, in the initial phases of the community, to make the streets wider than the developer originally desired. In the case of the alleys, plans for Southern Village had called for alleys to be 12 feet (3.6 meters) wide, but the engineering standards called for 20 feet (six meters) of width. Although the developer prevailed, the town mandated that the alleys had to remain privately owned —which meant that they would not be eligible for publicly provided trash removal, and that residents would be forced to put trash out for pickup in front of their houses. Currently, residents contract with a private trash removal company that is willing to pick up trash from the rear alleys.

Southern Village was organized around the village center, which contains the office and

Wide planting strips provide space for trees that will eventually create a canopy of shade over the streets and sidewalks.

retail components of the community. The development's first building permit was issued for the Corner Store, which established the mixed-use nature of the project. To meet the expectations of potential homebuyers, the development of Southern Village was strategically phased: the retail and office uses were established first, then the multifamily residential portion.

Like other mixed-use communities, Southern Village struggled, in the early stages, to maintain an appropriate balance of housing and retail space. It is difficult to attract retail uses to a development that still is under construction and lacks supporting residents. At first, the developer subsidized the Corner Store's rent to keep the operator solvent until the community became more established. Such a practice has actually proven cost-effective, because of the value that a mix of uses adds to the community.

Neighborhood commercial buildings blend seamlessly into the community.

Southern Village's office buildings, currently 100 percent leased, are structured to accommodate first-floor retail, and the developer has worked to attract office-associated retail uses to the existing office buildings.

Bryan Properties, Inc., donated land for the development of the Mary Scroggs Elementary School, a public school, and the Christ United Methodist Church. As it is often financially difficult for schools and religious institutions to obtain developable land, and the presence of an elementary school and a church on site is desirable for any community development, both transactions proved to be winning situations for all parties involved. The church is adjacent to the park-and-ride lot—which, given that there is virtually no overlap between the peak times for the two uses, allows for an effective shared parking arrangement.

Financing, Marketing, and Operations

The developer relied on financing from a local bank, obtaining a line of credit as well as limited partnership equity. Construction costs were increased by several factors, including the widely varying topography of the site, and the site analysis and preliminary engineering that were required by the town and by the zoning approval process.

Marketing the area's first new urbanist community presented some initial challenges. Although Bryan knew that people were willing to pay a premium to live in the older, traditionally designed neighborhoods that new urbanist developments emulate, he also knew that buyers want new homes. Thus, in order to sell the first units, Bryan had to educate potential buyers about the nature of new urbanist communities—which, essentially, offer new homes in "old" neighborhoods. Because there were no new urbanist neighborhoods in North Carolina to serve as examples, the developer drew comparisons to several older neighborhoods with which potential buyers were familiar. The combination of modern floor plans and features and the ambience of an established community was appealing, and the developer's initial assumptions proved correct: new urbanist communities can achieve premiums in resi-

The village center includes a mix of uses: shops and offices, a movie theater, a day-care center, a church, and the two-story elementary school (shown here).

dential sales. According to the local multiple listing service, Southern Village has been the top-selling community in the Research Triangle area since 1999.

As is typical with many new developments, particularly when they are of a type not familiar to potential buyers, Southern Village's residential sales began slowly, but they increased when the first neighborhoods and street networks were completed and people could actually see and experience portions of the community. During the first two years, Southern Village averaged 50 to 70 units in sales annually, a figure that increased to about 200 units annually for the remaining years. Lot and home prices have also increased significantly, benefiting both early buyers and the developer. Selling prices of the single-family homes, for example, began between $195,000 and $700,000; by the time the project closed out, prices ranged from $350,000 to over $1 million, averaging in the high $400,000s, which is about 10 to 15 percent higher than the average for Chapel Hill on a per-square-foot basis.

Experience Gained

- Close coordination between the local government and the developer makes for a better development process—and, ultimately, a better project.
- An appropriate regulatory framework is critical to the development of mixed-use new urbanist projects. Localities should review ordinances and regulations to ensure that they will facilitate—or at least not hinder—desired development patterns.
- People are receptive to the concept of new urbanist developments. By undertaking effective marketing and by increasing the number of successful new urbanist projects, developers can communicate the benefits of such developments over conventional subdivisions.
- While negotiation and compromise between the public and the developer are important, critical components of new urbanist development (e.g., narrow streets) should be protected.
- Mixed-use developments should be phased strategically in order to ensure that potential homebuyers have accurate expectations for the nature of the built-out community. Because the developer completed one street at a time, rather than building scattered homesites, buyers had a clear picture of what the community would look like.
- Public/private partnerships can work (e.g., Mary Scroggs Elementary School), creating a win-win situation for both parties.

Southern Village
Project Data

Land Use Plan

Use	Area (Acres/Hectares)	Percentage of Site
Buildings	78/32	25
Streets, surface parking	78/32	25
Open space	156/63	50
Total land area	312/127	100

Residential Unit Information

Unit Type	Unit Size (Square Feet/ Square Meters)	Number of Units Sold or Leased	Initial Sales Prices/Rents
Apartments	800–1,225/74–114	250	$865–$1,375/month
Condominiums	800–1,400/70–130	225	$77,900–$175,000
Townhouses	1,100–2,320/100–220	135	$155,000–$290,000
Single-family homes	1,600–4,000/150–370	525	$195,000–$700,000
Total		1,135	

Gross Nonresidential Building Area

Use	Existing Area (Square Feet/ Square Meters)	Planned Area (Square Feet/ Square Meters)	Total (Square Feet/ Square Meters)
Office	95,000/8,830	50,000/4,650	145,000/13,480
Commercial	30,000/2,790	40,000/3,720	70,000/6,510
School	90,000/8,360		90,000/8,360
Church	25,000/2,320		25,000/2,320
Daycare center	6,000/560		6,000/560
Total	246,000/22,860	90,000/8,370	336,000/31,230

Development Cost Information

(In Millions)

Site acquisition	$3.5
Site improvement	25.0
Estimated total development costs	$28.5

Development Schedule

Site purchased	December 1992
Planning started	December 1992
First approvals	July 1993
Construction started	March 1994
Sales/leasing started	August 1994
Phase I completed	August 1994
Project completed	January 2002

Development Team

Developer

Bryan Properties, Inc.
P.O. Box 728
Holly Springs, North Carolina 27540
919-552-4547

Site Planners

Stimmel & Associates
305 West Fourth Street, Suite 1A
Winston-Salem, North Carolina 27101
910-723-1067

Tony M. Tate Landscape Architecture
1912 East NC 54, Suite 202
Durham, North Carolina 27713
919-484-8880

Engineering and Construction Consultant

Blackmon Engineering
505 Benson Road
Garner, North Carolina 27529
919-772-8205

The site plan for **Southern Village** illustrates its interconnected streets, village center, and integrated open space.

Architects

Cline Davis Architects, PA
125 North Harrington Street
Raleigh, North Carolina 27603
919-833-6413

Looney Ricks Kiss Architects, Inc.
175 Toyota Plaza, Suite 600
Memphis, Tennessee 38103
901-521-1440
www.lrk.com

Murphy Garnow Design Group, Inc.
1140-300 Kildaire Farm Road
Cary, North Carolina 27511
919-481-9115

Omega Design Architecture, PC
1015 Aviation Parkway
Morrisville, North Carolina 27560
919-388-2500

Bahcesehir

Bahcesehir, Turkey

Nestled in the hills on the outskirts of Istanbul, Turkey, Bahcesehir will eventually be a community of 100,000 residents. Phase II features parks and other public facilities, as well as a mix of housing types to support retail and commercial development.

Taming a big city's suburban growth with satellite cities that offer the best of urban neighborhoods and amenities is a century-old dream. On the arid slopes of a green valley 40 miles (64 kilometers) from Istanbul, Turkey, the dream seems, at least in part, closer to reality.

When complete, Bahcesehir will be a city of 100,000 residents, linked to Istanbul via the Orient Express rail line and the main highway to Western Europe. Developed by a government-owned bank, Emlak Bankasi, Bahcesehir began with Phase I, 3,500 units on the valley's west side, made up mostly of uniform, high-rise apartment buildings that

follow the pattern of earlier Emlak Bankasi satellite towns near the growth centers of Istanbul, Ankara, and Izmir. In contrast, Bahcesehir's current phase, now in construction east of the valley, is a 170-acre (68-hectare), 2,300-unit mix that recalls an older urban order, offering a plaza with a rail station, stores, institutions, and parkland that serve the whole city; quarters with their own shops and schools; and walkable, mixed-use, low- and mid-rise urban neighborhoods providing a variety of housing types for people of varying income levels.

In their promise to save land and resources, give structure to regional development, and replace shapeless, single-use ghettos with diverse neighborhoods, pioneering new urbanist communities like this one have much in common with new urbanist projects in the United States. In fact, Bahcesehir (the name is being used for both the projected city and its current phase) is in many ways more advanced than some of its better-known U.S. counterparts.

Site Plan and Development

Bahcesehir is all about alternatives to sprawl. In modern Turkey, however, sprawl is of a different order. Greater Istanbul had 1 million people in 1950, had grown to 7 million by 1990, and has long since passed the 12 million mark. Many of the newcomers are rural migrants squatting on once-open land in *gecekondus* —literally, "overnight" settlements—which, because they destroy vegetation and lack runoff, erosion, and pollution controls, as well as sanitation, are as bad for public health as for the environment. Meanwhile, well-off buyers consume more countryside: both car sales and permits for American-style, single-family houses double every few years.

Maryland-based Torti Gallas and Partners, the lead architects and planners for Bahcesehir, admit that a satellite town for the middle classes can hardly curb this runaway growth; at best, the development can save its own open space and relieve some pressure on roads and on the city's older, affordable housing. The real hope is that, if Bahcesehir works, it will offer a strong alternative model for a generation of mixed-income new towns, where residents can work, play, worship, go to school, shop, and take intercity transit, all within walking distance of their homes.

The idea behind Bahcesehir, explains managing principal Tunca Iskir, of Torti Gallas, is that a town's form should support civic life as well as private life—a concept that is readily visible in historic towns and cities

near Istanbul and throughout the Mediterranean. In fact, nearby examples studied firsthand inspired many of the early design ideas proposed in meetings attended by local residents and Turkish and U.S. architects, planners, and developers. An important event in the early planning stages was a 14-person design charrette—a two-week crash program of study, consultations, drawing, and model making designed to give the project its basic shape.

As in traditional towns, the plan for Bahcesehir's current phase shows a hierarchy of scale as well as uses. Narrow streets and compact squares and parks make up neighborhoods. Neighborhoods connect at community focal points, such as a school or a mosque, to form quarters. Within a five-minute walk of each quarter are the central, terraced public park and the watercourse that cascades down the steep hillside toward the town square. This urban center—with its rail station, offices, shops, theaters, and cafés—opens, in turn, onto the regional "Tivoli Gardens" park and lake, the small lush valley shared by greater Bahcesehir. Throughout the city are different scales of transportation, from narrow paths to high-speed rail and freeways; and varied sizes and styles of buildings, from small

Narrow, tree-lined streets provide the framework for neighborhoods. Homes are a mix of attached and detached villas and mid-rise and high-rise multifamily units.

apartments over corner stores to luxury villas and a few high-rise towers.

At every scale, buildings are positioned in such a way as to define streets, squares, and other public and private outdoor spaces, giving each place a clear identity. As the town's official description says, "to know where one is and what activities are likely to occur . . . is a prerequisite for both civic and private life." In other words, Bahcesehir is seeking to provide a sense of place.

In contrast to some new urbanist planning processes, in which the designer's end product is a zoning code or a pattern book, Bahcesehir's developers contracted with the original schematic design team, Torti Gallas and local associate architect Oner Ozyar, of INAS, to stay involved throughout a detailed design development phase—and, working with Turkish engineering and construction professionals, to manage a fast-track construction documents phase. This approach allowed site planning, landscape design, and building design to go forward as a single process. "We try to combine urban design and architecture in every project," Iskir says. "But here it's especially important because of the topography."

With much of Bahcesehir occupying land with an average grade of 18 percent, it made sense to let the streets follow the hillside contours and to place concrete-framed "uphill" and "downhill" buildings—which double as retaining walls—between them. The cost of using stepped buildings to hold back the hillside is offset by several pluses, including

open views and distinct unit types that take the appealing and practical form of the traditional, breeze-cooled Turkish hillside villa.

Residential Design

For affluent homebuyers, Bahcesehir offers several actual villa plans: uphill and downhill, detached and attached, and stacked (entered individually from upper and lower streets). Most have a rear garden within one level of the street entrance, and under-building parking. Elsewhere, single-orientation rowhouses back up to a three-story wall to retain the steepest slopes. Similar "wall houses" alongside Istanbul's Topkapi Palace inspired this prototype—one of several instances in which Turkish and American architects working side by side traded cultural insights.

Mid-rise (six- to 12-story) condominium apartment buildings rub shoulders with the villas and share their siting strategy and architectural detail. Because of their size and uniform height, these buildings are used throughout the plan to shape the big spaces of the perimeter boulevards and main streets. Some apartment clusters are also designed to enclose private courtyards, complete with gardens and swimming pools; parking structures are below the courtyards.

The plan also includes four flat-slab, concrete-frame, high-rise condominium buildings. Two smaller towers frame the top of the central park's cascade, and, near the ridge of the hill, twin 34-story buildings frame the town's central axis and create a symbolic gateway to Istanbul—which, on a clear day, is visible to the east.

This variety of building designs yields a wide range of floor plans, from 650-square-foot (60-square-meter) efficiency apartments to luxurious, 5,800-square-foot (540-square-meter) villas, all with modern appliances and interior finishes, and amenities such as swimming pools and on- and off-street parking. Some apartment buildings incorporate "smart" system controls.

In their basic architecture, however, many of these structures would be at home in a 19th-century Istanbul neighborhood. Rooms tend to be separate, and are symmetrically and traditionally proportioned, with tall, multi-paned casement windows that often lead to a balcony or terrace. Outside, the concrete-framed villas and mid-rise buildings, finished with masonry and tile, combine with garden walls and street trees to shape the edges of old-fashioned, walkable streets and neighborhood parks.

The precise blend of new and old derives, on the one hand, from local social customs, notions of appropriate scale and character, and adaptations to climate—and, on the other, from the American architects' experience with historical styles as a proven tool for connecting people with their surroundings and smoothing transitions among income levels, uses, and building types. It is also a direct response to local market research, which revealed that modern homebuyers are strongly attracted to traditional lifestyles and architecture.

Local, project-specific market research is relatively new to Turkey. During the charrette and throughout the design process, the project team studied nearby communities from several eras and talked with potential owners (as is typical in European countries, Bahcesehir consists entirely of for-sale, market-rate units, about 80 percent of which will remain owner occupied). In the course of this process, the

local developers and the American and Turkish designers learned both from homebuyers and from each other, with the result that many preconceptions were changed.

In terms of geographic proximity, the closest market comparable is Bahcesehir's own 3,500-unit first phase, the conventionally modern group of identical high-rise blocks and villas across the valley. Experience there pointed to the need for a deeper sense of place; a stronger framework of neighborhood and town; and fewer large, high-rise buildings. The architects point out, however, that the density of the current phase is identical to that of Phase I, thanks to a marketable and well-tested model: the classic six-story buildings of European neighborhoods such as those of Rome and Paris.

The new phase does have a few high rises, and these, too, look to noteworthy urban models, such as 1920s Manhattan apartment buildings and more recent models in Battery Park City. In New York City fashion, these buildings are shaped to define the street and serve as orientation points on the skyline, without overwhelming small-scale neighbors.

Community Amenities

With respect to its public space plan, Bahcesehir's response to topography differs from

All housing in Bahcesehir is for sale at market rates. An estimated 20 percent of the units will be purchased by investors as rental property.

familiar new urbanist models. The radial main streets that might, elsewhere, bring pedestrians straight to a train station or town square are deflected here by steep grades and by a patchwork of fields, woods, streambeds, and rural lanes. As a result, walks to and from the town center are varied and picturesque, often cutting through neighborhood squares or following the central park's watercourse. As in many historic Islamic cities, the resulting richly detailed quarters and neighborhoods have a specific—and pleasantly disorienting—sense of place.

"We wanted each quarter to have its own distinctive open space, each roughly equal to, but different from, the others," says Torti Gallas design principal Rob Goodill. "Their shapes might seem arbitrary at first, but when you walk the site, you realize that they're a fairly straightforward response to the land."

The plan distributes community-oriented institutions near these local open spaces to serve as neighborhood anchors or focal points—a new urbanist signature that meshes well with regional tradition. Examples include a high school, an elementary school, several community preschools, and two mosques. Throughout the plan, small corner stores dot neighborhoods.

For the main town square, the design team looked again to Mediterranean history, comparing the shapes and proportions of famous Italian squares, such as those in Siena, Florence, and Venice. While Bahcesehir will have other big civic spaces, the principal one is designed, above all, for continuous street life, much of which will be generated by the rail station, post office, and municipal building, and will be reinforced by a 220-car garage and by bridges across the valley to the green "Tivoli Gardens" and to playing fields, the lake, and greater Bahcesehir. About 108,000 square feet (10,000 square meters) of commercial space—including offices, shops, restaurants, and a six-screen cinema—will

surround the main square. Beyond the landmark bell tower, arcaded cafés, and a large central fountain, residents will find other areas to explore: the stepped park, with its closely planted grove, and the shady loggia overlooking the lakeshore soccer field.

Marketing and Sales

More than a few residents of Phase I have looked across the lake and decided to trade in their units for one of the new villas. Despite high demand, however, and available labor from neighboring Russia, at the time of this writing a financial and political crisis, involving the government developer, had halted both construction and sales. Even under normal conditions, however, financing and development proceed at a measured pace; the current phase's first offering will deliver about 600 units. Although no firm timetable has been set, Iskir predicts that buildout of greater Bahcesehir may take 20 years.

Experience Gained

"What Bahcesehir shows is that new urbanism is much more than a magic bullet for American-style suburban sprawl," says Iskir. "It's really about some deeper values that affect people everywhere. Like the ability to live one's entire life within a town full of all kinds of people . . . the choice of large and small places and different ways to get around . . . having a sense of where you are, a clear idea of public and private . . . seeing houses and apartments at various economic levels." He adds, "There's a misconception . . . that the developing world is still rooted in wonderful villages and traditional cities where people sit in cafés all day. The truth is, growth and globalization are tearing the old urban fabric apart all over the world, with sprawl worse than anything in the U.S."

New developments designed along the lines of Bahcesehir can be truly valuable as a way of putting the modern middle class back in

touch with its own traditions—in Turkey, in the United States, or anywhere. Again, there is no instant remedy for Istanbul's population and settlement problems. Like earlier British and American new towns, Bahcesehir is relatively small and predominantly middle class, especially when compared with the vast public housing schemes that followed World War II in much of the developing world.

But Bahcesehir is more than an academic exercise. The largest and most centrally located in a program of satellite cities, it is being closely watched by the media and the general public. Bahcesehir will be among the first large-scale projects to realize an ideal: a walkable community large enough to support its own employment and community life, that also offers fast transit to a major city.

Bahcesehir's broad choice of housing types also bears watching. The picturesque one-block transitions—from luxury villas to small, mid-rise flats and high-rise efficiencies—promise a step forward from most suburban development. Although based on local tradition, these designs suggest how future urban settlements can reverse modernist, single-use zoning to allow different ages and income levels to share a single community.

Not least, Bahcesehir offers a practical example of international cooperation in town building. Turkish and American professionals collaborated throughout the process, from the first concept to the latest construction documents. And, through market research and design charrettes, many more people participated in the planning.

At its 2000 convention, the American Institute of Architects (AIA) gave Bahcesehir and Torti Gallas a national Honor Award in urban design. The AIA awards jury wrote of Bahcesehir: "In an era of almost universal acceptance of American models, this offers a more sustainable model. [It demonstrates that] the growth pressures on global cities can be shaped into beautiful, livable towns."

While the idea of managing growth through satellite cities is not new, living in one has often seemed more like a duty than a choice. The shapers of Bahcesehir hope to make good on the promise of creating a truly urban neighborhood, 40 minutes from a world center, so that global urbanization might someday take a different, better direction.

Bahcesehir: Phase II
Project Data

Land Use Information

Site area (acres/hectares)	170/68
Total number of dwelling units planned/completed	2,320/1,000
Gross density (units per acre/per hectare)	14/35
Average net density (units per acre/per hectare)	19/47

Residential Unit Information

Unit Type	Lot Size (Square Feet/ Square Meters)	Average Unit Size (Square Feet/ Square Meters)	Number of Units Planned/ Built	Current Sales Prices
Villa	8,600/800	4,400/409	160/80	$990,000
Attached villa	4,300/400	3,300/307	460/220	$660,000
Multifamily	N.A.*	2,200/204	1,700/800	$385,000

* Not applicable.

Land Use Plan

	Acres/ Hectares	Percentage of Site
Villas	32/13	19
Attached villas	46/19	27
Multifamily	56/23	33
Roads	16/6	9
Common open space	20/8	12
Total	170/69	100

Development Cost Information
(In Millions, to Date)

Construction costs	$235
Architecture, engineering services	6
Project management	10
Total development costs	$251

Overall site plan.

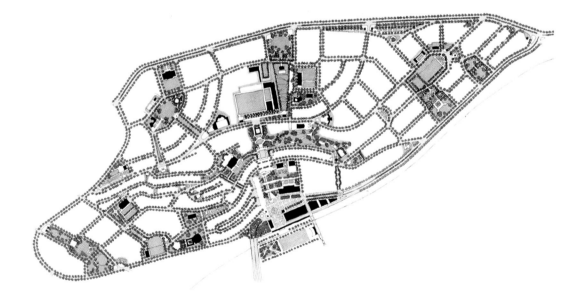

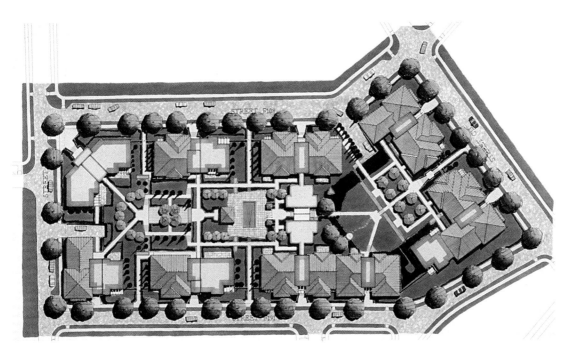

A neighborhood site plan shows how the buildings enclose squares and other public spaces.

Development Schedule

Site purchased	1986
Planning started	1995
Construction started	1998
Sales started	1999

Development Team

Developer

Emlak Bankasi
Buyukdere Cad. No. 43-45
80670 Levent
Istanbul
orgmd@emlakbank.com.tr

Architect and Site Planner

Torti Gallas and Partners
1300 Spring Street
Silver Spring, Maryland 20910
301-588-4800
www.tortigallas.com

Architect

Oner Ozyar
INAS Construction, Contracting, and Trade, Inc.
Cemil Topuzlu Cad. Tibas BL.
E2
Dalyan-Kadikoy 81030
Istanbul, Turkey

General Contractors

Nurol
Insaat VE Ticaret A.S.
Arjantin Caddesi No. 7
06700 Gaziosmanpasa
Ankara, Turkey

Mesa Housing Industries, Inc.
Abidin Daver Sokak No. 12 A-B
06650 Cankaya
Ankara, Turkey

Ladera Ranch

Orange County, California

Neighborhood as amenity. That is the proposition around which Ladera Ranch, a 4,000-acre (1,620-hectare) master-planned community in Orange County, California, is being built. Developed on land holdings that were once part of the massive Rancho Mission Viejo, the 8,100-dwelling-unit development has been thoughtfully organized and designed around a hierarchy of community, village, and neighborhood planning concepts. At the community level, all residents are linked by intranet. Within the community, six villages are planned, each with its own core of social and recreational facilities. Each village, in turn, consists of a number of neighborhoods, each with its own complement of open space and amenities, all of which are linked, via pedestrian pathways, to the village core and to the nonresidential districts of the community.

Beyond this carefully orchestrated hierarchy, Ladera Ranch is notable in another way: its developers have enlisted traditional, high-volume, production homebuilders in the cause of neighborhood building. Guided by detailed design criteria, these homebuilders are producing not merely houses but neighborhood infrastructure and identity. Subdivision builders have thus been made partners in community building—and, from all reports, have benefited from it.

Site Planning and Development

The site of Ladera Ranch is a 4,000-acre (1,620-hectare) parcel of greatly varying topography, ranging from rolling hills to steeply pitched ridgelines. Although the area was undeveloped before the establishment of

One way in which the automobile has been deemphasized is through the use of deeply recessed parking garages, which are screened by porticos on the street elevation.

Ladera Ranch, the site is just a few miles inland from the interstate freeway. It is surrounded by the cities of Mission Viejo and San Juan Capistrano, and by other suburban developments. Ladera Ranch is being developed by DMB/Ladera, LLC, a joint venture of Rancho Mission Viejo and Arizona-based DMB Consolidated Holdings, LLC. Rancho Mission Viejo, which is owned by the O'Neill-Moiso family and others, contributed the land for Ladera Ranch from the historic 30,000-acre (12,140-hectare) cattle ranch that the family has controlled since the 1880s. To create a buffer for the planned community—and to leave a legacy of the ranch—approximately 1,600 acres (650 hectares) of the site have been set aside as permanent open space. Paul Johnson, vice president for community development at Rancho Mission Viejo, notes that a visitor to Ladera Ranch "gets a sense of identity just by crossing through the open-space buffer."

In 1995, when EDAW, Inc., Ladera's master planner, was just beginning to formulate plans for the project, various "big bang" amenities were considered, including a golf course and artificial lakes. But the amount of earth-moving that would have been required rendered these amenities impractical and uneconomical. At that juncture, recalls Steve Kellenberg, principal of EDAW, the question was asked, "Could we make 'neighborhood'

the primary amenity?" Or, in marketing terms, could housing at Ladera Ranch achieve a price premium because of its neighborhood design? Positive results from market research inspired further research, which was used to formulate principles and guidelines for neighborhood design.

Out of this research came the community/village/neighborhood organization. Each village has its own design identity: one village is inspired by the Pasadena Arts and Crafts Movement of the 1920s, another by the revival styles of the 1930s, and yet another by the farming towns of Orange County and the Midwest. Although each village has a predominant design theme, housing in all the villages incorporates a variety of architectural styles.

When completed, each of Ladera's villages will have between 900 and 1,400 homes— a large enough number to support a Village Club as part of the village core, and a small enough number so that the club can be located within a short walk (12 minutes, maximum) of all homes. The Village Club, notes Kellenberg, is "like a private social club, but everybody [in the village] belongs." Typically, the clubs, which are architecturally in keeping with the village identity, will have social and meeting rooms, dining facilities, and outdoor recreational facilities, including swimming pools. Although the clubs' basic functions will be the same in each village, each club is expected to have a different social or recreational character—one club will emphasize sports and another aquatics, for example. Since all clubs will be open to all Ladera Ranch residents, this variation will expand the available recreational opportunities.

Neighborhood size at Ladera is limited to approximately 40 to 50 dwelling units, and typically represents the output of a single builder. If a production builder prefers to build a larger number of units, as is often the case, the builder is required to split its output between two smaller enclaves in two different

One of Ladera Ranch's guiding design principles is "architecture forward"—that is, focusing the streetscape on architectural design, not on garages. In this case, garages are set to the rear of the lot and accessed via alleys.

locations. What makes the builder's subdivision into a neighborhood, according to Kellenberg, are detailed urbanistic and stylistic requirements—which, instead of showcasing the work of a particular builder or offering the bland sameness that often characterizes new subdivisions, are designed instead to create a strong *neighborhood* identity. Further, builders are required to construct neighborhood-scale parks and to connect each neighborhood's open space to the larger open-space network. The requirement for neighborhood open space at Ladera is that usable open space must be located within two blocks of every residence. Kellenberg calls these spaces "formative" parks—that is, the parks or open space form the nucleus of the neighborhood, both physically and symbolically.

These small open spaces link up to an "activity spine" that connects the neighborhoods to the Village Clubs, recreation areas, and the open-space buffer surrounding the community. All together, the activity spine amounts to ten and one-half miles (17 kilometers) of hiking, biking, and equestrian trails. Part of this system, which cuts through the middle of the site, is the Sienna Botanica, a linear open space—and biofiltration system—that was designed to hold runoff from the adjacent hills, reducing the amount of rainwater that must be conducted away from the site.

In a departure from standard Orange County practice, Ladera's designers have reintroduced curb-separated sidewalks—that is, the sidewalk is separated from the curb by a planting strip, or tree lawn. Typically, Ladera's planting strips range from five to seven feet (1.5 to 2 meters) in width, and are planted with a variety of trees that were selected to produce an old-fashioned, continuous canopy along the streets.

Street patterns at Ladera Ranch vary within each village, depending on the topography and the village concept. Some neighborhoods have a fairly conventional cul-de-sac layout,

although they are updated with "eyebrows" (small diversions off a main street), roundabouts, and other elements to introduce variety and interest. Other neighborhoods, influenced by new urbanist practice, have continuous streets organized in more formal, axial plans. According to Kellenberg, the design team preferred street widths of 32 to 34 feet (9.7 to 10.4 meters); but, because of local fire department requirements, minimum street widths have been set at 36 feet (11 meters). To calm traffic and provide additional landscaped areas, the streets taper at the corners and at midblock (where street parking is not required). Street width at tapered areas narrows to 22 to 24 feet (6.7 to 7.3 meters).

In addition to the community/village/neighborhood hierarchy, the organization of Ladera Ranch includes one further element: the district. The district is a special-use area, usually with both residential and nonresidential functions but without a sufficient number of homes to support a Village Club. More urban than the villages, the districts have higher residential density and a larger share of attached and rental housing.

The Bridgeport District, the first district constructed at Ladera, is a 130-acre (53-hectare) neighborhood that includes a 10-acre (four-hectare), 100,000-square-foot (9,290-square-meter) neighborhood shopping center with a supermarket, shops, small businesses, fast-food outlets, and an outdoor dining area. A second district, the 88-acre (36-hectare) Township District, which will ultimately serve as Ladera Ranch's town center, will include a 15-acre (six-hectare) downtown with approximately 150,000 square feet (13,940 square meters) of main street retail and business space. Within the Township District, a 2.2-acre (0.9-hectare) town green, which will serve as the community's ceremonial center, has been completed, as has some of the district's housing. Among the features of the town green are a 250-year-old oak tree, a combination gazebo and bandstand, and a community rose garden.

About three-quarters of the housing in the Township District is planned as attached: apartments, townhouses, and courtyard housing. Higher-density housing is also planned for the Avendale Village Core, an area that will include a component of 22 home-based businesses, with live/work units grouped around a freestanding business center. Orange County had to develop a new zoning classification so that business signage and visitor parking could be allowed in the home-based-business area.

Residential Design

Three primary concepts have guided the residential design at Ladera Ranch: "architecture forward," "diversity," and "authenticity."

"Architecture forward" is the design team's shorthand for emphasizing and articulating the living areas of the homes and deemphasizing—and recessing—the garage. This design approach has been implemented in a variety of ways at Ladera: some units have shallow, recessed garages shielded with protruding balconies or other architectural devices; others have more deeply recessed garages screened by an arched portal along the front plane of the house; in still other cases, garages are split or turned; and, finally, several neighborhoods have rear, alley-loaded parking. The intention, notes Kellenberg, is to ensure that the view down the street is of houses and architecture, not garages.

"Diversity" is Ladera's response to the overwhelming sameness of Orange County's red-tile Mediterranean subdivisions. William Hezmalhalch Architects has identified and distilled 17 styles for use by builders at Ladera Ranch. In addition to the Mediterranean style, with its tile and stucco finishes, there are traditional styles derived from the midwestern precedents that influenced Orange County's early architecture, including American Farm, California Ranch, Cottage, Craftsman, Monterey, and Prairie.

A dominant style or group of styles has been identified for each village, and builders are

Ladera Ranch has an extensive off-street trail system. Over ten miles (16 kilometers) of hiking, biking, and equestrian trails link residential areas to community facilities, recreation, and open space.

required to orient their product to the village theme. Specifically, builders must provide three architectural elevations for each floor plan they offer, and at least one of those is required to be of a material other than stucco, such as Hardiboard (a cement fiber product) clapboard siding, or stone. Also, the community's design guidelines prohibit builders from using any elevation more than once within a block.

"Authenticity" refers to the accurate and appropriate incorporation of stylistic details and proportion throughout the design—as opposed to the superficial application of the features of a particular style. The problem, notes Kellenberg, is that housing designers typically design a floor plan first, then design the elevations to fit the plan. And where one plan is required to have three elevations, the

The architectural guidelines produce a wide variety of streetscapes.

required structural gymnastics sometimes result in expensive—but inauthentic—designs. In contrast, the developers of Ladera encourage the builders to design the house plan in the chosen style—that is, to create floor plans that are appropriate to the style of house selected.

Another example of authenticity can be found in the corner houses at Ladera. In many older towns, the houses at the ends of the block were typically larger and more impressive, and often sat on larger lots. This tradition has been incorporated into the Ladera lot-platting and design guidelines. Corner lots are ten feet (three meters) wider than other lots, and builders are required to design a house articulated on both street elevations, with the objective of making it look as if the house was designed for that unique site. Overall, the objective is to prevent the neighborhood from feeling mass-produced.

Community-level amenities at Ladera Ranch will include four schools (two of which have been built); 10.5 miles (17 kilometers) of trails; a regional sports park (on land donated to the county); sites for religious structures; retail and service facilities; and a communitywide intranet. The intranet, called LaderaLife, is available to all residences through an agreement with Cox Communications, Inc. A high-speed, high-capacity fiber-optic telecommunications network is being installed throughout

A 2.2-acre (0.9-hectare) village green, complete with bandstand, is the centerpiece of the Township District, and the symbolic and ceremonial center of the Ladera Ranch community.

2005. (As of December 2002, approximately 3,820 dwelling units had been constructed.) In order to meet this rapid pace of construction and sales, the developer undertook detailed market research, created a finely gradated program of market segmentation, assembled a wide menu of product types and builders, and matched builders to appropriate market segments. Some 15 to 20 builders are active at Ladera Ranch at any one time, providing a range of product types and prices—from single-family detached residences, to townhouses and apartments, to custom homesites. The formula appears to work for everyone involved—the developer, the builders, and the public. Kellenberg notes that the designs that builders are pioneering at Ladera are gradually being used by the same builders in other projects around the county. Maribeth Gunn Missico, Ladera's sales and merchandising manager, notes that the alley-loaded, small-lot homes are one of the hottest building types at Ladera Ranch. "We can't keep them on the market," she notes.

Experience Gained

The idea of "neighborhood as amenity" appears to be successful at Ladera Ranch. Ladera's organization into villages and neighborhoods, with Village Clubs and neighborhood parks, has been a strong selling point for the community.

Through appropriate design guidelines, new urbanist design principles can be successful in a high-volume, production-homebuilder environment. Shifting the builders' focus to the larger community context of their work is not an overnight process, however. "It's like turning the Queen Mary," notes Kellenberg. "A little bit each year."

As the information age reaches all aspects of family and business life, "soft infrastructure," including a community-based intranet system, is becoming more important as a basic amenity.

the community, allowing residents to be online 24 hours a day, connected to community schools, businesses, medical facilities, and other services. The mechanism for this connection is the Cox@Home Internet access service, which has been customized to provide a LaderaLife home page and related services. LaderaLife includes a directory of residents, a message board, volunteer sign-up locations, and connections to various clubs.

Paralleling LaderaLife is Ladera Ranch Community Services (LARCS), a nonprofit organization dedicated to promoting and supporting community participation through the formation of clubs and through alliances with outside organizations, and by hosting community-wide celebrations and events. LARCS is funded by a combination of contributions, user fees, fees on home sales, corporate alliances and partnerships, fundraisers, and endorsements.

Marketing and Sales

Conceived in 1995, Ladera Ranch is on schedule to complete construction of its approximately 8,100 homes and related facilities by

Ladera Ranch
Project Data

Land Use Information

Site area (acres/hectares)	2,400/970
	(plus 1,600 acres/650 hectares dedicated open space)
Total number of dwelling units planned/completed	8,100/3,820
Gross density (units per acre/ per hectare)	3.4/8.4
Average net density (units per acre/per hectare)	8.3/20.5

Land Use Plan

	Acres/ Hectares	Percentage of Site
Detached residential	620/250	26
Attached residential	350/140	15
Roads	520/210	22
Common open space	820/330	33
Other nonresidential	90/36	4
Total	2,400/966	100

Residential Unit Information

Unit Type	Unit Size (Square Feet/ Square Meters)	Number of Units Planned/ Built	Current Sales Prices/Rents
Apartments	700–1,200/70–110	880/420	$1,000–$1,400/month
Seniors' apartments	600–1,100/60–100	420/0	$1,000–$1,400/month
Attached	1,000–1,500/90–140	2,550/800	$190,000–$250,000
Single-family detached	1,300–4,500/120–420	4,250/2,600	$220,000–$750,000
Total		8,100/3,820	

Development Cost Information
(Anticipated Totals, in Millions)

Site Acquisition and Improvement Costs

Site acquisition	N.A.[1]
Grading	$155
Sewer, water, storm drainage	40
Paving, curbs, sidewalks, dry utilities	47
Slope landscaping, irrigation	56
Recreational facilities, parks	45
Fees, general conditions	36
Special costs	22
Subtotal, site acquisition and improvement costs	$401

Soft Costs

Legal services	$5
Urban design	26
Development	32
Design review	2
Fees, permits, bonds	170
Marketing, advertising	22
Finance, administrative, other	53
Subtotal, soft costs	$310
Total development costs	$711

1. Not applicable.

Development Schedule

Planning started	1995
Construction started	1998
Sales started	July 1999
First closing	September 1999
Phase I completed	September 2000
Estimated completion	2005

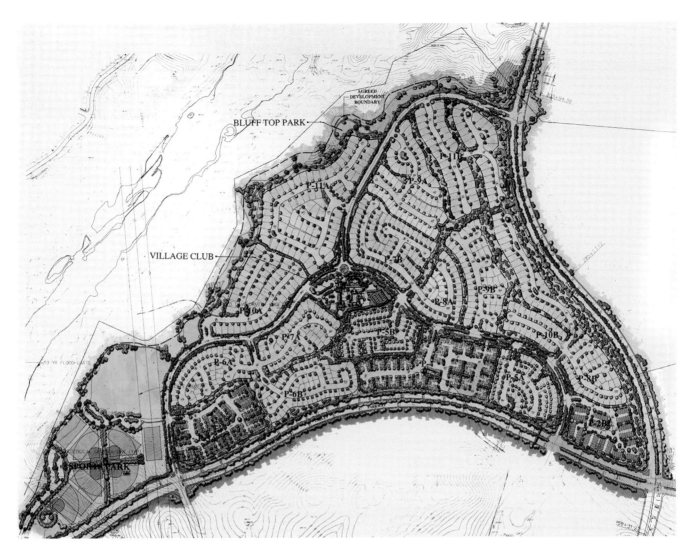

Development Team

Developer

Rancho Mission Viejo Company and DMB Ladera
28811 Ortega Highway
P.O. Box 9
San Juan Capistrano, California 92693
949-240-3363

Site Planner

EDAW, Inc.
17875 Von Karman Avenue, Suite 400
Irvine, California 92614
949-660-8044
www.edaw.com

Architect

William Hezmalhalch Architects
17875 Von Karman Avenue, Suite 400
Irvine, California 92614
949-250-0607
www.whainc.com

Landscape Architects

Land Concern Ltd.
1750 East Deere Avenue
Santa Ana, California 92705
949-250-4822
www.landconcern.com

The Oak Knoll Village site plan is one of six that make up Ladera Ranch. Each village has 900 to 1,400 residences clustered in neighborhoods of 40 to 50 units.

King Farm

Rockville, Maryland

King Farm is a 430-acre (174-hectare), mixed-use, traditional neighborhood development (TND) built on a former dairy farm in the northwestern suburbs of Washington, D.C. Its transit-oriented design uses the existing heavy-rail facilities (Metro) as well as private and public bus services, and is designed to accommodate a proposed light-rail system. The mix of housing types—which includes townhouses, condominiums, apartments, and single-family detached homes—is located within walking distance of the retail and office areas.

Site and General Description

As one of the last large undeveloped parcels in Washington's inner-ring suburbs, the project site was ideal for infill development. And its location—adjacent to the Shady Grove Metro Station, near the surrounding high-tech and biotech businesses, flanking busy Interstate 270, and between Gaithersburg and Rockville (Maryland's second- and third-largest cities)—made it a prime candidate for mixed-use, transit-oriented development.

King Farm sat dormant for more than a decade while the King family searched for a suitable buyer. Eventually, their bank had to foreclose to pay off a $36 million loan that the owners had used to pay inheritance taxes. In 1995, the Penrose Group, together with the Pritzker family, formed King Farm Associates, LLC, and purchased the property out of bankruptcy court for a total of $45.4 million.

At buildout, King Farm will have 2.5 million square feet (232,260 square meters) of office space, 130,000 square feet (12,080 square meters) of retail space, and 3,200 residential

The wide variety of housing options creates interesting streetscapes where townhouses, single-family homes, and multifamily homes are often located within a block of one another.

units. It will also include a daycare facility; a 300-room, full-service hotel; schools; and access to a future light-rail system. Over 100 acres (40 hectares) are dedicated to open space, including parks, ponds, and public areas. Amenities such as a community center, a swimming pool, and ballparks are already open. The residential and retail components of King Farm are expected to be completed by 2004.

Development Process and Financing

Cooperation between the government of the city of Rockville and the developer was essential to successfully "build a city from scratch." The developer initially invested more than $60 million in acquisition and development costs, and carrying costs were estimated at $24,000 a day—meaning that it was critical to keep the project moving expeditiously. The city had approved the developer's concept plan design (CPD) in 1996, and King Farm Associates was able to accelerate the permit process by using the already approved CPD as its final master plan.

King Farm Associates studied several already developed TNDs and transit-oriented developments (TODs), and incorporated the lessons that those developments offered into the plan for King Farm. Whereas other TNDs consisted mostly of higher-end, custom homes, King Farm was designed to offer more affordable homes specially designed for the project. King Farm particularly benefited from the lessons of the nearby Kentlands, one of

ANDRÉ BALD

the first new urbanist projects in the United States, designed in the early 1980s. By not requiring prohibitively expensive building materials or using excessively rigid architectural standards, King Farm Associates avoided some of the logistical and financial problems that the Kentlands had encountered. Further, because of the success and recognized benefits of the Kentlands, the local government was already familiar with the TND concept and supported its unique design standards and special permitting and approval needs.

One of the developer's strategies was to maintain as much autonomy as possible over the design and management of the community. After purchasing the property— which represented 19 percent of the land area of the city of Rockville—the developer worked with Rockville officials to have the city's boundaries enlarged to incorporate the property. The developer gained greater control by being under the city government, rather than under the larger county government. Annexation also meant that a larger share of the tax revenue from the project could be reinvested in King Farm, instead of being diverted to other areas of the county. King Farm Associates also dedicated land to the city of Rockville for parks and future elementary and middle schools, ensuring that

Two apartment units are stacked together behind a facade that creates the appearance of a larger row house. This design made it possible, from a marketing standpoint, for the developer to locate the affordable, "two-over-two" units adjacent to more expensive units, to meet the county's requirements for moderately priced dwelling units.

A neighborhood of single-family houses, with traditional picket fences and front porches, is adjacent to a neighborhood of multifamily residences with red-brick Colonial facades.

the locations and designs would coordinate with the community's overall theme and plan.

Planning and Design

Like other new urbanist developments, King Farm is pedestrian oriented, offering a mix of land uses, amenities located within walking distance of residences, a street plan in the form of an interconnected grid, and smaller lots and higher densities than are found in typical suburban developments. The design uses several methods to deemphasize automobiles: residential garages are located off rear alleyways; commercial parking structures are carefully screened; and a network of sidewalks and trails is integrated throughout the community. However, King Farm's transit-oriented aspect distinguishes it from other TNDs. The development is adjacent to the Shady Grove Metro Station, has county bus service as well as a community shuttle bus, and was planned to accommodate a future light-rail system.

Although the site provided a clean slate—an empty field with no existing structures or obstacles—the monotonous landscape also posed several design challenges. As Mark Gregg, president of the Penrose Group, noted,

"An advantage of the original site was that it was relatively flat with no trees, and the disadvantage was that it was relatively flat with no trees." To overcome the barren character of the landscape, the developer decided, despite the added costs, to plant larger trees than are typically installed in new residential developments. Numerous pocket parks—with gazebos, playgrounds, and gardens—were also located throughout the community.

The King Farm design guidelines shape the character of the community and ensure that

The townhouse facades borrow materials and design elements from the historic homes in nearby early-American towns.

every aspect of the development is consistent with TND principles. Homes are oriented toward the street and have shallow setbacks and narrow lots—a design approach that creates a more urban streetscape and encourages interaction among residents. Most homes have front porches, another element that encourages social interaction. Garages are accessed from the alleys behind the homes, except in areas where site constraints prohibited such an arrangement. The public spaces and civic buildings were designed as landmarks that would serve as focal points for the community. King Farm's overall plan creates a traditional atmosphere that is reminiscent of historic nearby communities such as Georgetown, Old Town Alexandria, and Williamsburg.

The land use plan partitions King Farm into three sections: Watkins Pond, Baileys Commons, and Irvington Centre. Watkins Pond is primarily residential, with a mix of single-family homes, townhouses, and multifamily residences. The focal points of Watkins Pond are the 12-acre (five-hectare) park, the site of a future elementary school, and a community center with a pool, exercise room, and meeting facilities. Baileys Commons, with townhouses, condominiums, and apartments, has a higher density than Watkins Pond. It also has retail uses and a 28-acre (11-hectare) site reserved for a proposed middle school and park. The 100-acre (40-hectare) Irvington Centre, which serves as the urban-style commercial office district, includes restaurants and a hotel.

At King Farm, the mix of housing types creates a varied streetscape. Forty percent of the total planned units will be rental apartments (1,200), with the remaining 60 percent divided among single-family units (366), townhouses (926), and condominiums (708). Although only a few of the single-family homes are custom designed, each home at King Farm appears unique because buyers can select from a wide array of house types, plans, and

TORTI GALLAS AND PARTNERS

facades. The developer selected five builders to construct the single-family homes, some of whom were not accustomed to the relatively strict design guidelines or to the challenge of having to ensure that construction would cause minimal disturbance to residents already living in the community. The single-family homes have been well received: over 300 of the 366 planned homes have been built, at sales prices ranging from $280,000 to $604,000.

Prices for townhouses range from $210,000 to $523,355. Of the 926 townhouse units planned, 415 have been built. Twelve percent of the total units at King Farm meet the affordable-housing requirements of Montgomery County's Moderately Priced Dwelling Unit (MPDU) program. In the "two-over-two" apartments, multiple smaller units were stacked and given a unified facade that creates the appearance of larger, individual row houses—a design that allowed the MPDUs to be integrated into neighborhoods with larger, more expensive ($375,000) townhouses and averted opposition from the owners of the larger units.

Most of the higher-density multifamily units (30 units per acre; 74 per hectare) are con-

The developer wanted to avoid the overly rigid design standards that had caused problems for other new urbanist projects. Although the design guidelines at King Farm called for porches, shallow setbacks, narrow lots, and rear parking, they did not require custom homes. Because the builders were able to modify many of their existing designs to comply with the guidelines, they saved time and money without compromising the aesthetic quality of the community.

The King Farm village center is located within a short walk of most of the residential neighborhoods. The community's large population base and easy access for residents of neighboring communities made the village center an attractive location for retailers.

centrated in Baileys Commons, which is only a five- to ten-minute walk from the Shady Grove Metro station and King Farm's retail core. Internal structured parking for the garden apartments is tucked discreetly between the buildings, away from the view of the street. The "Charleston-style" luxury apartment buildings contain three units, each with a direct-access garage and a covered porch. Baileys Commons also offers for-sale townhouses and nine-unit rental "manor houses."

In the Village Center, luxury two-story apartments were constructed above the retail space. Although they are now approximately 75 percent rented, demand for the product was not as strong as expected, partly because the retail portion is still in the early stages of development and has yet to be an attraction for residents. The condominiums and rental apartments have drawn a broader and more mature market than expected, appealing as much to buyers between the ages of 45 and 60 as to the 20- to 30-year-olds who were originally anticipated as the primary market.

King Farm Village Center is located within quick walking distance of most of the community. Three roads—King Farm Boulevard, Redland Boulevard, and Gaither Road—bisect the community and provide easy access to the Village Center for the surrounding population outside King Farm. The Village Center

consists of seven brick buildings that, collectively, create an enclosed space for Village Green Park. Currently, 92,319 square feet (8,580 square meters) of retail space has been constructed, and lease rates are $28 to $35 per square foot ($301 to $376 per square meter). The Village Center will have 130,000 square feet (12,080 square meters) of retail space upon completion. Current Village Center tenants include six dining establishments, two banks, and retailers and service providers. The largest tenant is Safeway Food & Drug, which has an in-store Starbucks, a dry cleaner, and a bank. King Farm's large population base and neighboring communities provide a good market draw for the retailers.

Irvington Centre offers residents the opportunity to work near their homes. Two office buildings are already occupied, and ten more (totaling 2.5 million square feet—232,260 square meters) and a 300-room hotel are planned. The two existing Class A office buildings rent for more than $30 per square foot ($323 per square meter), and have amenities such as conference rooms, gyms, and restaurants. The office buildings have structured parking—which, although it was considerably more expensive to construct than surface parking lots, increases density and results in a less sprawling, more attractive, and more walkable environment. The neoclassical-inspired design of the six-story office buildings gives them a strongly vertical, high-rise feel. When completed, Irvington Centre will be enhanced by a 22-acre (nine-hectare) park, tree-lined avenues, and plazas. A right-of-way has been dedicated on King Farm Boulevard to accommodate a proposed light-rail system linking King Farm to three other metropolitan town centers.

King Farm exemplifies many of the principles of smart growth. It was built on a suburban infill site using existing infrastructure. Its density, mix of uses, and walkable environment encourage transit, biking, and pedestrian trips. It is well served by both heavy rail and bus. The community-operated shuttle bus runs on a 20-minute circuit from Irvington Centre through the King Farm Village Center, the Shady Grove Metro Station, and the residential areas. The shuttle averages 6,000 transit riders per month—a significant

number for a new system, and considering that the residential and office space is not fully developed. Transit use, walking, and biking as commuting options should increase substantially as the residential, office, and retail components mature. It is still too early to gauge King Farm's success in shifting commuters from auto to nonauto trips, but the existing transit infrastructure and the pedestrian-friendly environment offer great potential.

Experience Gained

Cooperation, support, and flexibility from the government are key to designing and building large-scale TND and TOD projects. In the case of King Farm, the local government was already familiar with the nuances of TND development because of the nearby development of the Kentlands. King Farm also had the backing of the state government, which proactively supports smart growth through its policies.

To ensure a cohesive plan for all components of the project, the developer maintained control over as much of the design and management as possible. By striking a balance between high-priced homes and more moderately priced production homes, the developer was able to offer a range of products that appealed to a broad spectrum of customers, leading to more rapid sales than would otherwise have occurred.

Because the developer created appropriate design guidelines at the start, builders were not overwhelmed with overly rigid architectural standards and requirements for expensive materials; nevertheless, the homes and resulting neighborhoods have a high-quality look and feel.

TORTI GALLAS AND PARTNERS

Multifamily housing makes up a large portion of the residential mix at King Farm.

King Farm
Project Data

Land Use Information

Site area (acres/hectares)	430/174
Total number of dwelling units planned/completed	3,200/2,000
Hotel (planned)	300 rooms
Daycare (planned)	Accommodations for 200 children

Land Use Plan

Use	Percentage of Site
Buildings	75
Landscaping and open space	25

Gross Building Area

Use	Existing (Square Feet/ Square Meters)	Planned (Square Feet/ Square Meters)
Office	517,000/48,030	2,500,000/232,260
Retail	130,000/12,080	130,000/12,080
Total	647,000/60,110	2,630,000/244,340

Residential Unit Information

Unit Type	Number of Units Planned/Sold or Leased	Current Sales Prices/Rents
Single-family	366/325	$280,000–$604,000
Townhouses	926/415	$210,000–$523,355
Condominiums	708/265	$122,000–$380,000
Rentals	1,200/790	$1,200–$2,500/month
Total	3,200/1,795	

Retail Information

Tenant Classification	Number of Tenants	Gross Leasable Area (Square Feet/ Square Meters)
General merchandise	1	54,000/5,020
Food service	7	22,359/2,080
Personal services	3	6,173/570
Financial	3	6,094/570
Medical	1	3,693/340
Total	15	92,319/8,580

Development Cost Information
(In Millions)

Land and Construction Costs

Site acquisition	$45.4
Site improvement	66.8
Community buildings and pool	3.0
Subtotal, land and construction costs	$115.2

Soft Costs

Legal services	$4.4
Project management	10.3
Marketing	3.2
Financing	4.0
Construction and interest fees	6.5
Subtotal, soft costs	$28.4
Total development costs	$143.6

Development Schedule

Site purchased	June 1995
Planning started	June 1995
Construction started	November 1996
Sales/leasing started (grand opening date)	October 10, 1997
Estimated completion (residential component)	2004

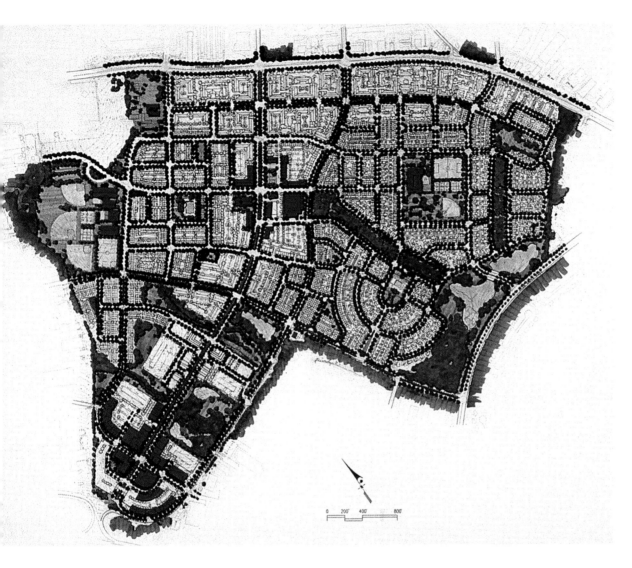

Development Team

Developer

King Farm Associates, LLC

8330 Boone Boulevard, Suite 460

Vienna, Virginia 22182

703-847-5270

www.kingfarm.com

Planner and Architect

Torti Gallas and Partners, Inc.

1300 Spring Street, Fourth Floor

Silver Spring, Maryland 20910

301-588-4800

www.tortigallas.com

Landscape Architect

Land Design, Inc.

1414 Prince Street, Suite 400

Alexandria, Virginia 22314

703-549-7784

www.landdesign.com

Engineer

Loiederman Soltesz Associates

1390 Piccard Drive, Suite 101

Rockville, Maryland 20850

301-948-2750

www.lsassociates.net